Clay
In the Potter's
Hand

By Dorothy Sun

Christian Aid Mission
Charlottesville, Virginia

CLAY IN THE POTTER'S HAND
© Copyright 2006 by Dorothy Sun

Published by
Christian Aid Mission
P.O. Box 9037
Charlottesville, VA 22906
USA

First Printing 2006
Second Printing 2010
ISBN: 0-9741325-3-5

Cover and Interior Design: John T. Sanderson

Printed in Canada

We are glad to send you *Clay in the Potter's Hand.* Though we do not charge for the book, it has cost Christian Aid to produce, publish and mail it. Offerings to support the China ministry are welcomed. We pray that our Lord uses Dorothy's message to encourage you in your walk with God.

IMPORTANT WORD OF CAUTION.

Please do not send this book to China or give it to someone who might take it to China. It is important that it not be given to any non-believer from China. This book should not be considered a tool for Chinese evangelism. If you have a Chinese friend who has shown an interest in the gospel and with whom you would like to share this book, use your God-given spiritual discernment to be certain they are born again by the Spirit of God before giving them the book. Water baptism can be a helpful indicator of true spiritual rebirth and repentance.

Foreward

Dorothy Sun's extraordinary testimony illustrates the transforming power of the Lord Jesus Christ, working in and through her. Every testimony is unique, but few are filled with the heart-rending events that mark Dorothy's life. Through this book, you will discover her love for God and how her call to His purpose was, and continues to be, realized.

In 1984, when a mutual friend introduced me to Dorothy, she told me what she had endured during the years since Communism overtook her country. At that time, her husband, Freddie, and their two sons were still being prevented from leaving China to join her in the United States. We spent much time in conversation and prayer when she attended Bible study at the church where I pastor. The Potter had dramatically molded Dorothy into the servant of Christ that she is today. And He continues to transform her.

One would assume that a person who had undergone such horrendous experiences would find life easier at some point, yet she continues to face difficulties as she travels the world to share the wondrous gospel of her Lord Jesus Christ.

As painful as these events have been, they have served to strengthen her, and to prove the truth of God's Word.

> *"And we know that all things work together for good to them that love God, to them who are the called according to his purpose."*
> (Romans 8:28)

Bruce Johnson, Pastor
Reedy Creek Baptist Church
Cary, North Carolina

Foreward

I first met Dorothy eighteen years ago when she spoke at our church. She greatly impacted our vision for missions. I had never met anyone with as deep a passion for the Lord as Dorothy; and until this day—eighteen years later—I have met only one other person who comes close to the selfless life that Dorothy lives, and that is her husband, Freddie.

She is a true disciple of our Lord Jesus Christ, and matches what I have read in the book of Acts about the disciples who set the world on fire.

I have witnessed how the suffering you will read about in this book has helped shape this beautiful vessel, who now accomplishes much for the Lord. Until now, very few have known of the extent of Dorothy's dedication and suffering. I am certain that, as you read this book, you will have an increased hunger for a closer relationship with the Lord, and a desire to participate in His work.

May the Lord bless this testimony, that it may plant many seeds in the hearts of those reading it—seeds that will be watered and grow to bring glory to our Lord and Savior, Jesus Christ.

Rev. Bob Atkins, Sr. Pastor
Greensprings Chapel
Williamsburg, Virginia

Acknowledgments

I am deeply appreciative and much indebted to several godly brothers and sisters in Christ who have strongly supported me in the translation and publishing of my Chinese autobiography, "Clay in the Potter's Hand" into this English version.

Without their contributions of time, energy, personal ability, financial support and many prayers, this book would not have been completed. I would especially like to thank Rev. Bob and Lawana Atkins, Senior Pastor, Greensprings Chapel; Rev. Bruce and Vickie Johnson, Senior Pastor, Reedy Creek Baptist Church; Jim Wright, President of FHG Inc, and his wife Nila.

Several sisters in Christ helped with different stages of editing. Leona Choy read and edited the first draft. Brittany West, writer and editor, also spent significant time in the early stages, for which I am most grateful. Patricia Taylor did the final edits and proofreading. My heartfelt thanks to all of them as well as to John Scully, Publications Director of Christian Aid Mission, for publishing and John Sanderson, cover and interior design. I am thankful to Freddie Sun, my dear husband, who did most of the translation of my book from Chinese into English.

Without the help of these precious people, and many unnamed prayer partners, the English edition of my book could not have been published.

Most of all, I praise the Lord for His spiritual leading, wonderful blessing and His abundant grace and mercy all the way in my life. He has kept me safe through all kinds of sufferings and tribulations. To God be the glory!

I pray that God will use this book to glorify His name and bless each and every reader.

— Dorothy Sun
    October 2006
    Charlottesville, VA

Dedication

This book is dedicated to my beloved parents, my husband, sons and my sister, Grace, who have been through all the sufferings with me and to all the saints who love the glory of God only.

Author's Preface

I was born into a Christian family that loved the Lord very much. I grew up in a special period of time witnessing and experiencing the great changes and turbulence of the national and church history of China from the 1930s to the present. As I recall my past life, our Lord is so wonderful. He has used all sorts of tribulations, trials and sufferings to discipline and teach me brokenness and to destroy my flesh and body, so that His life is able to grow toward maturity in me. From self-righteousness, I acknowledge I am a sinner. From pursuing personal dreams, I began to learn that His ways and thoughts are higher than my ways and thoughts. I grew from a naïve young girl, lacking the ability to distinguish true and false pastors and brothers, to know how to distinguish the deception of the anti-Christ. As I grew from all of these things, the Lord enabled me so that I could say: *"I have heard of thee by the hearing of the ear, but now mine eye see thee."* (Job 42:5)

From my own experience of His presence, with the faith of a mustard seed to a stronger faith that He bestowed on me, He has kept me. This lengthy pilgrimage interwoven with blood and tears is a testimony that I walked through in that special historical period of time. However, it is also full of joy in Him because He talks with me and walks with me all along the way. I must say, *"But by the grace of God I am what I am: and His grace which was bestowed upon me was not in vain."* (I Corinthians 15:10)

The memory and life span of a human being have some limitations. Many brothers and sisters in Christ urged me to share my stories and testimonies. My husband Freddie and I translated the manuscript into English and Sisters-in-Christ Leona Choy, Brittany West, and Patricia Taylor edited it into fluent English enabling eventually my autobiography to be published both in Chinese and English versions. I didn't keep diaries in past years and my parents' house was ransacked three times. Much precious historical family information, written materials of my parents' ministries and pictures were destroyed and lost during the times when the Japanese occupied China in the 1940s. From 1966 to 1976 the Red Guards also ransacked our home during "the Cultural Revolution" launched by Mao Ze-Dong. However, with God's help I have tried my best to bring all the scattered pieces together in order to share these testimonies of God's faithfulness to complete this book. May the grace, mercy and the boundless love of our Lord Jesus, which He bestows on me, be fully spread throughout this book so that all of the glory will be His alone.

Scriptures That Have Guided My Life

"The word which came to Jeremiah from the Lord, saying, Arise, and go down to the potter's house, and there I will cause thee to hear my words. Then I went down to the potter's house, and behold, he wrought a work on the wheels. And the vessel that he made of clay was marred in the hand of the potter: so he made it again another vessel, as seemed good to the potter to make it." (Jeremiah 18:1-4)

"But we have this treasure in earthen vessels, that the excellency of the power may be of God, and not of us. We are troubled on every side, yet not distressed; we are perplexed, but not in despair; Persecuted, but not forsaken; cast down, but not destroyed. Always bearing about in the body the dying of the Lord Jesus, that the life also of Jesus might be made manifest in our body." (2 Corinthians 4: 7-10)

"And He said unto me, My grace is sufficient for thee, for My strength is made perfect in weakness. Most gladly therefore will I rather glory in my infirmities, that the power of Christ may rest upon me. Therefore I take pleasure in infirmities, in reproaches, in necessities, in persecutions, in distresses for Christ's sake: for when I am weak, then am I strong." (2 Corinthians 12: 9-10)

"But by the grace of God I am what I am: and His grace which was bestowed upon me was not in vain; but I laboured more abundantly than they all: yet not I, but the grace of God which was with me." (1 Corinthians 15:10)

Table of Contents

III. Third Section – Rebuilding215

I. Chosen

1. Father David Chang

2. Mother Miriam Nieh

3. My mother worked with the Methodist Wesleyan Church in Tianjin city and also with the Young Women's Christian Association in China. She devotedly served the Lord especially in women outreach ministries.

4. Miriam Nieh, the chairwoman of the trustee board of YWCA in Tianjin (middle), Ru-Quan Zheng, the general secretary of YWCA in Tianjin (left) and Danny, an actor (right)

5. I am the first daughter of my parents

6. A picture with a girl of the neighborhood

7. I was taught to respect my older half-brothers; my 12-year old elder brother pressed my shoulder even taking a picture with me

8. I was taught to take care of my younger sister

9. I loved to go out with my mom to learn how to raise funds

10. I was learning how to serve

11. In the kindergarten of the church, among the children of the Sunday school it was I who received an honorable prize at the center of the front row

1

2

3

4

5

6

7

8

9

10

11

Chapter 1

Godly and Devoted Parents

I thank God for my parents. They strongly influenced and helped me in my spiritual life journey. I see my parents like bellwethers among the sheep who kept following the Lord as He went before us through "the valley of the shadow of death." My father, David Chang, was raised in poverty, as my grandfather suffered from tuberculosis and could do little more than selling salt, which he sifted from the sea. At this time in China, traditional schools were nonexistent, so parents would instead hire a teacher to instruct their children at the village's Buddhist temple. My father was not afforded the opportunity to attend this kind of private school, so he observed classes through a window outside the temple everyday. He faithfully attended his post, during both the bitter cold winters and burning hot summers. Moved by this child's eagerness to learn, the teacher, a knowledgeable Taoist monk, privately tutored him. Throughout the following years, my father's instructor taught him Chinese classics, language in characters, Chinese medicine and philosophy. A quick learner and deep thinker, my father was able to remember and incorporate knowledge into his life at an impressive pace. At age fourteen my father was granted aid and enrolled in

Hui-Wen High School, which was established by American missionaries. The evangelism and influence of western missionaries in China began in 1807.

Research of the Relationship between the Bible and the Chinese Classics, Characters and Culture

My father later dedicated his life to Christ at Hui-Wen University. He continued his studies at the University of Tokyo and University of Paris, later earning a degree in law from Michigan State University and a degree in political science at DePaul University in Illinois. Although spending a large portion of his youth in foreign countries, he did not become westernized, but kept his Chinese ethnic and cultural ties. His passion for the Chinese classics, characters and culture inspired him to write several books. Among those are: "The Role of China's Politics and Economy in the World"; "The Mystery of Chinese Characters in the Bible" and "The Comparison of Jesus' Teaching and Mozi's Philosophy." Along with these books, my father meticulously kept twenty-four volumes of diaries and thousands of documents, records detailing his thoughts and meditations. All these and 7,000 of my father's books, including all of the family pictures, were burned by the Red Guards in 1966, during the Cultural Revolution led by Mao Zedong.

About My Parents

As the only son in his family, my father was pressured by grandpa to marry early and have more children. When he was sixteen (before he was saved), he was betrothed to a woman whom my grandpa had chosen. She was a beautiful rich woman, but was physically weak. She lacked the strength to manage a household, because she was an opium addict. While my father was overseas for educational purposes, she even neglected the education of her five children. After nineteen years of marriage, my father's first wife died, leaving behind five uneducated children and a poor household. I remember my dad said, "I was born with nothing plus nothing and had to fight in this world. Then I lost my wife when I came back from America and I had to be both father and mother. It is only by my Heavenly Father's gracious love and mercy that I could endure these very difficult times."

After my father returned to China, he began to serve in many different political positions. He became General Yu-Xiang Feng's diplomat for foreign affairs. General Feng was a Christian and they often enjoyed good fellowship in Christ. My dad later held positions as the judge of Qingdao Municipal Court of Shangdong province; the director of Bureau of Land and Resources of Nanjing City, the director of Financial Bureau of Tianjin City, the director of Products Inspection Bureau of Tianjin City and the general manager of China Paint Company. My dad found it very hard to be a politician in these circumstances of corruption and turmoil because of his Christian conscience. He prayed often about leaving these positions.

In 1937, the Japanese invaded China and overthrew the government ruled by the Chinese Nationalists in Nanjing. As a result, my dad's political career came to an end. He was thankful to the Lord for answering his prayers. The Japanese quickly took over many parts of China and Asia and established a puppet government in China. In order to keep their lives and wealth, many Chinese politicians and wealthy people became traitors and cooperated with the Japanese. Two years after the Japanese occupation of our hometown, Tianjin City, when the Japanese authority discovered that my dad had previously studied in Japan, they intended to appoint him as the mayor. This was a strong temptation and also a life or death decision. Dad did not want to betray his country. He wanted to keep his integrity. My mom said to my dad, "If you become a traitor, we are divorced." Dad responded to the Japanese telling them that as a Christian, he would not be involved in politics anymore. His refusal to cooperate badly offended the Japanese and they sent a corps of military police with dogs to search our house in the middle of the night. They took away all the English books, letters, documents and radio. The Japanese were furious when the officials found out that my older brother and sister had left for Chongqing. Sichuan province, the home base of fighting and resisting the Japanese invasion of China, was the temporary capital of the Chinese Nationalists led by Chiang Kai-Shek. Then the Japanese handcuffed my dad and took him away. I can still remember that horrible night vividly even though I was only three years old. After my dad was taken away, my mom held me in her arms and cried and prayed to the Lord. It was known that once anybody was taken away by the Japanese military police, they would never return alive.

But, praise the Lord, my dad was released and came home after two weeks. It was amazing the way that God worked in that serious situation. The new Japanese commanding officer, who had just been transferred to

Tianjin City, was Mr. Nagai Santaro. An alumnus of the University of Tokyo, he knew my dad when they were both classmates there. He found my dad's name in the list of convicts and appealed to the authorities to release him. Explaining that he had known my dad in Japan, he told them my dad had the potential of contributing to the "Great East Asia Commonwealth". As a result, my dad was released. Since he disappointed Nagai Santaro by refusing to work with him, he was then put under house arrest. He was not allowed to leave Tianjin. For eight years he supported the family by selling hand-written calligraphy of Chinese characters. Nevertheless, God had great plans for my dad.

After the death of his first wife, my dad prayed that God would provide a devoted Christian wife for him. He wanted to have a wife who loved the Lord, loved him and also had the desire to help him restore the family. Tracing back, the man who would become my uncle, Pei-Yuan Nieh, and my dad met at the University of Paris. They became good friends. When my uncle returned to China, he learned of my dad's bereavement. He invited dad to his father's grand villa. My future grandpa on my mother's side was the biggest landlord in his hometown of Funing County, Hebei province. He was also the major shareholder in many businesses such as the East Asia Wool Company, Kailuan Coal Company and Tianjin Glass Company. He could afford to give his children a good education. He sent his son to France to study. After his daughters, Miriam and Vera, attended the Christian Keen's School run by American missionaries in Tianjin, he sent them to the U.S. to study. My mom and my aunt became born-again Christians through their schooling. Because of their witnesses, grandpa became a believer and made a commitment to follow the Lord.

After his conversion, he released the farmers from their tenancy contracts of the land he owned. He donated his money to build public schools, post offices, roads in the villages and even railways. Days later, he sold his land and donated the profit to several compassion and mercy projects. When the Communists took over China in 1949, my grandpa had already passed away. Yet, he escaped the condemnation of being a landlord, so the members and relatives of my mom's family escaped the disastrous fate of having a family association with a landlord: an enemy class that the Communists wanted to eradicate.

Vera Nieh, my aunt, was bright with a strong personality. She remained single all her life. After she graduated from a medical college in the United

States and returned to China in the early 1930s, she founded and became the principal of the China Nurse Institution that was affiliated with the well known Beijing Union Medical University and Hospital. She was also a member of the trustee board of the International Nurse Association as well as the founder of the cause of nurse and nursing management in China. After the Communists took over in 1949, she became the vice president of No.301 Hospital in Beijing and later the vice president of the Provincial Hospital in Anhui province. In 1957, she was wrongfully condemned as a rightist. She devoted her whole life to the medical cause. She went to be with the Lord at the age of 94 in 1997.

My Mother's Vision to Marry a Christian Warrior Called "David"

Miriam Yu-Ching Nieh, my mother, was a charming, elegant and sweet lady, who devoted herself to the Lord and His ministries. At school, an American teacher took mom under her wing and trained her in singing. She became a famous soprano vocalist. In 1923, she began to work with the Young Women's Christian Association (YWCA) in Beijing as a secretary. After she moved to Tianjin in 1932, she was promoted to the president and the chair of YWCA trustee board in Tianjin. She was also one of the board members of the National YWCA of China. She worked with YWCA for twenty-six years until 1949. She also served in Beijing Union Medical University and Hospital in the social work department when she was in Beijing.

My mom had a very close relationship with the Lord. God gave her a vision that she would marry a man named "David" who loved the Lord. During her younger years she had many reputable suitors who pursued her. She rejected them all, because some of them were non-believers and some were believers but they were not named "David". In 1931, when dad was first invited to grandpa's villa by Pei-Yuan Nieh, his good friend and classmate in Paris, and my mom's elder brother, he met mom for the first time. They immediately clicked with one another and had many meaningful conversations. My mom was overjoyed to find that my dad's Christian name was "David" and thought that this David Chang was probably the one whom God had prepared for her.

My dad fell in love with my mom at first sight, but was afraid to pursue her because their situations were so different. After many prayers and much soul searching, dad finally wrote a couplet of Chinese poetry to propose to her, which read: *"I do not own a house or a piece of land. All I have are five children and my hand. But I love the Lord and strive for the truth I stand."* My mom was touched by his couplet and especially my dad's sincerity, honesty and devotion to the Lord.

By God's gracious plan, dad and mom got married on September 5, 1932. Their marriage was sensational news in the area. Since then, on their anniversary, my dad would proudly repeat their love story. We children all know it by heart. Mom brought with her a good dowry to marry dad and all her friends admired her unselfish love and exceptional courage in wanting to be a good stepmother. Mom not only bought a new house, but also sent all five children of dad's first wife to a private Christian school to be educated. Every Sunday my parents took the whole family to church. My two older half brothers served zealously in the church choir and the whole family had an entire new look. Mom gave all she had in raising her five stepchildren. She was attentive and compassionate to them all. She took them to church every Sunday and faithfully discipled them in the Christian faith. She enthusiastically assumed the role of a mother, transforming her home into a warm and welcoming haven. My father truly adored her.

I was born three years after my dad and mom married. From the time I was very young, mom kept telling and reminding me that I should respect my older brothers and sister because they had lost their own mother. She also said that I should love my younger sisters because they were little. We were all very close and in harmony within our family.

During the eight years of Japanese occupation from 1937-1945, when my dad was under house arrest by the Japanese, we had very little income. My mom sold the jewelry from her dowry to support our big family of eleven members. From 1944-1954 she also financially supported my dad as he started the "Chinese Christian Self-Governing, Self-Supporting and Self-Propagating Million-Pound Foundation" and a Christian newspaper called "Tianjing New Life Evening Post."

After the Communists took over China in 1949, since my parents had contributed all their financial resources to the church and mission, our family was short of money. We couldn't even afford to buy Christmas gifts. When my dad's buddy found out our difficulties, he donated 800 silver dollars to my parents to buy Christmas gifts for us children. However, my dad had a plan to celebrate Christmas in a Chinese way in our church. There would be no Christmas tree. He planned to decorate the church with Chinese lanterns wrapped with beautiful silk and brocade. Long couplets written with Chinese characters of scriptures in golden color were hung along with big red balls of stripes of silk. All the decoration surely would cost a lot of money. My dad asked mom, "Shall we buy gifts for our kids or buy gifts for Jesus?" Without hesitation my mom gave all the 800 silver dollars to my dad to celebrate Christmas in the church in a Chinese indigenous way of decoration. We children felt so sad since our Christmas gifts that we had dreamed of for so long vanished like bubbles.

At the end of 1955 my dad was arrested and suffered for Christ until 1979 when he got his "rehabilitation" and later he went to be with the Lord. "Rehabilitation" is the term the government used to distinguish between real criminals who were released, and those innocent people wrongly charged. During this long period of suffering, my mom was always his faithful companion as they experienced the water and fire trials together. How precious was this holy marriage that was arranged by God! It makes me think of the words in a beautiful love song, "Because God made thee mine...."

Chapter 2

A Golden Childhood

Though I am the firstborn child of my parents, my mother was a stepmother to one older daughter and four older sons from my dad's previous marriage. So, in the family, I am the sixth child. After me my mother had three more daughters. We were a big family of nine children. My childhood was joyful and abundant. We had four servants: one chef, one houseboy and two babysitters. My parents provided us the best education and wealth materialistically. They also set up strict family rules for us to obey, especially for me.

My oldest sister is twenty years older than I am. She was very beautiful and smart, a favorite of my parents. My mother also paid special attention, care and love to my two youngest stepbrothers. Correct manners, behavior and proper appearance were taught and emphasized by my mother. Our dining table was long enough to seat comfortably fourteen people, but no matter how delicious the food was, we had to listen to my father's lengthy prayers of giving thanks to the Lord before eating. We were not allowed to stretch our arms for food or make noise when we ate. Sometimes when my parents went out for dinners and parties, we children would make a big mess on the dining table. The troublemakers were usually my two youngest stepbrothers. We had fun and I also enjoyed the little bit of freedom.

Unforgettable Lullabies – Beginning Love of Christian Music

My parents' three-story mansion had eight bedrooms and long stairway banisters. Instead of walking down the steps, my brothers taught me how to slide down these banisters. When my mom found out our naughtiness, I was the only child to be blamed for my bad behavior, not my brothers. Because my mom had more tolerance and patience for my stepbrothers and sister and my own sisters who were still very young, sometimes I felt jealous. Hence, all my childish complaints were only to my dad. I sought his love and protection. My mom always told me that because my stepsister and brothers had lost their own mother, she needed to give more love to them. Since my own sisters were younger than I was, she also needed my help. As I think back now, I thank God that He gave me a godly mother who gave sacrificial love to my stepsister and brothers.

I learned to play the piano when I was five years old from pianist, Myrtle Liu, a famous Chinese pianist. I loved music very much, but I didn't like boring skill exercises. I only loved to play pieces. But, my mom strictly coached me for the basic training in these hard piano lessons and later the vocal training when she found that I loved singing. When I lost my freedom from 1960 to 1980 while in prison, I temporarily lost my skills in piano and my voice. However, God mercifully restored these gifts after I came to the United States in 1984. Now I can still pick up my piano skills and with a re-born voice, I can sing again to serve the Lord. I praise the Lord that I had a very disciplined mother. I also miss the lullabies in English and Chinese my mom sang to us when we lay down in our beds every night. All the old hymns and folk songs of African Americans are very inspiring and sweet for me. Those hymns and folk songs impacted me greatly. They became my only companions twenty years later when I was locked up in jail and experienced much loneliness.

Our choir of the Wesleyan Methodist Church in my hometown of Tianjin was very large and of professional quality. Among the seventy members there were well-known pianists, soloists and conductors. The weekly choir rehearsals were always practiced at our home. That was my happiest and favorite time, because the heavenly melodies, the harmony chorus and beautiful solo pieces lifted my heart to God. Even though I was too young to be qualified to join them, I couldn't help but follow them with my childish voice. This is where I got the dream to be a gospel singer at an early age.

I Grew Up in Church and in the YWCA

When I was growing up, my personality was a little different from that of other young children. I loved my parents, the bishop, pastor and other older learned and well-educated people, such as Bishop Jiang. I loved to listen to their talks, discussions and meetings for ministries, evangelism, church planting and administration and prayer meetings held at our home. Sometimes the gatherings extended late into the night, especially when they were discussing how to establish the "Chinese Christian Million-Pound Foundation" to help Self-Governing, Self-Supporting and Self-Propagating Indigenous Evangelism in China. I loved to listen to their humble prayers, and their zeal for God's kingdom. I also loved to join all the evangelistic conferences, parades, concerts and fund raising events for charities. Because of my interest I got a nickname, "little enthusiastic co-worker." From the time I was very young, God's Word, *"As for me and my house, we will serve the Lord."* (Joshua 24: 15), was very clear in my heart and in my family. That is why I still remember that part of church history in China that is purposely blotted out by the Chinese Communists. God has preserved me as a little remnant to be His witness.

My mother was the chairwoman of the Trustee Board of the YWCA in Tianjin when I was young. I loved to go with my mother to fund-raising and charity ministries and listen to their meetings. They held a lot of meetings at our home as well. When I played house with my younger sisters, we would dress up like our mother wearing her dresses, shoes and jewelry to imitate her image when she preached during her ministries.

Back in the 1920s to the 1940s, the YWCA was a real Young Women's Christian Association, whose theme was, *"And you shall know the truth, and the truth shall make you free."* (John 8:32) I liked the way they emphasized Christian education among teenagers and children. They often had summer and winter Bible schools and weekly Bible fellowship. For young adults they had gospel concerts, all kinds of seminars given by well-known pastors, ministers and missionaries as well as celebrations on Christian holidays such as Christmas and Easter. For the poor and needy people and victims of natural disasters, they had many relief works. For instance, when in 1939 a severe flood hit Tianjin, the YWCA immediately called up people to help. They supported building shelters for more than 10,000 households of victims. These shelters later became a village in the suburb of Tianjin.

The YWCA also taught women how to sew and make food to sell, and trained men to learn all kinds of skills and crafts to make a living. The YWCA had evangelistic meetings and crusades right among victims in these villages and a great number found the Lord. I became busy and so excited that I could help my mother in many ways. At meal times I helped distribute food and clothing and took care of the little kids. Actually, I was having fun and even making a mess, but I learned that people need love. I thank God through these experiences and my upbringing that Christ's love was deeply rooted in my heart although I was only three to four years old.

After the Japanese surrendered in 1945, the YWCA headquarters in Shanghai sent several young female secretaries to the Tianjin YWCA. My mother soon found out that they were not really Christians. They had no interest in all the Christian evangelistic activities. They were interested in student political movements opposing the Nationalist government that was ruling China and gave freedom to Christianity at that time. Some of them came and went and some stayed for a longer time. They were actually Communist secret agents infiltrating into the YWCA. They planned to take over the leadership of the Christian churches and organizations after the Communists took over the country.

After the Communists took over Mainland China in 1949, the YWCA actually became the "Young Women Communist Association" and they had no more Christian ministries in the communities. So my mother resigned her position in the YWCA. She said, "No Jesus Christ, no Miriam Nieh." I lost my garden, too, where I grew up in the love of Jesus. Through my mother's association with the YWCA I had learned a lot about Christ and had a lot of joy and fun. Many years later, these secretaries in the YWCA exposed their Communist memberships. They all became the officials of the religious bureau of the Communist government and the leaders of the so-called "Chinese Christian Self-Supporting, Self-Governing and Self-Propagating Patriotic Movement Association" (TSPM). This became a Communist puppet tool used to control the Protestant Churches and Christians in China.

Chapter 3

A Carnal Teen-Age Christian

I graduated from a private grade school in Tianjin in 1947 and enrolled in the private Christian Keen Girls' School, also in Tianjin, that same year. This school, established by Methodist missionaries, I liked the best. It was a boarding school and most of the teachers were American missionaries. My mom sent me there because back in 1923 my mother and my aunt had also graduated from that school. She knew that I would receive a very good Christian education.

My grandpa had found the Lord through these Methodist missionaries and had been saved. He faithfully and constantly supported this school. The school emphasized the Christian education of a whole person, spirit, body and soul. All students could be well trained especially in English and music as well as other regular courses. We sang songs, laughed, had parties and fun, but were disciplined whenever we broke the rules. I loved the life at the school very much. There was amnesty, however, if we begged for the missionary's forgiveness. We would often say, "We're sorry, we have been tempted by Satan." Then we would be permitted go free. The headmistress, Miss France, often encouraged me to be a gospel singer and to consider the leadership in the YWCA. I dreamed one day of becoming my mother, Miriam Nieh, the Second. Her encouraging prediction laid the foundation of my willingness to serve the Lord, but also inflamed my carnal pride and arrogance.

Defending the Truth – The Cause of My Later Accusation

During the eight years from 1937 to 1945, the Japanese invaded and occupied China. Western missionaries planted Christian churches in north China that were closed down by the Japanese. Many believers left the churches and the congregations were in extreme poverty. The churches were incapable of supporting the pastors and ministers, these faithful servants of God. Our Methodist Wesleyan Church was one of them. Out of Christian compassion, my father shared his vision and burden with Bishop Chang-Chuan Jiang that churches in China should be "Self-Governing, Self-Supporting and Self- Propagating" and financially independent from any Christian churches and missions from the West. Bishop Chang-Chuan Jiang, Bishop Hua-Qing Wang and my father often prayed together for revival in the missionary-planted churches and to regain the freedom of China as a nation from the Japanese occupation. The Lord gave them the Word, *"Strengthen ye the weak hands, and confirm the feeble knees. Say to them that are of a fearful heart, Be strong, fear not: behold, your God will come with vengeance, even God with a recompense; He will come and save you."* (Isaiah 35:3-4). Praise the Lord for the victory of World War II and from 1945 to 1949 we enjoyed the freedom and spiritual revival nationwide for four years.

In 1950, the TSPM "Chinese Christian Three-Self Patriotic Movement Association" a puppet tool of the Communists was founded. It intended to cut off the relationship of the churches in China from the Western missionaries, churches and Christian organizations. They advocated the principle of so-called "Self-Governing, Self-Supporting and Self-Propagating." Actually, the TSPM has been totally controlled and sustained by the Communists from the day it was founded. In 1955, the TSPM forced my father to hand over his ministries – "Chinese Christian Self-Governing, Self-Supporting, Self-Propagating Million Pound Foundation" and the newspaper called "Tianjin New Life Evening Post" to the Communists. My father's answer was, "I'm sorry, I can't do that, the owner is God and I have no right to give it to you!" Nevertheless, they took everything away and later put my father in jail.

After my father rejected the Communists, they confiscated everything including property, title and the facilities of my father's ministries. In 1955, my home church, Methodist Wesleyan Church in Tianjin, joined the Communist TSPM. The church became controlled by false brethren who bowed down to Baal. The Communists took over the leadership of the church. Pastors' sermons became political lectures praising the Communists. The adult and children Sunday schools became a flower shop. One pastor even said: "Jesus came for the poor; if He lived today he would be a Communist." They watered down and twisted Biblical truth.

This church used to have a congregation of 800 or more and had women fellowships, Bible studies, Sunday schools, prayer meetings and pastor visitations. But now they were all called to a halt. Many believers stopped coming because they were not properly fed. Some were too intimidated to come. The congregation dropped to around twenty people and most of them were seniors. I cried many times for my church where I grew up. Out of my Christian conscience, I went to the senior pastor face to face to defend the truth, asking him the following questions:

1. Our church had been the mother church and headquarters of the "Chinese Christian Three-Self Million-Pound Foundation (CCTSMF)." The principles of CCTSMF are "Love the Lord faithfully and evangelize the people extensively": The Lord is the Head, "Self-Governing" used to mean that Chinese Christians are governing and managing; but now it became the Communists and unbelievers who governed and led the church.

2. "Self-Supporting " used to mean that God's children paid tithes that provided the needs of the pastors and other church expenses; but, now it was the Communists paying pastors' salaries and becoming their boss.

3. "Self-Propagating" used to mean "Love the Lord faithfully and evangelize the people extensively", but, now the pastors did not evangelize and care for the people, nor share the gospel and visit the congregation anymore. The principles of the TSPM led by the Communists became quite different from those previous ones.

The Communist principles were, "Love the country, be patriotic and then love the church." "Pastor," I asked, "why you don't care about us anymore, don't you see that the Lord's sheep are scared, scattered and lost? You are supposed to be the shepherd!" ʹ

The pastors and the responsible persons of the TSPM led by Miss Jing-Juan Sun, (not related) a Communist, who was a secretary of my mother, were all present. But, nobody answered my questions. I left the office in tears. My questions about defending the truth and the principle of the church and true TSMF stating that the Lord is the Head of the Church offended the Communists and their false TSPM. Unknown to me then, my statement would become one of the accusations and reasons that the secret police arrested me a couple of years later.

After our church joined the TSPM led by the Communists, all the devoted Christians in our church began to be watched and even persecuted by the Communists. Mao Ze-Dong and the Communists initiated political drives not only in the societies but also inside the church through TSPM. Many of God's faithful servants became the targets of their accusations and denunciations. My father became one of the victims. He was arrested at the end of 1955 because of his faith in the Lord. Many pastors, some of them quite well known, bowed down to the Communists and began to praise them and betray the Lord. Our pastor Ching-Fen Liu even said, "Now I know I was deceived by the black book (the Bible), only the Communist Party is my parents." All the traitors later became leaders of the TSPM led by the Communists.

The Lord Himself Began the House Church Movement

Right after the beginning of the persecution, I began to turn my eyes upon the Lord Jesus. I read the Bible seriously and prayed fervently. Since my father's arrest, most of our church friends dared not visit us, although they used to come often. Only brother Ding-Zhe Lu and beloved sister Fu-Ran Zheng still visited us. We prayed and had fellowship together as we comforted each other. This became our essential need and helped to keep our faith in the Lord.

It was during the persecution that we began to suffer. We were led by the Lord to understand Biblical truth more profoundly. The Lord used persecution and tribulation to gather His sheep into small fellowships to preserve their faith on the foundation of His faithfulness. Those attending these secret fellowships were church members who had stopped attending the Communist-controlled TSPM churches. The house fellowships among family members and close friends started the house church movement in Tianjin and also in other cities as well as the countryside all over China. This goes on even now. This movement began right after the Communists initiated the persecution against Christians in the fall of 1955.

At the same time during 1953 to 1955, while I was studying in Beijing Medical College, I attended another Methodist Church in Beijing. There I saw the same betrayal of the Lord as they participated in the Communist-led TSPM. I stopped going to that church which was the sister church of my home church in Tianjin. Instead I attended Pastor Ming-Dao Wang's church. I loved Pastor Wang's bold preaching of God's truth. He ignored the Communist threat and refused to join the TSPM. Pastor Wang proclaimed that their church had always been indigenous and pursued the principle of "Three Selves-Self-Governing, Self-Supporting and Self-Propagating". Therefore, he insisted that his church did not need to participate in the communist-led TSPM.

His church was not a missionary-planted church, so he didn't need to cut off any relationships with the West. Pastor Wang believed: "The head of the church can only be Jesus Christ and the church can only be led by the Holy Spirit, not by any men or secular worldly organization." Pastor Wang's faithfulness to the Lord won the hearts of many believers in China. He became the Lord's trumpet and the Lord's flag waver in China for all time.

I had two intimate schoolmates in the Beijing Medical College, Miss Daisy Lee and Miss Martha Kang, both Christians. We studied together and stayed in the same dorm. Daisy Lee graduated from a missionary-planted Christian girls' school in Beijing and Martha Kang graduated from a missionary-planted Christian girls' school in Shanghai. Martha Kang was an orphan, rescued and brought up in an American missionary-planted orphanage in southern China. They both suffered persecution from the Communists for their faith, so we had the same suffering experience. We often hid ourselves somewhere for fellowship. We loved each other in Christ and spent a lot of memorable time together sharing sorrow, happiness and fun. I praise the Lord for our intimate friendship in Christ that has lasted almost half a century. At present, as they both also immigrated to the U.S., we often keep in touch.

During the tribulation time, especially after my father was put in jail, we had faithful friends. We also had false brethren who betrayed us to please the Communists. They loved the benefit from the Communists and the glory of man. My parents' closest friends, Mr. and Mrs. Bao-Lin Young and Dr. S.K. Kwan, often came to our house to comfort and care for us. There was a Mr. Liang, my brother's friend, who also joined our choir. He frequently came to our house for meals and fun. But he betrayed us. My parents supported him financially because he was a poor student. This man was very smart. I would never forget his furtive big eyes. He made the acquaintance of many close friends of my parents through contacts at our home.

Among our guests were a number of returned students from the U.S., well known medical doctors, musicians and professors. Many years later after my father and I were arrested and put on trial by the prosecutors, one of our crimes was that we had organized "a reactionary cultural club" at Dr. Kwan's and our home. We were shocked! When many of these past events happened, Mr. Liang was always present, so we knew that Liang must have been the reporter. He fabricated many accusations and related many untrue stories to please the police and betray us, to whom he should have been grateful.

While we were suffering, our friends found out that Liang was promoted in his teaching post from a teacher in an elementary school to be an assistant professor in an English department in a college. During the Communist crazy political drives, one after another especially from 1950s to 1970s, tremendous pressure twisted the hearts and deceived the minds of many Christians. Church friends like Liang and others were some of those. They quickly deserted the Lord, abandoned their faith and even betrayed us.

As I look back on my past easy and comfortable life, I see I was but an immature Christian with insufficient Biblical knowledge. I didn't understand that I should deny myself, bear my cross daily and follow Jesus. I just enjoyed the sweetness in the vineyard and did not recognize the foxes and wolves under the sheep clothes. It was the persecution and tribulation that taught me to grow spiritually.

Chapter 4

A Young Lady's Dream

Every girl has her own dream and I dreamed of becoming a successful woman, even better than my mom. I believed that if I could use all my talents and do my best with the help and blessing of God, I would accomplish my goal and wouldn't disappoint my mom.

God blessed my mother with the gift of giving. A great number of people from church and from the YWCA received financial support, help, comfort, counseling, intercession, love and encouragement from her. My mother owned a lot of precious jewelry, gold bars and valuable stock in big enterprises that were given to her by her wealthy parents, my grandparents. I often noticed my mother giving my older stepsister permission to select any jewelry she wanted to keep for herself.

During the eight-year Japanese occupation of China, my father was held under house arrest because he refused to cooperate with the Japanese. Since he had no job and no income, my mother often sold her jewelry willingly to help support our large family of nine children. In 1944, when the "Chinese Christian Three-Self Million Pound Foundation" was founded, my mother donated a great deal of her own money to help get it started. She saved the only blue-light diamond she had left for my oldest stepbrother and his bride as a wedding ring for them. Even my nanny, our baby-sitter, got gold and silver birthday presents on her birthday. But my mom did not think about or prepare any jewelry, property or money for her own four daughters' weddings and futures.

I dreamed that someday I could have all the money my mother had and help the poor and needy. What I didn't know was that I could help the poor even without money. I dreamed I would become a respectable professional woman with an admirable career, but I had never dreamed to be God's servant living by faith.

I Loved Beauty, Arts and Music

To be pretty and have pretty things is the natural desire of every woman. When I was young, I didn't look pretty. I had a flat nose and small eyes. My stepsister and brothers often humiliated me and made fun of me because of the ugly way I looked. I had to cry out, "I look like my daddy!" to make them stop. As a matter of fact, my father looked very handsome in his younger days. I enjoyed playing with my mother's jewelry box. I would put lots of things on my neck, ears, fingers and hair, heavily decorating myself to look prettier. But, when I looked at myself in the mirror, I was still very disappointed.

My father often gave big banquets at our home inviting many VIPs in political and business circles. One evening a grand party was being held and many ladies dressed up elegantly in evening gowns. I was eager to help my mother to be the hostess, so I searched my mother's drawers and found one of her best long black silk nightgowns with beautiful lace. I put it on and walked down from the stairway like a noble lady to join the party. Of course, I caused both tremendous laughter and applause from the distinguished guests. Judging people by their outward appearance beginning in my childhood brought me trouble as I grew up.

I loved drama very much. My younger sisters and I played together, and we particularly loved to play with paper dolls made by my own hands. I would draw all kinds of stage figures for our playtimes. Kings, queens, princes, princesses and beauties with their colorful costumes were the kind of paper dolls I would create and cut. We would perform all the ballets and classic dramas on our big dining table such as "Swan Lake", "Sleeping Beauty", "Snow White" and others. We accompanied them with classical drama music. We enjoyed ourselves very much. My home would actually become like an opera house. Of course, I was everything: I was the designer, the producer, the conductor of the play and the stage manager. Every year we added and renewed more beautiful things to our plays, which we stored in many big boxes. I kept these boxes at home even when I went to college because I still loved them. Sadly, the Red Guards burned them all when they ransacked our home during the so-called "Great Cultural Revolution."

Strongly influenced by my mother, who was a Western-style opera singer, I loved to play the piano and sing songs, especially hymns and sacred and classic music, even Chinese Peking opera. There were a lot of opportunities for me to give performances at the YWCA, so I dreamed I would be a soprano soloist. If the audience gave me an enthusiastic "bravo" or "encore" after singing at the children's concerts, I would start singing again and bow again, non-stop until someone carried me down.

When I was studying and boarding at the Christian Keen Girls' School, many of my schoolmates attended Sunday school at our church. Every night in the dorm, while we lay on our beds, we would sing lullabies, hymns and masterpieces of classic music together before we went to sleep. After I was old enough, I joined the church choir and became the leading soprano. But all my dreams were shattered, and my Lord allowed it to happen, because I didn't have the desire to glorify only His name. I desired to have praise and glory from man for myself. Many years later I served Him as a broken vessel. After I was released from jail, He knew my heart had changed. He could use the gifts He had granted me to serve and to sing for Him and to glorify His name only.

My Ten Requirements for Dating

To love and be loved are beautiful dreams everyone possesses. And of course, it was a dream of mine. I didn't want to be a stepmother. I didn't have the great sacrificial love that my mother had. I had ten requirements for anybody who wanted to date me and I followed them closely:

1. He should be intellectual and I should admire him as a learned man. He should not be a medical doctor. Based on my experience, medical doctors are easily tempted by female nurses and patients.

2. We ought to have the same family upbringing; otherwise, we could not have a common language within our home.

3. I cannot live joyfully without classical music, so he should be able to at least comprehend music.

4. His height should be at least 1.7 meter or 5 feet 9 inches, because among the Chinese women, I am a tall woman and I like to wear high-heeled shoes.

5. He should be manly, courageous and responsible, not a coward or a sissy.

6. He should have a gentle and caring temperament and know how to give love to me, because I grew up in a loving and harmonious family and church.

7. Economically, he should have ample income, because I honor my parents and would like to support them even after I am married. Otherwise, we would have quarrels because of finance.

8. I would like to see my husband honor my parents as I would honor his and be a good daughter- in-law.

9. I would be afraid to marry a man with a big family because it would be hard for me to please all the in-laws.

10. I would never marry a man who was divorced.

All these showed that I was very picky, arrogant, proud and prejudiced. On the other hand, I totally forgot the most important requirement: that he should be a committed and mature Christian.

In my church several good Christian young men expressed the desire to date me seriously, but I refused all of them whom I thought did not meet my requirements. This was not because I became prettier. I was young and in my prime. Besides, all the church people said, "Chang's girls are all charming and decent, they are well-educated and well-brought-up and serve the Lord devotedly." And the church people especially spoiled me, which encouraged me to be even more arrogant.

My mom had a rule that no matter who was chasing after us, the daughters, we had to bring our boy friends home to know our family members and vice versa. Mother didn't want us to date rashly nor act first and report to parents afterwards. Actually, I had so much fun with my family, good friends, schoolmates, in church and at school that I felt dearly loved by many people. I didn't really need a boy friend.

Soon dreadful storms of political drives in China broke the tranquility of my private life. In 1959 my two younger sisters enrolled in colleges and left home. My stepsister and brothers had been married for quite some time. They left home long before and were now afraid of political accusations because of my father's arrest. They gradually came less and less and soon they stopped visiting us altogether. After my father was put in jail, I had to work to support my mom and three younger sisters. I was expelled by the Beijing Medical College for defending my innocent father and came back home in Tianjin. I had to take miscellaneous part-time jobs to bring bread home for our living.

My father suffered from heart disease in jail and was about to die, so he was released after thirteen months arrest. He was then put under house arrest and forced to do penal manual labor under surveillance by the masses of neighbors. After doing the forced labor daily, my dad had no energy to write confessions and reports to the local authority regularly, so I had to write for him. We prayed often together and had sweet fellowship. However, I still felt lonely for the first time and nobody could help me. A few other brothers and sisters in Christ also suffered from the attacks and accusations in the political drives. They lost their freedom, so they too were unable to communicate or visit us. Martha Kang was put in jail just because she was an orphan raised in an American missionary-planted orphanage and refused to malign the American missionaries as spies. At that time my mother had a stroke and was partially paralyzed. I felt heavily burdened and often cried out to the Lord that the cross was too heavy for me to bear.

The Engagement that Displeased God

During the time of loneliness and pressure, a young engineer appeared and chased after me ardently and we dated. He met almost all my requirements, but he was not a Christian. He loved me and showed deep compassion and sympathy for me as well as my family. His father, who had owned a big pharmaceutical factory in our city, committed suicide during the political drives earlier. He really took good care of me and said often, "Making you happy and contented is all my desire."

After a year, being with him became a refuge for me to get away temporarily and forget all my troubles. Despite my parents' protests about our relationship, I was comforted by his total loyalty and tender love to me. I tried my best to share Jesus with him but his answer was always, "I would believe and get blessing because of you after we are married. Don't force me, let me believe Jesus on my own will." I hoped that he could be saved before we got married. I was struggling in confusion just like playing a symphony with several notes missing.

Out of my Christian conscience, finally I told him frankly that I did not want to displease my parents and that my marriage would not be blessed by them or God. I told him that I would not contact him anymore and I knew that he could find some other girl to suit him better. I felt so relieved after I made this decision. But, how could I have known that this man would try to commit suicide three days after I rejected him? His mother begged me to save her eldest son by accepting his proposal. This widow put all her hope into her eldest son. I was in a very fierce spiritual struggle. I was still a carnal Christian and so I found many excuses to persuade my mom to approve of our engagement and I intended purposely to ignore God's principle about Christian marriage, *"Be ye not unequally yoked together with unbelievers;"* (2 Corinthians 6:14). I used, *"Believe on the Lord Jesus Christ, and thou shall be saved, and thy house."* (Acts 16:31) wrongly seeking the Lord to permit me to proceed. We were engaged later and set the wedding date for October 1, 1960. During the period of time that we were dating, in the depth of my heart I had been hesitating, struggling and having doubts, but I tried to convince myself to believe what he said many times, that he would accept Jesus Christ as his Savior after we were married.

However, God's power, mercy and grace again and again did not abandon me and His will wonderfully worked on me to fulfill His plan. On July 9, 1960, three months before our wedding date, two Communist secret policemen in plain clothing came to my working unit and took me to a secret place to question me. From that day on I was detained and disappeared from the community and I lost my freedom for twenty years. When my fiancé learned that I was arrested he quickly broke off his relationship with me. He was scared to death that he would be jeopardized by my case that could bring him trouble. This was the end of my engagement that God disapproved of and my worldly dream was shattered and finished. Many years later I was told that this man became a Communist. Oh, my Lord, I want to praise and thank you for your interference to hinder my own will to marry him.

Chapter 5

Father Jailed in Disgrace

The sound of heavy knocking on the door of our house woke my mother up in the middle of the night on December 20, 1955 right before Christmas. Half a dozen policemen with guns intruded into our house shouting: "David Chang you are under arrest for being a counter-revolutionary!" They didn't show us any warrant. Three of them just pulled my dad from the bed, handcuffed him and dragged him to the police car. All this happened in about ten minutes. My mom ran to my dad to give him a padded cotton jacket because he was wearing only pajamas. But, since both of his hands were already handcuffed, he was unable to put it on. In a bitter cold winter night my dad disappeared into the heavy snow and the darkness. Due to fright, worry, agony and hurt cutting into mom's heart, she was partially paralyzed the next day.

After my father was taken away, my mother and three younger sisters were all forced to stay in our sitting room and they were forbidden to move around. When they had to use the bathroom, they had to leave the door open. The police began to search our whole house intensively until dawn. Even our cotton quilts were cut open and searched. The police took away all my father's handwritten manuscripts of books and articles, letters and old pictures. When they left they charged my father with being a counter-revolutionary, a tool working for the U.S. Imperialists and Nationalists in Taiwan committing crimes against the government and the Communists.

When the police first questioned my mother, she couldn't speak a word, her lower jaw crooked and her mouth slobbered incessantly. They didn't realize that she had a stroke. So, they turned to my younger sisters. The police said that the dependents and family members of counter-revolutionaries should stand on the side of the government to report all of David Chang's wrong doings and crimes and thus win the trust of the government. My younger sisters were trembling to death but the oldest among them, Margaret, still had boldness to defend my father. "I respect my father very much and he is an honest man!" I praise the Lord for her courage in front of the evil ones, since she was only seventeen years old. She later told me all this with a painful and pale face. When this incident happened I wasn't at home because I was studying in Beijing Medical College. I felt guilty that I couldn't be at home to be their companion to comfort them, especially my sick mother.

Two days after my father's arrest, the Communist secretary at the Beijing Medical College called me to the office to question me. A man with a long, cold face said, "Your father is a counter-revolutionary, you ought to break away from him and be loyal to the government and the Communist Party. You have to report against your father the best you can to prove this." He never looked me in the eyes.

My heart was tight and my head was numb and heavy, but I defended my father right away: "Your accusation of my father is not true. My father is a committed Christian. He was also a patriot when the Japanese invaded and occupied China for eight years. My father refused to serve the Japanese and was under house arrest. He has kept his faith and is loyal to the Lord and to our nation. He has never joined any political party nor done anything wrong against the government. I believe his case must be wrong. Somebody may have maligned him on purpose. I will wait for the results of the government investigation."

The iron face of that official turned green and he said: "Go back to your dorm and think it over. If you change your attitude, we will allow you to go back to your class. Otherwise, you will have to drop your schooling."

Nationwide Persecutions Spread to Protestant and Catholic Christians

Before my father was arrested, the Communists had already initiated the persecution against the Catholic Christians, loyal to the Vatican. The true Protestant Christians and evangelical Protestant churches, always non-resistant and peaceful were also persecuted. The Communists maligned the Catholics as spies and lackeys of the Vatican and Protestant Christians as spies and puppy dogs of American and Western imperialists. Pastor Ming-Dao Wang, Watchman Nee and Catholic Bishop Ping-Mei Gong, and a number of others who refused to bow down to the Communists, were all arrested. They were charged as "counter-revolutionary cliques."

A widespread political drive of persecuting Christians quickly followed. In Beijing Medical College, strong Christian Bible study fellowships and prayer meetings, planted and led by young devoted Christians from Pastor Ming-Dao Wang's church, had existed long on campus. After Pastor Wang was arrested, all the Christian fellowships and meetings were forced to stop. The Communists watched every Christian closely and separated them to brain-wash them individually. The authorities pressed them hard "to draw a line between themselves and counter-revolutionary Ming-Dao Wang" which meant to deny him and give up their Christian faith.

Many weak carnal Christians denied the Lord Jesus and maligned the Western missionaries as imperialists, invaders, or spies right before my own eyes. They falsely testified against other believers to the government and exaggerated the facts for their own security and benefit during those repeated non-stop crazy political movements.

I also personally witnessed a small number of strong Christians standing firm for the Lord and for Biblical truth in a mass meeting. A violent and disorderly crowd of thousands shouted at them with unrestrained hatred. The police cars were waiting there. The Christians knew that if they denied their faith they could go home, but, if they proclaimed the name of the Lord and stood up for Jesus, they would be imprisoned right away.

The Communists even mobilized one brother's wife and child to come to the front to persuade him to denounce publicly the Lord for the family's sake and practice his faith secretly at home. This brother held his head up to control his tears and kept silent. These courageous brothers moved to the right side of the stage and signed their names on a statement that they would neither deny the name of the Lord Jesus nor malign God's faithful servants. Those who denied Jesus moved to the left side and were cheered by the crowd.

I was an open Christian and everybody knew that. I was scared, so I stood behind those courageous brothers. At that moment of faith testing, "Oh, Lord, please help me!" was the cry of my heart. The atmosphere of the angry rioters was scary. Finally, at the end of this mass meeting these faithful brothers were all arrested and taken to the police cars, and I was the only one left on the stage. The authorities treated me differently because my mother church, the Methodist Wesleyan Church in Tianjin had joined TSPM. As I was one of the church members, they did not arrest me right away. But, they separated me from my classmates, stopped my classes and questioned me day and night hoping to force me to testify falsely against God's faithful servants. But I refused to cooperate. Worse accusations and severe persecutions were yet to come.

Enjoying Intimacy with the Lord

After I was put in isolation by the authorities of Beijing Medical College, one evening I received a letter from my sister Margaret. It read, "Daddy was arrested and mom had a stroke and couldn't eat or drink. Are you coming home?" When I learned this news I couldn't stand it anymore. I ran out to find Daisy Li and Martha Kang, my best friends whom I hadn't seen for days.

Fortunately, I found Daisy in the girls' washroom. My family news shocked her and she asked me with eyes filled with fear and confusion, "What will you do next?" Her hands were full of soap bubbles and her body was shaking.

"I have to go home right away to take care of my mom and younger sisters," I answered. "I know if I apply to the college authority asking for leave, they would reject me and I have no time to lose!"

Daisy gave me two yuans (Chinese money), all she had in her pocket. She said, "I'll go with you to the bus station."

I ran back to the dorm and quickly picked up my belongings. As everybody was still in the classrooms, nobody was there to see me. We left the campus and rushed to the bus station. It took me two hours on the bus from the suburb of Beijing to arrive the railway station in downtown area. It was too late for me to catch the last train heading for Tianjin, my hometown, and the next available train wouldn't be until early the next morning. In the bitter cold winter night I shivered in the big empty hall for passengers waiting for trains. Huddling on the hard bench I prayed, "Lord, help me, please take me home!"

I took the first train to Tianjin early the next morning and finally got home. Because of the stroke, my mom's jaw was twisted to the left and her face was deformed, so she could not properly eat and drink. Her right arm and hand could not move so she was struggling with a spoon and tried hard to use her left hand to put food into her twisted mouth. The food always dropped. My three younger sisters were still in school and they also had a hard time with the school authorities, especially since they defended our father by saying, "We respect our father!" Their lives became miserable and fearful too.

Our house, having been ransacked by the police, was in a big mess. But, nobody was in the mood to clean it and put things back to order. All of a sudden I realized that all the burden of the family fell on me, and I had to take up all the responsibilities. First, I had to care for my mother and three younger sisters financially, because all of my older stepsiblings had already married and had families of their own to support. Besides, because of the political pressure and fear, they broke the family relationships with our parents and dared not come home to visit us.

I wrote a formal letter to the Communist authority of Beijing Medical College apologizing for my sudden leave without their permission. I explained that my mother was seriously ill and could not survive without my help. However, Daisy wrote me a letter saying: "Don't come back to the college, the authorities spread bad rumors about you and they are going to expel you because you escaped with serious problems that you didn't confess."

One month later, I received a formal letter from the Communist authority of Beijing Medical College. Instead of accusing me as a counter-revolutionary, they wrote: "Because you had too many absences from classes, we have decided to stop your enrolment, effective immediately." So, my dream of being a medical doctor was smashed and my happy, easy and naïve college life as a student with Daisy and Martha abruptly ended.

There was no income and no money at home. Because of my father's political status of being a counter-revolutionary, there was neither hope nor help for me to get a job. My Aunt Vera Nieh supported my mom generously for her medical bills but her gift wasn't enough to support a family of five. I cried every night after mom was sound asleep and prayed, "Dear Lord, You tell us that to honor parents is the only commandment with promise in the Ten Commandments, but now I am only a drop-out undergraduate medical student. Who could hire me and offer me a job? I have to support my mom and three younger sisters, and I don't want them to drop out of their schools. Dear Lord, what shall I do? Please give me a job so I can support the whole family and please comfort my dad, your faithful servant and protect him from brutal torture, coldness and starving. Please heal my mom." I prayed in tears. But I knew my Lord was listening because He gave me peace.

The next morning, I saw my mom staring at the sky through the window and her left hand was slowly mopping the window, which was clean and shiny enough. I knew what was on her mind. I slowly approached her and said, "Mom, I am your first daughter and I have already grown up. I will do my best to help you and Margaret, Betty and Grace because I love you all. Regard me as your son, maybe even better than a son, I want to support the family and take up all the responsibilities. Mom, take heart, I mean it!"

My Lord answered my prayers very soon and He opened a side door for us. My parents' close old friend Mr. Bao-Ling Yang and choir member Brother Ding-Zhe Lu visited us fearlessly and insisted on helping us financially. They kindly brought us everything we needed. They respected and loved my father very much, and they knew the real reason of his arrest. My mom was recovering from her stroke and she felt better everyday. Despite the promise I made to my mom, I still needed a job and was waiting. I prayed to the Lord every night and He comforted me with an old song, "His eye is on the sparrow and I know He watches me." It was the first time in my young life that I felt I was a sparrow and He was watching, caring and touching me. During the hard times and under such difficult circumstances, I could feel the Lord so close to me. I could still sing often since we still lived in a large three-story house by ourselves. We enjoyed the privacy and convenience. So we sang all the beautiful old hymns and folk songs: "I know that my redeemer lives....", "Our father which art in heaven..." My mom murmured the songs and accompanied me with her twisted lips.

Praise the Lord for Daisy Li. The Lord used her to find a job opportunity suitable for me. Daisy knew there was a "governess wanted" job at the Indonesian ambassador's home in Beijing. They offered U.S.

$50.00 for monthly wage and I would be the one taking care of house phone messages, the home expenses account book and four naughty, undisciplined Indonesian kids. Since mom's health was recovering rapidly and there was no other choice of work, I went to Beijing for the interview. Praise the Lord, by His grace I got the job.

Chapter 6

Chinese Church History Blurred

Why didn't the Communists arrest my father right after they took over the power of mainland China in 1949? Because before 1955 the Communists were busy in land reform, suppressing and killing the landlords, crushing and putting to death those Nationalists who were loyal to Chiang Kai-Shek, the president of the Republic of China. Fighting the U.S. in the Korean War and confiscating capitalist properties in China took much energy. After the cease-fire of the Korean War in 1954, Mao Ze-Dong and the Communists began to launch crazy political drives, one after another suppressing other social groups which they thought could be a threat to their rule and power. The persecution of Catholic and Protestant Christians and churches began from 1950 and worsened after 1953. The victims were God's servants and believers who would neither bow down before the Communists nor betray Jesus.

My father, David Hsiao-Chuan Chang, was born again while he was studying at Hui-Wen High School in Beijing, a school founded by the missionaries of an American Methodist church. From 1922 to 1932 when he studied in Japan, France and the U.S. pursuing his degrees at Michigan

University and DePaul University, he had been devotedly serving the Lord, involving himself in church activities. During this period of time he kept writing spiritual diaries in a total of twenty-four big notebooks. He was so hungry and thirsty for God's Word that he recorded all his learning through the Bible and his personal meditation with inspiration from the Lord.

After he returned to China, he became a high-ranking official in the Nationalist government under Chiang Kai-Shek's rule. He was appointed to several high positions: Judge of the Municipal Court of Qingao, President of the Financial Bureau, President of the Commerical Produce Bureau. At the same time he was still devotedly serving the Lord in his mother church – the Methodist Wesleyan Church in Tianjin. Whenever the church had any needs in finance or personnel matters he was the one ready to donate, to help and to offer.

The years from 1928, when the Chinese Nationalists headed by Chiang Kai-Shek made Nanjing the national capital, through 1937 when the Japanese invaded were a period that China saw the first wave of Christian revival among indigenous churches in China. In 1807 Robert Morrison came to China, translated the Bible into Chinese and began mission work. China Inland Mission founded by Hudson Taylor followed, as well as many missionaries of different denominations from the west such as Methodist, Presbyterian, Episcopal and Baptist. They planted quite a number of churches, schools, hospitals and charities throughout China.

After the Boxer Rebellion in 1900, the western missionary-planted churches began to emphasize indigenous mission movements and encouraged Chinese Christians to become involved in spreading the gospel and church planting. Quite a number of God's faithful servants emerged in China during the period from 1928 to 1937, such as Pastors Ming-Dao Wang, Shao-Tang Yang in the north and John Sung and Watchman Nee in the south. They were devotedly committed to pioneering, evangelizing, church-planting, discipleship training and other mission work. Many Chinese indigenous churches were planted, while thousands of Chinese came to the Lord.

During this period of time, the Methodist Wesleyan Church in Tianjin was very active in evangelism. My father helped the pastors, bishops and deacons to organize many evangelistic meetings and activities such as retreat conferences and crusades, Youth for Christ, prayer meetings, etc. The Lord added new converts to the church daily. Our church used to have one service on Sunday with a congregation of around 800. But so many streams of people kept coming to the church that they had to keep adding pews and chairs. Very often people had to sit on the windowsills. Western missionaries witnessed the soul harvest, saying that for generations they sowed in tears and now they reaped the fruits with songs of joy. They also beheld the growth and maturity of Chinese indigenous churches and the faithfulness of God's Chinese servants. Praise the Lord for the revival!

Indigenous House Churches Emerged

The Japanese Fascist military invaded China in 1937 and an all out war broke out. In those eight years of flames of war and brutal, savage and inhuman rule, the Japanese slaughtered over thirty million innocent Chinese people including women and children. Some were buried alive and beheaded and the land of China occupied by the Japanese was sacked in bloody suppression until 1945 when the Japanese surrendered. During this period Chinese churches went through a severe trial of water and fire.

Especially after the Pearl Harbor incident on December 7, 1941, the Japanese occupied the concessions of my hometown, Tianjin City, where westerners lived and missionary-planted churches were located. They closed down all the western missionary-planted churches and put all the westerners and western missionaries into concentration camps. Some were expelled and deported from China later. All the support of my church from the West was cut off. Chinese indigenous churches in the villages and cities still continued their worship services despite all of the pressure they were under. They stood firm in their faith and looked to Jesus.

My father saw the tremendous hardships of the pastors of all the churches due to the unstable situation and the shortage of provisions. Some pastors had to work for a living by selling hot tea and food at the stalls by the roadside. Many believers and families escaped from the Japanese occupied areas and fled to southwest China where the Chinese Nationalists initiated and led the anti-Japanese war. So the number of the church congregation was reduced and ministries and activities shrank. My father prayed everyday, sometimes with bishops and pastors, asking God, "Return our homeland from the Japanese occupation and grant us a great Christian revival of the church!" God enlightened my father to read the Book of Acts. After Jesus was resurrected and ascended to heaven, the believers of the New Testament churches were scattered and met in homes and in secret places. They prayed in faith and broke bread with one accord. They praised and thanked the Lord with joy and singleness of heart. God blessed them abundantly. My father received the vision from God that, "We can do the same!"

Very soon believers began to gather at our home. At first they came to pray on weekends and then quickly Sunday worships, Bible studies and communions were also frequently held at our house. The Japanese were afraid of American bombing at nights so they strictly ordered all civilians to shade the windows with heavy curtains and dim their lights in houses when evening came. Any light that leaked out from the house would attract Japanese military police and bring upon them big trouble.

The Japanese tried to control churches by asking all the churches to register to their puppet Christian organization and they also had many tough restrictions for meetings. Therefore, all the Christian gatherings in our house were in darkness, praying in low voices and everyone was very alert to the circumstances. They even alternated the dates for gathering. But people needed Jesus so they jammed in every corner of our house and brought some food to help my mom to serve them. All our cups and bowls were used for guests. As a kid, I was interested and busy and enjoyed helping my mom to serve the congregation. My mom had to do a lot of cleanup afterwards, including the mess I made.

Quantity Decreased but Quality Increased

The situation was getting worse as the persecution intensified and hardships increased. But under tribulation believers felt the touch of the Holy Spirit and they prayed fervently serving the Lord zealously. Christian growth was slow in number, but their faith grew stronger, their love for the Lord deeper, and their spiritual lives became more mature. Praise to the Lord, right under the nose of the brutal Japanese, a considerable number of Chinese indigenous house churches of good spiritual quality emerged from western missionary-planted churches without the presence and help of any western missionaries under very special tribulations and trials!

During the same period the Lord enlightened my father with Colossians 1:27 *"To whom God would make known what is the riches of the glory of this mystery among the Gentiles; which is Christ in you, the hope of glory."* Many years ago American Methodist missionaries planted our Methodist Wesleyan Church of Tianjin. The activities, services, fellowships, celebrations, music, hymns, customs of the church, almost everything to run a church were copies of the Methodist mother church in the U.S., following western culture in a high class way. No wonder the ordinary Chinese, especially the poor and uneducated people saw us as semi-westerners. They despised us as pseudo or half-foreigners who forgot our Chinese ancestors and abandoned our traditional culture to believe in a foreign God.

"Oh, Lord, My God" my father cried out, "I don't think so. Thank you, dear Lord, for giving me a special childhood. You sent a Taoist to teach me the Chinese language and the original pictures, structures and meanings of many Chinese characters. Oh, Lord, it is now probably the right time to study, 'The relationship between Chinese characters and the Bible'. I believe that the make-up and the structure of the Chinese characters reveal the stories, events and history told by the Bible." My father walked back and forth in his study murmuring prayers. Sometimes he would sit me on his lap and cry out, "I know what I have found! It is the time to do it!"

I still remember when my father studied some antiques made out of rock and discovered the structures of the numbers of "one, two, three, four, five, six, seven." in Chinese written in the style that exactly fit in "God's six days of creation and on the seventh day He rested" which were revealed in Genesis Chapter One. My dad clapped his hands and jumped up from his chair laughing and shouting out: "Oh, Lord God, YOU ARE WONDERFUL!" He was so excited.

My father also shed light on almost all the Chinese characters that are composed of the pictograph of a "lamb" depicting the meaning of "blessing". "The lamb from God is a blessing!" Especially the Chinese character of "righteousness" is written as "Lamb cover me" in pictorial structure. My father's eyes beamed with joy and he kept saying: "Oh, Lord, YOU ARE AWESOME!" He looked at me, despite the fact that I was too young to comprehend his discovery or share his insight. I was the only listener and student in his presence at that moment of his discovery.

As I was my father's tail and rarely out of his presence, he taught and showed me a lot. The marks, strokes, structures and pictures on those pieces of rock became Chinese characters and those characters reveal God's message, stories and events in the Old and New Testaments. Several years later, one of my father's closest friends, Professor Yu-Ru Wu, joined in his study to find out the original meaning of Chinese characters. Prof. Wu was an expert in Chinese literature and linguistics and the head of the department of Chinese literature and linguistics of Jinggu (Tianjin) University in Tianjin at that time. He came to our house almost every evening and helped my father finish a book entitled "The Chinese Characters and the Bible".

My sisters and I learned Chinese linguistics from Prof. Wu for three and four years. We admired his wealth of learning and knowledge of the Chinese written language and enjoyed his vivid and interesting teaching. Prof. Wu was also encouraged by our thirsty and hungry attitude to learn Chinese literature, language and linguistics so he did his utmost to teach us wholeheartedly. Unfortunately, my father's book was totally burned by the Red Guards in 1966 during Mao Ze-Dong's Cultural Revolution. Not even a single page was left. Thank God, some of my father's writings and Prof. Wu's teaching are deeply imprinted on my mind that I can still rack my brain and recall it.

Chinese Christian Three-Selves Ministries Started in Western Missionary-Planted Chinese Churches in North China

My father was so on fire for the Lord that not only did he keep doing research on the Chinese characters, but he also would put it into practice to serve the Lord and show God's love to the Chinese in the Chinese indigenous way. He invited a Chinese calligrapher, Dr. Lei-Chuan Wu to begin hand-copying the Chinese Bible with brush-stroke Chinese characters. Dr. Wu completed a few books of the New Testament before he passed away. Pastor Zhen Wang was his successor.

During that time, a publishing group of the Bible in Chinese calligraphy was organized and it was widely known that Bishop Chang-Chuan Jiang, Mr. Xiao-Chuan Chang (my father) and Dr. Lei-Chuan Wu had partnered together to start the Lord's ministries. Since their first name all carried the character "Chuan" which means "river" in Chinese, they were well known as "Three Rivers have joined to flow the Living Water of Jesus Christ into Chinese people's hearts". I remember my father often said: "Buddhism entered China from India, but no Buddhist monks have ever asked support from India. Why can't Chinese churches and Christians survive and operate without American missionaries and U.S. dollars?"

As the Holy Spirit urged and the Chinese churches cried out for the need loud and clear, my father shared his vision and burden with bishops, pastors and Christians in 1943. He maintained that we Chinese churches and believers should advocate, practice and follow the indigenous principle to love the Lord, be faithful and widely evangelize for Christ. That is Biblical and was practiced among the churches during the New Testament age. As no support, aid or funds came from any western mission or church at that time, my father and other Christian leaders consulted with each other repeatedly. Finally, they decided to build up a "Chinese Christian Self-Governing, Self-Supporting and Self-Propagating Million Pounds Foundation". They called all the Chinese churches, whether Chinese indigenous churches or western missionary-planted churches, to unite on the basis of Jesus Christ. Taking Biblical truth with one Lord, one Spirit and one faith, to stand up for Jesus, spread the gospel and evangelize people through extremely difficult times was the call, despite the Japanese fascist, brutal occupation.

This calling like a huge trumpet to wake up the believers echoed widely and the Foundation received unbelievably warm responses from all the pastors and relevant churches crossing all denominations. So the ministries of Chinese Christian Self-Governing, Self-Supporting, and Self-Propagating Million Pound Foundation started secretly and the office was set up right in our house until 1945. After the Japanese surrendered and the Chinese and the allies celebrated the victory of World War II, the office of the Foundation was moved to our Methodist Wesleyan Church and a big sign board of the Foundation was hung at the front gate of our church.

During all these difficult years from 1943 onward through 1954, even after the Communists came to power, many pastors, ministers, and indigenous missionaries of the churches all over north China were greatly supported by this Foundation. Dr. Rong-Fang Liu was among the members of the board of trustees and Bishop Chang-Chuan Jiang was the chairman. They were in charge of the spiritual leadership with many teachings, trainings and church planting evangelism. From 1945 through 1950, a spiritual revival of Chinese indigenous churches and missions spread over China, which was the second wave similar to the Christian revival of indigenous churches and missions that spread over east China back in the 1930s through the1940s.

The first big donation given to this Foundation came from my mother, Miriam Nieh. She sold all her jewelry, including her wedding ring. Praise the Lord for giving my father a devoted, godly and gifted wife who came from a wealthy family. She was willing to sacrifice again to give back every possession she had to the Lord and help my father to fulfill his dream and start the indigenous evangelism and church-planting by the Chinese ourselves.

The Lord also gave my mother the gift of creativity. She encouraged the church congregations and YWCA people to offer the best of their ability to develop financial resources for the Foundation. The YWCA started a "hand crafting, sewing, and tailoring class". Sisters in Christ contributed their talents to make embroidered cushions, purses, shoes, tablecloths, pillow cases, dolls and other decorations to sell in charity sales to raise support for the Foundation. Some brothers in Christ had the skill to make Chinese snacks and all kinds of goodies such as egg rolls, dumplings, sugarcoated sweets and other things to sell. Every three months my mother arranged a big charity sale for fund-raising. Sometimes she invited musicians to give charity concerts to support the ministries. In a variety of ways, funds flowed into the Foundation to support the native churches, pastors, preachers and God's servants who were in poverty. I remember how happy I was, busy and excited during those charity sales and concerts while I served customers and guests as a young volunteer.

At the same time, we organized retreat conferences, revival crusades, evangelistic meetings, seminars of Bible teachings and Christian women's conferences! All of these activities educated and encouraged Chinese believers that God widely opened their spiritual eyes and led them to know that, *"Three-Selves principles and ministries are really God's will!"* The foundation and center of the "Chinese Christian Indigenous Three-Selves Evangelistic Movement" are and will always be to exalt and glorify Jesus Christ. Jesus is the only Head and the Lord of the church and the goal is to spread the gospel and win lost souls for Jesus.

After the Japanese surrendered in 1945, western missionaries came back to China right away. All western missionary-planted churches recovered and the financial situation improved. New western missionaries were sent and came to China and funds and support from western mother churches flowed back. Thus, the "Chinese Christian Indigenous Three-Selves Evangelistic Movement" that started in the darkest hour and most difficult time during Japanese occupation was facing new challenges.

Chinese Christians and churches should stand up and grow up and mature. However, a bunch of so-called "Christians" such as the general secretary of the YMCA in Tianjin, Mr. Xiao-Pang Yang and other pastors who were all very liberal and actually "non-believers" admired and gave warm welcome to U.S. dollars. They did their best to flatter westerners and tried to control the YMCA. They operated the YMCA as a social club to entertain and serve the rich with many secular activities instead of spreading the gospel to the poor and helping the needy. As for the YWCA, my mother was still the president of the Board of Trustees and she resisted all the challenges and temptations to keep the YWCA loyal as the Lord's instrument.

The Birth of "Tianjin New Life Evening Post"

The revival of the Chinese Christian indigenous evangelistic movement continued. It started in 1943, despite different denominations coming back with the western missionaries when they returned to China in 1945. All the charity sales and activities stopped but the Chinese Christian Self-Supporting, Self-Governing and Self-Propagating Million Pounds Foundation kept on operating well. Their priorities turned more toward indigenous churches, ministries and Christian workers in small cities and in the countryside in North China.

The Lord touched my father's heart by the story told in Matthew 25:14-30, *"Well done, thou good and faithful servant."* God gave him the vision that we should start some profitable business to support those native churches and pastors. We should not only use our mouths to spread the gospel but also pens to propagate the Good News of the Lord Jesus. He asked the Lord to help him start a Christian newspaper with a special "Christian Forum" for the readers. The Lord blessed him and answered really quickly and far greater than his dream.

The "Tianjin New Life Evening Post" (TNLEP) was founded in 1945. It consisted of three pages of fast and updated news amply provided every evening. A Christian Forum covered one whole page with solid good sermons, Biblical teachings, touching testimonies, and guides to lead a Christian life. Miracles happened as the answers from the Lord to my parents' and other believers' prayers and support produced needed things.

From the beginning the Lord provided for building facilities, machines, printing costs, hiring reporters, editors and personnel for the newspaper.

First, God provided a big vacant building right on Roosevelt Road in the downtown area and my father leased it for a cheap rent. After the war, the Japanese left a huge number of collapsed air-raid shelters dug for civilians to hide in when U.S. B-29s bombed the Japanese military facilities in our city. Rubble, trash and filthy water were everywhere causing widespread environmental pollution. My father was inspired and got the idea to clean up all the shelters and collect the bricks and useful material to build a print shop for the newspaper. He got permission from the municipal authority to clean up the whole city and would get all the bricks and other useful materials free as a part of the deal. A great number of believers responded and immediately went into action. All the participants received two meals a day and a little pocket money. Several months later, a print shop and some other facilities were ready for the "Tianjin New Life Evening Post."

The "Tianjin New Life Evening Post" gained in popularity daily and it was warmly welcome by the citizens of Tianjin City. The newspapers were published and sent to the hands of eager readers at four o' clock every afternoon. Because it was daily, fast, true, attractive and with updated news, it won many readers. Its sales volume even prevailed over the two well-known morning newspapers of the city and the income of TNLEP kept increasing. Periodically TNLEP donated a large amount of funds to the Million Pounds Foundation, which kept the Foundation operating well. The Gospel was widely spread through "Christian Forum" daily.

Starting in 1945 the annual conferences of the Foundation were held in its headquarters at the Tianjin Methodist Wesleyan Church. I remember every year there was a grand opening and closing ceremony for the Foundation annual conferences that included great concerts. Well-known vocalists, singers, pianists, orchestras, conductors, and our choir all performed together sacred operas such as "The Messiah", "Creation" and "Elijah" and Chinese traditional classic music. The Methodist Wesleyan Church became the gospel music center in Tianjin and some choir members went on to become famous vocalists.

The number of subscribers to the "Tianjin New Life Evening Post" increased tremendously, so delivery of the newspaper to the subscribers became a problem. God gave my father a creative mind to start a delivery team of high school students. He called on and encouraged high schools kids who had needs for living and tuition to come and help after school. Each one received quite good pay and a free bicycle for delivering the newspaper.

Unfortunately, due to the traditional consideration of losing-face, not even poor students would show up to help at first. So my father persuaded my two elder brothers who were in high school to be first to take the job as leaders and organizers to head up a big crowd of delivery boys. Another problem was the boys who were selling the newspapers on the streets were composed of hundreds of poor kids who had poor upbringing and the bad habits of street boys. Many of them were uneducated or homeless and some of them didn't even have names. Every afternoon in front of the newspaper building when they were waiting for the newspaper to be ready for them to sell on the streets, they fought, smoked, gambled and made noise and huge messes. When my father noticed this situation he prayed for a solution to provide some help and education for these poor newspaper seller kids. God answered his prayers.

Right behind the TNLEP office building, there was a small church. My father rented their Sunday school area to use as a classroom. He invited several teachers to teach Chinese, English, mathematics and sports. My parents were the first two to join and help teaching. Lunch, uniforms, stationery and other daily use articles were provided. They called it the "News Boys' School." Every day these boys had to come and attend four classes from one to three-thirty in the afternoon. They also had to learn good manners and behave well. Each day when the class began, my father would ask these kids three questions to encourage them and the kids enthusiastically shouted loudly the answers.

> Q: *What was the first job that American President Hoover had when he was a boy?*
> A: *Newspaper boy!*
> Q: *Whom does God love the most?*
> A: *God so loved the world, especially me!*
> Q: *Whom do you praise and give thanks to?*
> A: *Praise and thanks be to God!*

Not very much time passed before the manners and attitude of these newspaper boys completely changed. My father had given them a priceless gift. They gained their dignity. When they lined up in front of the newspaper building, each dressed in TNLEP uniform vest and carrying a bag, they looked like students patiently waiting for the papers to be distributed. They were reading, singing and laughing. When they were selling the newspaper they were yelling loudly, "Tianjin New Life Evening Post, update news. Have a look!" Their voices became pleasant and polite, attracting a lot of buyers on the streets.

Sometimes after they learned some hymns from the church, many of them would sing; "This is my Father's world" and other sacred songs, forming a choir on the street!

My father saw himself as the "humble little donkey colt that carried Jesus into Jerusalem". He didn't want any title or position, and invited Bishop Chang-Chuan Jiang to be the chairman of the Chinese Christian Self-Supporting, Self-Governing and Self-Propagating Million Pounds Foundation. He just prayed that the Foundation and TNLEP dedicated as God's instrument would glorify Jesus' name and His kingdom. Then the Chinese Christians and churches could grow and be mature to the measure of the fullness of Christ by being Self-Governing, Self-Supporting and Self-Propagating.

This Foundation in Tianjin operated continually until 1954, even after the Communists took over China in 1949. Since the Korean War broke out in 1950, the Chinese Communists cut off all the relationships with the United States. Ties were severed between the Chinese churches of all denominations and their mother churches or missions in the west, especially in the U.S. They appointed Mr. Yao-Zong Wu to start a Communist puppet organization. This was called the "Chinese Christian Self-Governing, Self-Supporting and Self-Propagating Patriotic Movement Association." It was to take over the leadership of all the churches and their activities in China.

Mr. Wu, an extreme liberal and a non-believer, was affiliated with the Lingnan church, a Cantonese church in Shanghai. In his book he claimed that he disbelieved Jesus was born of the Virgin Mary. He denied Jesus' resurrection and His second coming. He continued saying all he believes in the Bible is the teaching of Jesus Christ from Matthew Chapter 5 to 7. Mr. Wu also advocated that the accomplishment of Communism is the realization of paradise on earth. He welcomed the Communists to China to fulfill the task.

Under the direct order of Chinese Communist Premier En-Lai Zhou, Mr. Wu stole the name of the Christian "Three-Selves" from many indigenous

Chinese churches. They had practiced and followed the principle of "Three-Selves" for decades from my father's "Chinese Christian Indigenous Self-Governing, Self-Supporting and Self-Propagating Evangelistic Movement." It started during the Japanese occupation of China in World War II. Mr. Wu and a whole bunch of phony "Christian leaders" in China founded an organization of so-called "Chinese Christian Three-Selves Patriotic Movement Association" (TSPM).

First, it was not a Christian organization but a clumsy political tool. Added to its name in 1950 during the Korean War was, "To Resist the U.S. Aggression and Aid Korea." Later, it was changed to "Patriotic" in 1954. This does not mean love your mother country, but love and be loyal to the Communists! Second, it was totally controlled by Communist theological ideology both pastorally and administratively. Third, it was completely supported and fed by the Communists from the first day it was established. Fourth, no evangelism, gospel outreach or church planting was allowed.

The Chinese Communists were smart enough not to close and burn down the churches in China in one day, like Lenin and Stalin stupidly did in Soviet Russia. Mao Ze-Dong and En-Lai Zhou fabricated their "Three-Selves" to deceive Chinese Christians. Their aim was also to deceive the naïve foreign believers by taking over the leadership and totally controlling churches in China. This amounted to a "window fashion show" to the West. The Communists became the head and the lord of the church, replacing our Lord Jesus Christ. The Communists strongly believed that Christianity and other religions as well would gradually die out in the face of the progress of socialism carried out in China and other Communist countries. Their utopian thought was that when the old religious and superstitious people died, all their beliefs and religious faith would be buried with them. Fifty years later, to the surprise of the Communists, God still exists. Christianity in China survives and grows tremendously while Communism is dying and on the way out.

In early 1950s TSPM began to demand that all the Catholic and Protestant churches participate in TSPM and submit to the communist leadership. All the churches had to hand over their properties and authorities to TSPM. In 1955, the Communists confiscated the Chinese Christian Self-Supporting, Self-Governing and Self-Propagating Million Pound Foundation. They forced my father to hand over the leadership of "Tianjin New Life Evening Post." My father replied, "I don't have the authority to hand it over. This newspaper belongs to the Lord Jesus."

He also refused to join the Communist "Three-Self" puppet organization. He proclaimed, "We have long been 'Three-Selves'; your slogan is 'be patriotic, love your country, love the church'. But, our principle and goal is "Love the Lord, Be Faithful to Him and Spread the Gospel!" So the Communists put my father in jail. My father was in and out of jail for twenty-four years from 1955 through 1979.

Nevertheless, a great number of so-called "Christian leaders" quickly and flatteringly bowed their knees to Baal, among them many bishops and pastors of churches planted by western missionaries. Bishop Chang-Chuan Jiang, the original chairman of the "Chinese Christian Self-Supporting, Self-Governing and Self-Propagating Million Pounds Foundation" right away handed over his authority of leadership to Mr. Yao-Zong Wu. He was the chairman of TSPM. My father was forsaken.

Before the Communists came the secretaries of YMCA in Tianjin such as Mr. Xiao-Peng Yang. They strived for and coveted U.S. dollars from missionaries and churches from the West. They strongly opposed the churches in China being indigenous and following the "Three-Selves" principles. After the Communists took over power in China, they changed their loyalty overnight to their new lords. They begged the Communists for their survival and benefits. Not for thirty pieces of silver but for millions of dollars, they sold Jesus Christ, His churches, their brothers and sisters in Christ in China and their own pitiful souls. This power for evil is characteristic of antichrists that come and go swiftly on the stage of human history.

II. Molding and Shaping

12. *I dreamed of being a vocalist (3 pictures, same captions)*

13. *A young girl with arrogant eyesight*

14. *Taken in 1959 just before I was arrested*

15. *Love in the violent storm*

16. *The next day after our wedding we went to the "Fragrant Hill" to pray*

17. *God blessed us with twin boys, Daniel on the left and Joseph on the right; Joseph, his Chinese name means the morning star in the darkness and Daniel, his Chinese name, the joy in the tribulation for us (2 pictures, same captions)*

18. *Our family picture, Joseph on the right and Daniel on the left*

19. *Mama, where is papa, we want papa!*

20. *On May 1, 1974, a family reunion every two months for us, Freddie was secretly arrested after this reunion*

12

13

14

15

16

17

18

19

20

21. We were waiting for Freddie's release

22. After our rehabilitation, our whole family went to Shanghai to see grandpa and we also met Freddie's uncle (2 pictures, same captions)

23. Before I was leaving for the U.S. our whole family stood in front of the "Temple to Pray for Good Harvest" at the Temple of Heaven Park

24. After rehabilitation we three intimate schoolmates of Beijing Medical College had a happy reunion

25. My passport picture when I was 48 years old

26. Mom's five daughters with mom before I left for the U.S.

27. Before I left for the U.S., I visited the cemetery, where my father's cremated ashes were placed to say goodbye to him

28. Mom, we miss you!

29. Mom, don't worry, Lord Jesus is taking care of us!

30. Father and two sons staying in Beijing

21

22

23

24

25

26

27

28

29

30

Chapter 7

A Servant is Not Greater

The aunt of my good friend, Daisy Li, worked with the Indian embassy in Beijing. She learned that the Indonesian embassy in Beijing needed a governess. She must be someone who knew English so as to be a receptionist for phone calls. She also had to take care of four children. At that time I had no other offer or choice, so I went to Beijing for an interview. I was hired as a "live-in" governess to take care of four unruly children. Given free accommodations, I was paid monthly fifty U.S. dollars.

Lord, Why are You So Hard on Me?

The Indonesian embassy was located in the eastern part of Beijing city. The building was a former royal court of a prince in the Qing dynasty. It was Chinese style outside and renovated into western style inside. The compound was divided into two parts. In the front was the office area of the embassy, and in the rear was the residence of the ambassador and his family. Despite their having other servants to do the cooking, cleaning and other housekeeping, my responsibilities were heavy. According to the expectations of the ambassador and his wife, I had to answer telephone calls in their house and take care of four young children, ages seven, five, three and one and a half years of age. I had to feed the baby, give piano lessons and supervise their homework.

Almost every day the ambassador and his wife had many social activities outside the house and often they entertained many guests at home. Sometimes Mrs. Ambassador had to attend several parties and banquets in one day and I had to help her get dressed. I was inexperienced in this kind of housework; yet I didn't feel it was too big a deal for me at first. After awhile problems came one after another and I was in trouble. Mainly, it was the children. I quickly found out that these Indonesian children were much naughtier than the Chinese kids I knew. They didn't behave well at all. They had never been trained to have good habits or manners nor did they care to listen to my instructions. The young maid, just fourteen years old, whom they had brought along with them from Indonesia, knew no English. The Indonesian maid was supposed to help take care of the children also, making sure they had their meals. She failed. It was why they needed to hire me. The house was in a great mess.

I was required to eat and stay with the four kids. At mealtime the servants would send the food to the kids' dining room and the maid and I would make sure they ate the meals. At first, I instructed them in table manners according to what I learned in my family since my early childhood. But none of them understood, paid attention or seemed to care. At the table, the two older girls often had fights. They would throw bowls of soup or pieces of butter at each other.

The third child was a boy who was rather timid but naughty as well. Whenever he was frightened he cried out aloud. The only thing that the Indonesian maid could do was to shout and scold. Even the youngest baby who had to be fed rebelled either by throwing food on the floor or putting his bowl upside down on his head. They were all constantly shouting and made huge messes on the table and the floor at mealtime. I was at my wit's end. There was no peace during meals and I felt uneasy at every meal.

The four children had different schedules for going to bed and napping. Before sleeping, the three older kids always had pillow fights. The accompanying shouting and yelling usually woke the baby, who had just fallen asleep. Then the baby would begin to cry. In the daytime, the older kids might run, fall and hurt themselves when they played outside in the garden or the youngest one crawled away and sneaked near the pond to try to catch goldfish. Day and night I was with these problem kids who left me exhausted and nervous. I had to play with them, watch and care for them while protecting them from any accident that could harm them. In the meantime I had to be ready always to help Mrs. Ambassador dress. She was sometimes impatient and scanned me with a long face.

Although the Indonesian ambassador and his wife were polite to me, I could clearly sense that they were strongly influenced by the Indonesian ideology of status differences between classes, ranks and race. I was only a governess, not one of them, even though I was educated as they were. I did my best to teach, educate and discipline the children to behave better, but often I failed.

The kids were extremely spoiled, especially by Mr. Ambassador. Whenever he was at home, the kids were even worse behaved and disobedient beyond my tolerance. Every night after everyone was asleep, I cried out to God, "My Lord, why did You put me here, in such a tough spot, to be embarrassed and disgraced? Even in the novel, Jane Eyre, the orphan girl was teaching and taking care of only one little girl in a wealthy mansion. But You gave me four undisciplined and restless monkeys!" I had never before taken such a tough job of house duties or dealt with such naughty kids.

When I was young, we had four servants, attendants and cooks plus two maids. Now I was on the opposite side of the fence. I had to serve four little lords! I was a governess, but this spelled out that I was only a servant of a higher rank. "Oh, Lord, I can't stand any more! I feel bitter and humiliated, please, would You take me out of this and give me some other job!"

I wanted to escape from this circumstance because I thought I could not handle it any longer, especially when I saw the faces of my bosses becoming longer and more ugly. At that time a monthly salary of fifty U.S. dollars was a large amount of money and a great help to my family, so I had to obey and tolerate it. I was so childish that I unreasonably argued with God during my prayers at night. God did not answer me directly, but I heard a small voice reminding me through verses that:

> "The disciple is not above his master, nor the servant above his lord." (Matthew 10: 24);

71

"I can do all things through Christ who strengthens me." (Philippians 4: 13);

"My grace is sufficient for thee." (2 Corinthians 12: 9)

Oh, Lord, let me try to do better for several days to see what would happen!

The Door Opens for the Obedient

Indonesians believe in Islam, so I was unable to share Jesus with the children. But, I modified a few of the hymns I learned from my childhood and taught them to sing. I also told them stories from the Old Testament. The oldest daughter was the most naughty and the leading troublemaker, so I taught her and her younger sister piano and dancing. I taught the three-year-old boy to play games with me to keep him busy, and let the Indonesian maid hold the baby. So, my policy was, "Divide them and rule or separate them and treat each differently," and it really worked. Sometimes, I taught them to play dramas and ballets. I dressed and made them up for roles on the stage such as "Sleeping Beauty", "Swan Lake," and "Nut Cracker." The girls wanted to be pretty and loved to be made up, so I did my best to decorate them. I taught them how to have the manner and appearance of the ladies in the royal palace who behave elegantly.

I also recalled that when I was young I played a lot with my sisters by drawing all kinds of noble figures of princes and princesses on paper and then cut them into paper dolls. I produced a whole drama or ballet and instructed the children each to hold some of these paper dolls to play their parts as if they were really playing on the stage. The children loved this and concentrated their minds and attention on these plays. Sometimes, I took them out to the garden to play games to use up their energy. Gradually, I realized that all the kids began to love me. They called me "Auntie Dorothy" as I required and they did so politely. The three-year-old boy pronounced it "Dendi Dordi!" while the baby called me "Dor, dor, dor!" Whenever I become obedient and submissive, the Lord opens the door and paves the way for me.

After a period of time I began to have fun with the kids. We pretended to attend grand parties and magnificent banquets where we would meet many distinguished guests. Of course, in the play, they had to behave well since they themselves were dressed up. Acting like some kind of prince and princess required a dignified manner and noble attitude in a royal palace. Soon I moved the playing and acting to the dining table where the children had real food and meals. They totally changed and behaved so well sitting at the table that even their parents, especially Mr. Ambassador, were astonished. It was novel to see their children sitting quietly and speaking respectfully at mealtimes. He was also very pleased to see that his children could draw a marvelous series of pictures telling a whole children's story. The children finally had a regular schedule of a normal life and I could catch my breath!

I now had more time and energy to take care of Mrs. Ambassador's dressing and jewelry matching. When she went out for parties and banquets, she would win the admiration, applause and popularity in her social circle. Both Mr. and Mrs. Ambassador were pleased at how I was handling the job, so, they raised my monthly salary from fifty to eighty dollars. Praise the Lord, my income totally provided the urgent needs of my family of six members.

I recalled how generous and kind my mother was toward the servants, maids and attendants who served our family at home. It wasn't until I became a servant myself during the beginning of my spiritual pilgrimage that I learned my first series of lessons of obedience, humility, endurance and patience. Serving anyone should be just like serving the Lord. I began to realize my Lord's amazing grace, ample provision and abundant blessing in my heart. This was preparation for the trials to come. Eighteen months later, the Lord provided me another job in Tianjin and finally I went back home.

Chapter 8

Twenty Years in Prison and Hard Labor Camps

In 1960, one of my father's close friends, Mr. Bao-Ling Yang, was suddenly arrested even though he was seriously ill. He was accused as an "American spy" and a "counter-revolutionary" because his children all lived in the United States. Mrs. Yang was scared to death and struggled with sleepless nights. Our whole family cherished Mr. and Mrs. Yang's friendship and their concern and help to us in those days when my father was put into jail. My mother, since she could hardly walk, urged me to visit and help Mrs. Yang. Almost every evening I went to the Yang's household to comfort Mrs. Yang and keep her company. I hadn't the slightest idea that Yang's house was being closely watched by secret police. Before long, they followed me too.

In the morning of July 9, 1960, two men dressed in neat Mao' suits showed up in the clinic where I was working at that time. They came for me and said, "We need to talk to you about something. It will take about one to two hours. Please come with us to the office, and we will send you back when we finish." I wasn't alert or suspicious of them, so I followed them to a black car and then the car was heading toward the downtown of Tianjin

City. Finally the car stopped in front of a villa with a big yard. The two men led me to the sitting room to wait and they left.

It was a normal furnished residential sitting room and I waited for about two hours. Nobody showed up. I walked around the room and saw that there was a military guard at the front door of the room. I asked him where the two men who brought me here were, but the guard without any expression on his face just ordered me to wait.

I began to sense that something was wrong. I looked through the windows and saw that surrounding this big house and the yard were high walls. Several cars were parked there and occasionally some military men came and went. I kept nervously looking at my watch. I was as restless as ants on a hot pan. Around five or six o'clock in the afternoon, when someone gave me some food for supper, I asked again where the men who brought me here were and, "What am I waiting for?" I still got no answer.

I had an ominous premonition but didn't have a clue about the disaster to come. I sat alone nervously until eleven o'clock that night. Finally, three men walked into the sitting room. Besides the two men who brought me to this big house there was another short, thin man. They didn't introduce themselves, or tell me to what organizations they belonged. Under the dim light I had a chance to look at them. One of them with a long horse face full of pimples paced back and forth in the room and the fat guy was a chain smoker. He sat on the sofa with the short thin man, who never lifted his eyes to look at me.

I began to ask them questions: "You said you want to talk to me and I have waited for eight to nine hours. It is getting late. Can we continue our talk tomorrow? What is this all about? What kind of organization is this place anyway?"

The fat man answered, "This is an organization of proletarian dictatorship. As for other things you need not to know."

I said, "An organization of proletarian dictatorship is used to suppress enemies, but I am only an ordinary citizen and also a government employee. I have never offended any law. Why do you detain me here?"

The guy with a long horse face answered in a cynical tone, "You have to correct your attitude. Without evidence the proletarian organ does not carelessly bring people here to question them."

"Very well," I said, "Go ahead and question me!"

So, they began to question me one after another like an automatic gun firing, such as: "When your father David Xiao-Chuan Chang was on parole because of his illness, he was under surveillance by the masses. Tell us whom did he contact? Whom did you communicate secretly as your father instigated you? What information did you pass over to these people? What is the relationship between your father and counter-revolutionary Bao-Lin Yang? What counter-revolutionary activities are they involved in? We, the government authority, have investigated and know about your father Xiao-Chuan Chang's counter-revolutionary guilt. You have to make a clean breast of your involvement in all the crimes. We know you well and that you have viciously attacked "Chinese Christian Three-Selves Patriotic Movement". You must confess to us within 72 hours. Then we might treat you with leniency. Otherwise, you will be sorry...."

The shorter thin guy suddenly spoke out slowly in a mystic tone, "You are still very young and you were raised under the red flag. You are only brainwashed and poisoned by the U.S. imperialists and influenced by your father. He is a counter-revolutionary opposing the government. You could change. The government authority believes that you are able to make a clear line of demarcation from them and draw close to the Communists and the people. Our party's policy always is, 'Expose and denounce the counter-revolutionary. You will not be found guilty if you report and inform on them to the government. This will prove further your innocence and even gain merits.' Think it over carefully, as it is your future. Otherwise, the consequence will be...."

When I heard what they said, I felt I was being treated unjustly and wrongly and became very angry. My heart agonized and my head was dizzy and my scalp was numb. I defended myself and my father right away: "First, what do you mean by U.S. imperialists, who are they? During my childhood, my parents only received American missionaries at our home, and what they did was only to share the gospel with us. My parents had no dealing with any other Americans. Besides, those American missionaries left China a long time ago. Second, you accuse my father of being a counter-revolutionary. If he is, why did the Communists and the government appoint him as the deputy of the First Tianjin Municipal People's Congress a couple of years ago? Third, you say that I viciously attack 'Chinese Christian Three-Selves Patriotic Movement', but these allegations are not only false but also are aimed at my father's integrity. You are trying to malign him and fabricate a charge to bring him down!"

I suddenly realized those traitors in our church, who had been the opponents of my father for long had reported everything including my private words and deeds to the Communists. Then I boldly made a statement about my father's integrity, "My father David Xiao-Chuan Chang came from an extremely poor and destitute family. He fought his own way to success. When he went overseas to study in the United States, France and Japan, he worked part-time for his schooling. During the eight long years of Japanese occupation of China, our whole family was under pressure, but my father would not betray his mother country to work with the Japanese to gain power and prosperity. He kept his national confidence and self-respect."

I continued, "Before the Japanese came, even though my father had many high-ranking jobs and positions, he did not join any political party and remained clean-handed and uncorrupted. When he was in the position of the director of Tianjin Municipal Bureau of Finance, he exempted 239 taxes. This offended corrupt officials of the Nationalists and he was brought down from his position. After the Japanese surrendered and World War II ended, my father remained a professional, running a newspaper by himself that was recognized by the government. He is also the true founder of 'Chinese Self-Supporting, Self-Governing and Self-Propagating Christian Million Pounds Foundation' and a persistent true advocate who practiced the principles of "Chinese Christian Self-Governing, Self-Supporting and Self-Propagating Movement" in northern China. How could he oppose 'Three-Selves?'"

Gaining momentum, I went on, "As for me, after our Methodist Wesleyan Church joined the government-sponsored "Chinese Christian Three-Selves Patriotic Movement", I still attended church services. How could I be opposed to the 'Chinese Christian Three-Selves Patriotic Movement'? I fully respect my father because he keeps his national integrity and would not compromise with any forces of darkness. He advocated the independence of Chinese churches from western missionaries, refusing to rely on U.S. dollars. He has followed the principles of Self-Governing, Self-Supporting and Self-Propagating to plant and run churches. If you think he is wrong in his political behavior or stand, then why was 'Tianjin New Life Evening Post', allowed to resume publication under its original title in 1949 after the liberation of Tianjin? This was founded and then still being run and directed by my father, approved by our government. At present, my father suffers from heart failure but he is still forced to do hard physical labor in the neighborhood for seven to eight hours a day, and when he gets home he can barely breathe. Even the doctors dare not say how long he will live. How could he be involved in any counter-revolutionary activity? Since his arrest and now on parole due to being seriously sick, I have never heard him complain about the government to anybody. As a devoted Christian, he has faith in God's righteousness and the justice of the government toward his case."

My passionate speech and questions fired back at them like a machine gun. This overshadowed their questioning which greatly infuriated them. They talked to each other in a low voice for a few moments and then the short, thin guy declared, "You are under detention. You will be responsible for what you said and your future will depend on your attitude toward the party and the government."

"You can't do this!" I cried out. "You have to notify my parents. They don't know where I am!" But, the three secret police ignored my request, just walked out and left. The military guard at the front door pointed his gun at me and ordered me to follow him. I had no choice but to obey him. The blood in my head flowed swiftly to my feet and a huge vacuum was left there. I was terribly confused and upset. In front of me was nothing but darkness. "Oh, Lord, deliver me from evil!" I was thinking of my aged parents, as they would be worried to death if I suddenly disappeared. Nobody could rescue me nor could anyone care for or help my parents.

The guard used his gun to direct me as we left the sitting room. The guard led me to the basement and we passed a narrow stairway from another door and came down to a very long and dark concrete corridor. There was no light in the ceiling, the floor was concrete and dim lights came out on the floor from both sides. I couldn't see or hear anything clearly. I hesitated a moment but the guard pushed me immediately and shouted, "Move!"

When I adjusted my sight to the darkness, I realized there were many doors with big iron locks, one next to the other along both sides of the corridor. After a long walk following the soldier, he finally stopped in front of one iron door and spoke through an opening on the door: "New prisoner arrives. Her number is '917.' Check her through."

The soldier unlocked the door and pushed me in. The door slammed closed behind me and inside the cell was only one dim lamp on the floor.

There were also three female inmates. One was standing and the other two were lying on the floor and did not even bother to move or notice me. I totally lost my freedom, disappeared from the community and departed from the world suddenly. My parents didn't know where I was and I couldn't even keep my name. All I had was an inmate number "917."

I was rudely and thoroughly body-searched by one of the female prisoners from hair to toes and my hairpins, shoelaces, necklace, watch, handbag and other belongings were all confiscated and thrust out through the small opening in the door to the guard. This inmate ordered me to lie down. I suddenly realized this was a small square room and none of us had a bed. They were lying on some kind of thin mattresses. I had no quilt nor sheet and mattress. Near the door there was a bucket for us to urinate.

The concrete cement floor was cold and damp and my heart and body felt the same. I sat down in a corner of the cell, and kept a distance from the inmates, whose faces were pale as ghosts. I was frightened, homesick, trembling and I didn't know what to pray. Facing this unexpected incident and terrible circumstance, my lips were dry, tears fell and even my heart was crying. From the bottom of my heart I could only cry out, "Lord, where are You? Lord, save me please!" This was the first night that I was in prison and the beginning of a special period of twenty years. I lost not only my freedom, but nearly everything else during this time. I suffered from many brutal persecutions and tortures.

However, praise the Lord, during my tremendous fear, He gave me hymns that I learned from my childhood to comfort me, *"I pray my Lord to take over the helm to sail on the bitter sea and high waves. Great surges attack me, and many hidden reefs bring calamities. But, my Lord has the compass and the sea chart and He guides me through. I pray my Lord to take over the helm."* I sang this song repeatedly from the bottom of my heart and a verse of Psalm 23 sparked out, *"Yea, though I walk through the valley of the shadow of death, I will fear no evil: for thou art with me ..."* The verse kept echoing in my heart. But, my heart still cried out, "Lord, this valley of the shadow of death is so scary. Lord, please rescue me!"

Chapter 9

First Vision Revealed

In the cell there was a strong moldy smell and the concrete cement floor was cold and wet. My heart kept crying out to the Lord, "Why, why me? My father is so devoted and committed to You and loves You, yet he suffers and has been humiliated. Today the tribulations fall on me. Those who give up their faith and even betray and criticize Christianity seem to walk a smooth path. Wicked ones face no bad luck, but God, we who believe and trust in You end up in such dreadful and pitiful circumstances. It's not fair!" I couldn't sleep and my eyes were wide open staring at the wall in front of me. It was totally dark and I could see nothing that gave me any hope for my future. My watch had been taken away so I didn't know what time it was.

A Shining Picture Suddenly Appeared on the Wall

Suddenly, a shining picture appeared on the wall in front of me, like a scene in a movie flashes on the screen. It was like an oil painting that hung on the wall of my father's study. In the picture the Lord Jesus knelt down in front of a big piece of rock in the garden of Gethsemane to pray to God and a great light from heaven shone on His face. Behind Him was only a deep dark forest. Around Jesus' feet, His disciples were lying sound asleep. But, this scene wasn't a still picture. It moved like characters acting in a movie. The Lord Jesus was talking to His Father God, *"Oh, my Father, if it be possible, let this cup pass from me: nevertheless not as I will, but as thou wilt."*

This vision totally grabbed my attention and answered immediately and directly my cries and questions, "Why is it me?"

The Lord Jesus said to my heart, "Child, I could have freely asked my heavenly Father to change His plan and give me an easier and more bearable way to save sinful souls, to save you, not being crucified on the cross, but I didn't. I just obeyed and relied completely on Him. When I was in desperate solitude, I was alone and nobody was with me, neither to pray with me. Now, at least, you have me abiding with you." His intimate touch was something I had never before felt.

The vision of this vivid scene remained there for quite awhile. The Lord Jesus appeared alive in the picture. But I continued arguing with the Lord, "I am too young to tolerate all this, I am only a girl. How can I walk through all this just as You did? I am only a baby Christian spiritually."

I saw Jesus' lips moving and it seemed that He was praying or trying to speak to me. I couldn't hear clearly, but His word kept reminding me, "Don't forget, I am with you!" Some moments later the vision disappeared. I was still crying, but I had never experienced that the Lord was my companion and I was His companion in the dark and how close we were! Then my heart became warm and peaceful and I fell asleep.

The next morning a sharp siren screamed. I was awake immediately. I could see light shining through a tiny window on the upper left corner of the wall, but I couldn't tell what was outside. My three cellmates quickly started removing the wooden boards they used as beds in the night. No one paid any attention to me. Then I heard someone opening the iron locks for each cell. When the sound came to our door, the small window on the door was opened, and the prison guard yelled, "Latrine time!"

The cellmate who frisked me took us three to the restroom at the end of the hallway. As we walked, I took a closer look at my cellmates. The one who had frisked me looked like a worker, but I couldn't tell about the other two. One of them was No.150. She had silvery white hair, and looked very peaceful. I asked her, "Can I ask the guard when I can go home?"

She said, "Write a note and pass it through the small window on the door."

After I returned from the restroom, my cell looked totally different. There were three sewing machines, scissors, needles, threads, cloth, and police uniforms. The guard ordered the head of the female cell, "Close shop at five o' clock and don't forget to check the work. The paper and pen are for the new convict No. 917. She has to make a full confession within the seventy-two hours." Then the door closed again. The other three sat down at their sewing machines and started working. They seemed very skillful. Later I heard the chain on the door being pulled. It was mealtime. All the meals came in from the small window. Breakfast was rice gruel, steamed corn bread and salted pickles. I couldn't eat anything and didn't want to. The others started eating as they worked. No one talked.

The one who frisked me said to me, "If you want to go home, you have to confess."

I curled up in the corner close to the older one. The white haired cellmate whispered in my ear, "If you want to leave this place alive, you have to eat." I could tell that she was concerned about me, which made me feel close to her. I held the pen, but I didn't know what to write.

I was reminded of the Lord's word, *"Do not fight with your flesh."* So, instead I started to write to confess my attitude was not proper to the authority, etc.

Out of curiosity, I wrote a note to the silver hair cellmate, "Why are you here?" She whispered, "Catholic nun." And then put my note in her mouth. Immediately I felt as if I had met a member of my family.

The Lord was right. He was really lonelier than I was. He had put a nun, No. 150 with me. Although I thought of my parents every minute, I had a nun who was nice to me, and my loneliness diminished a lot. I wrote on a tiny strip of paper, "I am a Christian." After I showed it to her, I put it into my mouth too. Later I found out that I was in a preferential working cell and we were to make police uniforms everyday. They could use scissors, needles, thread and cloth. They had to finish the quota every day and close shop at 5:00 p.m. We had three meals a day and after 5:00 p.m. we had to sit still and read political books and newspapers.

I Could Not Hold Back My Anger

Despite all the suffering I endured in prison, each time we were released to go to the toilet and washroom, which were huge, I felt some kind of relief. While the head of our cell was washing and water was flushing, I would quickly move closer to the nun and we washed our faces, combed our hair and used the toilet together. If other cellmates weren't paying attention, we would recite the Lord's Prayer simultaneously in a very low voice: *"Our Father which art in heaven, Hallowed be Thy name."* However, we were unable to say more because we had to part quickly to avoid suspicion.

Sometimes the nun shook my hand softly, which became a sweet way, and the only way, of fellowship between believers. Under that kind of persecution, the wall or separation between Protestant and Catholic Christians was all removed. When we said, *"Our Father which art in heaven,"* just that one phrase, we felt that our lives and spirits were so close and we belonged to the same Heavenly Father.

About a week later, the police called me for another interrogation, since I had not written anything to expose what they called the "counter-revolutionary crimes" of my father or Bao-Ling Yang. As the interrogator who was both big and tall looked at me with a murderous look, the spotlight was aiming straight at me so brightly that my eyes could not open. He said, "You confess nothing and your attitude is arrogant and dishonest. Don't you want to be released?"

I answered, "Of course I want to be released right away, but my father and Bao-Lin Yang are not counter-revolutionaries. They are only returned students from the U.S. and they are Christians."

"What did they talk about when they met?" the interrogator asked.

"I don't remember. Uncle Yang loves to tell jokes." I replied.

This man took a stack of paper and threw it in front of me shouting, "See, these are tons of accusations of their crimes reported by the masses. Read them carefully. If you think they are true, sign your name and we will release you immediately. This is a way out of here for you granted by the party and the people. If you don't behave well and refuse to sign your name, we will have to punish you severely."

I took the papers and look them over. They were well printed and there were over ten items of accusations listed.

"No. 1) When David Chang was the judge of the court in Qingdao, the provincial capital of Shandong province, he brutally killed countless innocent

people;

No. 2) During the period when David Chang studied in the United States, he collaborated with American special agencies and reactionary religious organizations and has served them ever since;

No. 3) David Chang was conniving with the Nationalist (Kuo Ming Tang) and Chiang Kai-Shek Regime over a long period of time, oppressing and exploiting the people;

No. 4) From 1945 to 1949, David Chang collaborated with the Relief Bureau of the United Nations;

No. 5) As founder of the Tianjin New Life Evening Post, David Chang took advantage of the cultural activities, the media and publications acting as the mouthpiece of the Nationalists."

The accusations went on to say that when my father was the general manager of the "New Life Post" newspaper in Taipei, Taiwan, he founded the "Tianjin New Life Evening Post" in Tianjin to echo the reactionary Taiwan regime. That my father used the "Tianjin New Life Evening Post" to propagate religious superstition to poison the people and he closely colluded with hidden counter-revolutionaries in the communities and viciously attacked the "Chinese Christian Three-Selves Patriotic Movement" supported by the Chinese government. That he publicly opposed the people and looked upon them as enemies, and on and on.

I could not keep reading. I was so furious that they had made up these lies about my father. Despite the Lord's reminding me in a small voice that I shouldn't fight back by my own passion of flesh and blood, I failed and could not control my anger. Facing a killer-like interrogator, I looked at his eyes and was courageous enough to defend my father. I spoke up and argued once again. "I don't know where and from whom you got these so-called 'reports', but they are all false! I am very clear that somebody with ulterior motives attempted to malign my father and deceive the government." Of course, I knew from the beginning that whoever produced this did so on purpose. "This report is totally fictitious, lies and without any grounds. The government may continue to investigate, but right now I can not sign my name to agree!"

The interrogator was so furious that he struck the table in anger and shouted, "You alienate yourself from the people. You will behave someday!"

Two weeks later, a police guard called my number: "No. 917, get out!" The nun, No.150 used her gentle eyes to encourage me and say "goodbye." I left the cell thinking the police were going to release me and send me home. But they didn't. They transferred me to some other place. The police gave me a piece of paper on which was written: *"Dorothy Chang is an ideological reactionary and is sent to the camp of education through hard labor for one and a half years."*

I was taken to a car. I asked them, "Where are you taking me?"

"You don't need to know!" was the reply. So, they drove the car out of the city of Tianjin for quite a few hours to the suburbs. Finally, we reached our destination and entered a huge courtyard with a big red gate surrounded by high walls. After I got out of the car, I noticed that the name was "Liqizhuang" where I was put into custody in "Tianjin Municipal Hard Labor Educational Camp."

The police gave me two cloth wrapped packages with sheets, blankets and clothing that were sent by my family. I learned that the police had informed my parents and they knew something bad had happened to me. But they didn't know what caused it, or where I was. My head began to hurt and I felt numb. I knew now I was not allowed to go home.

The huge door of the red gate was shut behind me and I became a prisoner of conscience in a hard labor camp. What would the future be for me? What would be my destiny and fate? I could not predict and nobody would tell me. During this period of one and a half years how would my parents and my three younger sisters survive? Who was going to support and take care of them? I felt lost in the darkness.

Chapter 10

Hard Labor Educational Camp

The tall man with a long horse-like face who interrogated me led me into the Hard Labor Educational Camp with high walls and a big red gate. The camp is in the suburb of Tianjin about two hours driving distance from the city. Outside the camp there are rice fields and some village huts. The interrogator left after the police of the camp went through all the procedures of receiving me.

Another policeman came out from the office and shouted loudly in the yard, "Receive new one!" A short, fat woman ran out from one of the red brick dormitories in rows. She reported to the police and they exchanged a few remarks. I noticed the woman had a big hair bob at the back of her head, her teeth were all gold capped and her face was ugly and ferocious, similar to a hag described in a novel. When she talked to the police her face was so obsequious and obedient, that it made me sick and shocked. Would this woman be in charge of and discipline me?

This witch with gold teeth stared at me and said, "Follow me!" I followed her mutely and we passed a long courtyard and went into another courtyard with a huge single-story dormitory separated by high walls. That was the jail for female prisoners. Inside the house it was very noisy with a foul and filthy atmosphere. Many women were smoking. Some were humming local Chinese opera melodies and ditties. Others were quarrelling.

The atmosphere and circumstances were entirely different from the detention house that imprisoned special agents of enemy and "counter-revolutionaries" in the city. It was in the middle of a very hot summer and many female prisoners wore shorts and vests and had a flippant attitude. As soon as I stepped into the room, they immediately surrounded me, talking to me in the typical Tianjin slang of villains and wicked gangs. I couldn't understand them at first. For instance: "Where did you lose?" "Are you a playboy case or a grab case?" They looked me up and down from head to toe. While the gold-teeth witch was checking my belongings, I took advantage and suddenly ran out of the room as if a host of demons was after me. A military guard soon stopped me.

At the same time, the gold-teethed witch also chased and grabbed me: "Where do you think you are running?" she shouted.

I turned to the guard, "This is not the place I should stay. Send me back to where I came from!" I thought in my heart "I would rather stay with that nun in the dungeon than here with these demons."

The gold-teeth witch shouted at me continuously, "Follow me back to the cell, behave and obey!"

The armed military guard didn't look malicious and was very young, not even twenty years old. He spoke to me gently, "From now on, if you intend to say or do anything, you have to talk to your cell leader first if you want to contact the office and officers. You are not allowed to run around."

Then the guard escorted me back and the witch fiercely grabbed my hand. I realized that this little witch had a pair of big hands that did not match her stature. After I entered the room, she forced me to read the forty disciplines and rules of the cell, written in big characters on the wall. Some of them were related to crimes that I didn't even recognize. I felt deeply insulted so I refused to read, and immediately I was severely criticized by the witch, "You are already here in the cave. You have not behaved. Don't you even think about trying to get out!"

Right then the military guard who escorted me into this cell called my name from outside the wall, "Officers in the office are calling you!" I felt I was rescued and ran to the office. The officers there were quite different from those policemen who locked me in the dungeon in the detention house.

The atmosphere there was a little more relaxed. Several men wearing police uniforms were talking and laughing, but when they saw me, they abruptly stopped talking and told me: "From now on you shall call us 'captain'. If you have any matter to talk to us about, you have to report to the military guard first. You have just arrived and you ought not to run around disturbing people and making trouble. You have to learn obedience and accept your reeducation."

When I was locked up in the dungeon, I already understood that I should not use my flesh and blood to resist, so I determined I would behave this time. So I took out the "Notice of Education through Hard Labor" to show them. "Captain," I said, "Please re-examine my case and send me back where I came from."

The captain looked at me but did not return the notice to me. He said: "You don't need this anymore. This notice will be stored in your personal file."

And then all the military men gathered around the table and told me: "We don't have the authority to send you back."

"What is this 'education through hard labor?" I asked.

They answered: "This is the highest administrative discipline, not a legal punishment. You still have civil rights but your civil rights are suspended temporarily."

I was thinking in my heart, "What kind of 'civil rights'? You deceived and hijacked me to the dungeon detention house and then here. I didn't commit any crime against any law." So, I raised my voice a bit and said: "Captain, I couldn't stand those women who are locked up with me, especially that gold-teethed woman. I already read your disciplines and rules of the cell, which are all about forbidding adultery, stealing, and other crimes. What do these have to do with me?"

I didn't expect what one of the captains, one with white cheeks, cold eyes and a villainous looking stare spoke cynically to me: "Here is better. You can work hard while you do the labor and make a confession, so that you may try for earlier release. You should contact us, the captains, frequently to confess about yourself and accept the ideological reformation which is your only way out in the future."

Another captain fiercely spoke to me, "Don't think of your self as still being pure and clean. All the others are 'contradictions among the people'.

They are people who made mistakes and are locked behind bars. They are all of the proletarian class origin coming from poor family backgrounds and are easily reformed. You come from the high and disgusting intellectual class. Go back to your cell and accept the reformation of the government and the surveillance of your cellmates. Get rid completely of your disgraceful intellectual attitude and strive to remold yourself ideologically, just as you cast off your old spine and change to a new one!"

After these rebukes I was sent back to the cell at the big house. I realized that, as an educated individual coming from an upper-class family, I was considered a blemish in the Communist system. It was hopeless to protest. I retreated to the hellish prison cell and my heart sank to the bottom of the dead valley. The gold-teethed woman was called right away to the office after me. She was ordered to arrange for me to sleep beside her. I, just like the other cellmates, received a straw mattress and I put my belongings sent by my family on the mattress to make a bed.

When I saw the things from my family, I couldn't control my tears. I didn't know how my father and mother and younger sister would live. And this gold-teeth vixen, whom I hated, was less than one foot from me. Day and night she and I had to stay and sleep together. She constantly kept her eyes on me watching and reporting about me. I lived with a witch as my neighbor and I couldn't escape for a long time!

This "camp of education through hard labor" was also a detention house and a distribution center for detainees. Whenever a political drive or movement was launched in China at that time, trucks of detainees of "political criminals" would be escorted here. So, this camp was always a full house jammed with all kinds of criminals. Often we heard the whistles of the police. These signaled truckloads of detainees would be dragged out and sent to other hard labor prisons in the great wilderness of northeast China and other remote areas. Sometimes four or five truckloads of detainees were sent into the camp and several months later, we could see many of them were pulled out. It was estimated there were around 1,000 people in and out of there in a year.

One morning, while I was making my bed, a teen-age girl was looking at me and I asked her, "How long have you been here?"

She replied, "Two years. How long are you sentenced?"

"One and a half years," I answered.

"Don't be naive. 'Education through hard labor' is actually another term for minor life-sentence. You just wait and see," she cautiously said.

Later on, I was aware that some detainees were sentenced to one or two years, but several months later they were released. Some were also sentenced to the same term, yet they were still here for over three years. Every evening between seven and ten, we were ordered to read and study newspapers, pamphlets and other materials that were full of political content.

At ten-thirty sharp, it was our bedtime. However, the lights in the cell were always on, so that the police could frequently return to check on us. I wished the lights would be put out so I could enjoy a little quiet in the darkness. It was not like in the dungeon where I was first detained, which was gloomy and dreadful. Here, it was the opposite. It was always noisy. Many women were nearly naked, chain smoking, in a frivolous manner. They hummed ditties, sang cheap songs or chatted, telling dirty jokes filled with foul words.

All the women made efforts to serve the gold-teethed witch well by lighting cigarettes for her and giving her a cup of tea and making her bed to please her. The witch always wildly laughed at them for a while and then went to sleep. Sometime later, I learned that this gold-teethed witch was a murderer. Before the Chinese Communists took over China in 1949, in the old society ruled by the Chinese Nationalists (Chiang Kai Shek's time), she had been a prostitute for decades. She even became a madam running a brothel. She was involved in killing those prostitutes who became old or sick, because they would be useless for earning money for her anymore. She was accused and found guilty.

I tried my best but I was unable to close my eyes and turn deaf ears to their vulgar conversations, lewd stories, raucous laughter and screaming. I often felt like my head was about to explode! Each night, about ten or more women among our over fifty cellmates were called to the clinic for shots.

I asked the teenaged girl sleeping by me, "What kind of shots are they taking?"

She answered, "Shots to cure gonorrhea."

I was so scared because every night we all used the same hot water from one big barrel to take a bath and wash ourselves at the same time. I was afraid that I could be easily infected by sexual disease! My heart was caught in my throat. Lying on the straw mattress bed at night, I felt like I was lost in a huge forest surrounded by roaring lions, biting mosquitoes and scorpions. I feared being swallowed by beasts, or bitten by bugs. I had nowhere to hide and no one to rescue or help me.

My heart sank to the bottom of the valley of the shadow of death. I was so homesick! "Do I need to endure one and a half years like this?" Just as in the African American ballads I used to sing, "Deep River." The words were: *"Deep, deep river, my home is over Jordan,"* and *"Nobody knows the trouble I've seen, but Jesus."* I prayed, "My Lord, forgive me. I am unable to cry out 'O, yes Lord!' now. I don't even have the slightest strength to talk to you. Where are you Lord? Please hide me in your bosom. I don't want to look at these wicked women. I don't want to be here!"

I couldn't sleep at all. However, it seemed that God sent an angel to put hymn after hymn in my heart, plucking at my heartstrings and moistening my totally dried and broken heart. A song the Lord wanted me to sing was, *"In the secret of His presence, how my soul delights to hide…. O, how precious are the lessons that I learn at Jesus' side. For earthly cares can never wax me, neither trials lay me low. When Satan comes to tempt me, to the secret place I go!"* This hymn of "Hiding Place" is a very old song my mother taught me to sing. I didn't realize the meaning of the words before. Now the words were just like the living water of a stream, clean and clear, flowing into my heart to comfort me so I could fall asleep.

Chapter 11

A Bosom Inmate in Tribulations

One day when we began to work we noticed there were several cellmates missing, including the gold-teethed witch who always had indiscreet remarks and criticisms. The teenaged girl who slept beside me told me that they were having time off and allowed to go home to visit their families. Among them was a Communist with heavy features who was originally the wife of some bureau chief, another woman who has a nickname of "a fake guy" and two other women who were doing some sewing work for the police guards. Then I suddenly realized that all the detainees whom the police thought had behaved well were being allowed to take turns to go home and visit their families.

But, not I, I was not allowed to go home, since my case was related to my family. On the same day, I discovered that among the new detainees there was a quiet, slim Shanghai girl from the well-known Nankai University in Tianjin. Police announced that nobody should ask about her case and why she was there. Since we were the only college girls and intellectuals, it was very natural that when we labored together we found it easy to understand each other. Sometimes we just exchanged glances of compassion because the police forbade the cellmates to talk to me too much. However, one thing happened which gave us more opportunities to know each other.

It was 1960 when I was detained and lost my freedom. There was a nationwide famine in China. Over 30 million Chinese, especially in the rural areas, died of starvation. Of course, for prisons and hard labor camps there was insufficient food. Every month, in the society, each family was given a paltry amount of food to be divided among the members. On average each person had only half a pound of food to eat per day. Grain was carefully measured with each person allotted only a few grams of vegetable oil, pork and sugar each month. A package of lard, sent from an overseas friend or relative, was a precious luxury.

For the six week days, the meals for us, the prisoners, were only black and bitter steamed bread, of the size of a child's fist, made from the powder of sunflower seed husks, mixed with onion and potato skins from the garbage can of the police kitchen. We also had a little corn powder, plus leftover food from feeding army horses as well as a bowl of cabbage root soup. For breakfast we were given a bowl of very thin rice gruel with a piece of dried, salted pickle. At that time tons of vegetable oil made from sunflower seeds was transported to the Soviet Union to pay the national debt that Chinese owed them for the Korean War.

I remembered what the nun told me, "No matter what kind of bad food they give you, you have to eat in order to be released and go home alive." But, this college girl could not swallow the black and bitter bread and she refused to eat anything. Within several days she lost consciousness because of lack of food. A policeman from the office showed special consideration for her and cooked her noodles, a special treat for the patient. However, one or two meals of noodles would not be enough to save her life. Her frail body could not digest the bitter sunflower seed husks. She often fainted and was sent to the clinic.

A male medical doctor who was a counter-revolutionary suspect was practicing in the clinic, but the police ordered that when he checked and treated female prisoners, he must be in the presence of two to three other female prisoners. Since this college girl's (simplified as Ms. P) veins were so deep and shriveled, it was hard to give her an infusion. So the police often asked me to help this male doctor. Whenever they rescued Ms. P by giving her some shots, they asked me to help. This way we had more contact and got to know each other better.

On Sunday, we ate only two meals but with two real soft white steamed bread rolls as a treat. These two white bread rolls were just like cream cake to us and we were reluctant to eat them all at once. We ate the real bread by little pieces with water to fill up our stomachs. Some even preserved them for later days to remember the taste of real bread. After I finished the vegetable root soup, I saved two of my real bread rolls and secretly put them under Ms. P's pillow on Sunday nights. In exchange she gave me her bitter black bread. That was the only way to help her and the only thing I had.

Even though we were watched by the cellmates and unable to talk or make contact very often, we could still shake hands sometimes and exchange our glances to comfort each other. Ms. P never flattered anyone, as she was an honest and upright person. She didn't cover up her own ideas, opinions and dissatisfaction and would argue if it were necessary. She seldom contacted or talked to those filthy women. However, she regarded me in a favorable light. I regarded her as my very own "Jane Eyre" (in Charlotte Bronte's novel).

Once in every two months, family members of the cellmates were allowed to visit. In our cell more than fifty cellmates were waiting anxiously to see their folks. Only Ms. P and I had no family members to visit us. For me, it was because the authority disapproved. For Ms. P, her family was in Beijing. When the cellmates took turns to meet their folks, I saw her sadness and loneliness, which I also felt. I had compassion for her. As a matter of fact, I was more pitiful than she was.

Our cellmates reported to the police the little contact we did have. This caused the police to call us to the office individually. In order to prevent our further contact, the police told her that I was a counter-revolutionary, which was very bad. The police told me that she disclosed some state secret. They also attacked her personally with many bad words. Obviously, the police tried to separate us. On the contrary, we got closer. Every time we were in the clinic with only three of us, including the male doctor, Dr. Young, we could enjoy some privacy.

We talked, since we had the same mind set. I told her, once a week, my two real white bread rolls would not be enough to feed her and she had to eat. Otherwise, she would die. Ms. P thought of her parents very often. I said I would pray for her early release and family reunion. It was amazing that her father came from Beijing to visit her the same week I began to pray for her!

I didn't have any privacy to share Jesus with her, however I told her many times that, "The Lord Jesus loves you!" Sometimes she saw that I closed my eyes and she knew I was praying.

She asked me, "What are you praying for?"

I said: "Asking my Lord to rescue me from all the disasters and tortures and telling Him my desires, dreams and necessities. Whenever I feel lonely and sad I talk to my Lord Jesus." In order to comfort her, I told her I prayed that she would have a Christian husband. I said also I prayed for a Christian brother willing to suffer for the Lord to be my husband.

Several months later, we heard the police whistle again and a large number of prisoners were relocated. Ms. P was among them. After you heard your name called, the police gave you only ten minutes to pack up your belongings and nobody knew where one would be sent. I worried about Ms. P who was so thin and feeble that if she were sent to the northeast wilderness, she would surely die. I helped her pack.

For us, it seemed that we would bid farewell forever and that we would never meet again. Nobody knew when we could regain our freedom, and how we would find each other even if we were free. I stood in the courtyard and sadly watched her leave in the big truck of prisoners heading for far away. "Oh, Lord, help her please!" Even though Ms. P and I were only cellmates for a few months, we established trust and affection.

I thank the Lord when I was in the dungeon detention house, He gave me that nun, a sister in Christ with whom I could share some compassion and fellowship in that terrifying darkness. Here the Lord gave me "Jane Eyre" who became my bosom friend to enjoy a little clean privacy in filthy circumstances. Later, after I became a "night parolee" I was allowed to go home and stay overnight with my parents. Ms. P and I met each other miraculously, and little did we know that she would become my matchmaker! I found out later that her first name in English is "Jane!" Eventually, she was saved and converted to Christ and we became good friends and sisters in Christ forever!

Chapter 12

Starving and Hard Labor

Mao's crazy and wrong policies caused a devastating nationwide famine that began at the end of 1958. Over thirty million people died of starvation all over the country. In the rural areas people even ate tree bark and leaves. One could see dead trees everywhere. No dogs were barking and no roosters were crowing in villages. They had all been consumed by the starving people.

Because of this situation, there was not sufficient food for prisoners and hard labor camps. Sometimes our breakfast became a bowl of what we called "four eyes congee", because in the bowl there was hardly any rice. It was only very thin rice soup. You could see the shadow of your own eyes reflected from the bowl. The soup was served with one piece of dried, salted pickle. We not only drank all of our soup but we had to drink more water to feel even half full. If the intensity of our hard labor increased, for instance, during the harvest of rice, one sweet potato was added. We ate the whole sweet potato including the skin. Our lunch and supper were similar, one black steamed bread and cabbage roots soup.

We were hungry and starving all the time. Most female prisoners' monthly-menstruations stopped. Mine stopped for four years. Everyone's eyesight diminished and in the evening our vision was blurred. We lacked all necessary vitamins including vitamin A. Because there was no food in our stomachs, many suffered from stomach cramps. Many drank water to fill up their stomachs, so almost everyone suffered from dropsy. One woman's leg even swelled like an elephant leg.

Some cellmates could meet their family members and receive some more food, but not I. I had to suffer and endure to the extreme. When I was starving, I recalled how picky I had been about food when I was little. I disliked too many kinds of food, embarrassing the servants very much. I didn't cherish all the plenty that God granted to me, so now God let me experience hunger.

It was the hardest for us to endure the nights, especially winter nights. Fifty of us were locked up and jammed into one big room over twenty meters in length and over ten meters in width. The only heat in the winter came from a small coal briquette stove. The house was old and shabby and there were cracks in the walls and corners. The temperature inside the house dropped to below zero Celsius at night. The water in everybody's cup was frozen.

Big empty bottles of glucose liquid enjoyed by police for their health from the clinic were given to us to have some hot water to warm ourselves in our quilts. Every night when we slept we bundled ourselves in the quilts and in the middle of the night we had to take out the bottles which had already become cold. Because of the freezing cold and drinking too much water, many had to get up for the rest room several times a night, so no one got too much sleep.

The kind of hard labor we had was different according to seasons. In summer, we worked in the rice fields. We opened up the wastelands, picking out stones and planting seedlings. We hand softened the mud for the rice seedlings to be planted and picked out the tares. Then we harvested the rice, threshing the grain and storing it in the warehouses. Under the instructions of some aged farmers, we did all of the physical and manual labor. When we plowed the water wasteland to cultivate rice fields, of course we had to be bare-footed. There were a lot of sharp stones in the field that often cut the soles of my feet. In the muddy water the pain of the wounds pricked to my heart. When we transplanted the rice seedlings, we had to bend at our waists for over ten hours. My waist was almost broken in half. Old farmers got used to this kind of work, having done it all their lives. Some prisoners from poor families had done this hard work even during their childhood. They were all stronger than I was.

After the hard labor of the whole day, my face was swollen like steamed bread just taken out from the hot pot. My eyes were squeezed narrow so that they were hard to open. Even though I worked as hard as I could, I failed to meet the quota assigned to me by the police. When softening the mud and getting rid of the tares, we were unable to use any tools other than our fingers. After several days, my nails were ground to half and the skin on all my fingertips was broken. As I persisted in laboring like this, my fingertips slowly and painfully became calloused. Gradually my finger joints became swollen and deformed. I was unable to clench my fists. I knew from then on, I would be unable ever to play the piano again.

The Lord Taught Me to Kneel Down and Harvest

July was the harvest time for rice. Afraid of the rain, we had to get the harvest done quickly. Quotas were assigned to each of us, telling how many strips of land we had to complete in three days. We had to work harder and longer in the field from ten hours extending to fourteen hours. Even physically strong cellmates were barely able to finish the quota. Physically feeble ones like me without any experience in harvest, fainted many times under the burning sun. My underwear and shirt were drenched thoroughly and then dried up again in the heat of the scorching sun. On the front and back of everyone's clothes there were circles of salt "maps" drawn by dried streams of sweat alkaline.

The gold-teethed witch reported to one guard that my complexion and face were too white and pale, that I needed to turn tan under the burning sun. So this cunning and fierce guard did not allow me to wear a straw hat like everybody else. This was what they called "the reformation of a new life" for me. My face had to be tanned and black so that I would no longer be a bourgeois young lady.

We were doing these heavy jobs with empty stomachs, yet we were all doing our best. Your hard work and good behavior showed how successful was your ideological remolding and gave you better relationships with the government officials. All these were conditions to qualify you for a possible earlier release.

One day, I bent down to harvest the rice and couldn't stand anymore after less than one hour. I collapsed under the heat of the sun. When I recovered a bit, I saw all my cellmates were a long way ahead of me. They were all very professional and the rice straw root cuts were neat. Yet, for me my left hand had no strength to grab the rice straws tightly, while my right hand often failed to properly cut them with a sickle. Others cut the straws quickly with sharp sickles, while I was slowly hand-sawing them.

Behind me all the straw roots were uneven. Standing behind me were overseers monitoring the quality of our labor and they were abusing and cursing me from time to time. I raised my head and saw the endless stretch of rice field ahead, the quota for me to harvest that day. I was so desperate and feeble while I remembered that when I was little I loved to write compositions, such as "the beautiful blue sky and the green trees afar, the rippling rice in golden color…." But, now I was almost drowned by the rice billows. I lifted up my head to the sky and sighed, "Lord, rescue me, because You say You are my refuge and my help at all times." I suddenly felt dizzy and had faulty vision and a terrible headache. I fell and passed out.

I didn't know how long my faint lasted, but when the breeze awakened me, I found out that I was kneeling instead of lying flat. The rice plants were very high and nobody discovered that I had fainted. As I was kneeling, the tallness of my stature was cut in half. I found that in a kneeling position, cutting the rice plants was much easier, faster and labor-saving. I was so amazingly happy that I quickly cut the plants and reached the end of a strip of rice field and then started back.

I felt some new physical strength filling me, so that I gradually caught up to the rest of the team ahead of me. Because of the kneeling position, my knees were skinned and the knee parts of my trousers were all worn out. But there were first aid kits at both ends of the fields. Then I simply used some medicine and wrapped them with some gauze and bound my cotton shoes to my knees. As I knelt down on the ground, I used my knees to move forward instead of my feet.

I surprisingly found that since I had a pair of long legs, kneeling down to cut the plants saved me a lot of strength. Praise the Lord, God really humbled me so that I continued to harvest in a kneeling position and changed my "knee-shoes" from cotton to rubber sneakers. Not only did I catch up with everybody, I also met the quota and quality of harvesting. After the rice harvest, I was among the few whom the police praised for their hard labor.

This was the first time in my life that I experienced that in total desperation and almost dying, God would help me at all times! He used the breeze to wake me up from fainting and taught me to use a kneeling position to humbly fulfill my job. I received the appraisal from the guards: "Her attitude toward reformation through hard labor is correct, and a good result is achieved." Since then, during my twenty-year hard labor in prison, no matter how strenuous, hard, dangerous and filthy the work and tasks were, God gave me strength and wisdom miraculously. He protected me at all times and led me to walk through the valley of the shadow of death. And I was always able to do well in hard labor, receiving good credit.

After the harvest, we returned to our cells and in front of a piece of a broken mirror, I looked at my own face and was shocked. My face was full of suntan freckles. My skin was black, scarred, wounded and swollen similar to the black and bitter bread we had in every meal. I felt ugly and horrible.

After we harvested the rice grains, we had to winnow the chaff, and thresh the grain. The awns of rice were flying everywhere like thorns, hurting the wounds on my face and making my whole body itch. Later, I was ordered to go out to the countryside to collect human, cow, and horse manure and waste to be used as fertilizer. So, my whole body always smelled badly.

In the winter times according to their needs, likes and dislikes, the police assigned who should go out to do heavy, filthy jobs and who should stay in the hard labor camp for light jobs. For instance, those who were good at flattering and fawning on the police and skilled in sewing and knitting would stay to clean the police dormitories, wash clothes and knit sweaters for them. These female prisoners became their special close servants. However, no police paid much attention to me, so I was sent to another workshop to grind saw blades. Iron saw blades produced in male prisons were sent to us to polish. This was a kind of half-manual and half-mechanical labor. To polish saw blades we needed a special grinding wheel wrapped up in hard cloths with adhesive hot sand. When working, we simply had to hold these saw blades with two hands to polish them. Red-hot sand with black adhesive oil splashed out showers of sparks attacking my face and adding numerous wounds and dark pits, which I was unable to wash clean. The more saw blades we polished, the blacker and darker our faces became.

When operating the machine, our hands and fingers were very close to the spinning grinding wheel and we took a risk every second that our fingers or hands could be cut off or burned. After the work shifts, when we looked at each other's "dignified countenances," we would just laugh and laugh. "Are we prisoners being reformed through hard labor? No, we are simply a bunch of female black slaves from Africa now."

However, God is awesome. Joseph eventually said to his brothers: *"But as for you, ye thought evil against me; but God meant it unto good, to bring to pass, as it is this day, to save much people alive."* (Genesis 50:20) How could I imagine that my ugly, black face and extremely filthy, dirty and smelly body was actually a mask that God prepared for me to wear and a shield for me to use. Those wicked police disdained even to look at me or pay any attention to me, let alone take a fancy to me. God protected me from their obscenities and sexual insults. Some professional prostitutes flattered the police or through the gold-teethed witch were selected as their close servants. When the wicked policemen had enough sexual satisfaction with these adulterous women, they would quickly be released, because these bad policemen were afraid their scandal would be exposed.

Later, the whole prison was shocked when the news spread and we learned that some wicked police were punished by legal sanction for raping female prisoners. Some wicked police even hung themselves because they found out that they suffered from serious syphilis. Others tried to escape to avoid being sentenced and locked up behind bars.

Chapter 13

A Sinner

We were all totally exhausted after a whole day of hard labor. Yet, everyone had to attend the political indoctrination class for two hours everyday. Every day some cellmate was ordered by the police to make a self-confession related to the nature of the crime she committed and mistakes she had made recently in the cell. Daily, monthly, and yearly these self-criticisms were routine. Every two to three months the police ordered us to strengthen discipline, encouraging us to report on and accuse each other, and expose each other's so called "mistakes and violations of discipline." In order to protect themselves and hoping to get an earlier release, many accused others to prove that they were loyal to the government.

During this kind of political criticism and drives, one's family background and class origin meant a lot. Even in the prison there were different ranks of social strata. The first rank of prisoners was called "contradictions among the people." Many thieves, gangsters, murderers, drug dealers, prostitutes and other criminals were categorized in this rank. In the second rank were those classical counter-revolutionaries, who joined the Chinese Nationalist Party (Chiang Kai-Shek's Kuo Min

Tang) or other pro-Nationalist parties. The third rank was active counter-revolutionaries of reactionary religious believers, including Catholic and Protestant Christians and those who put up reactionary slogans, posters and other anti-government insurgences.

Among the reactionary religious believers there were "Yiguandao," a polytheistic religious sect, Catholic Christian priests, nuns and Catholic believers, Protestant Christian pastors, preachers and Protestant believers. Chinese Catholics who are loyal and related to the Vatican of Rome, denying the Communist-controlled Catholic churches in China were regarded as reactionaries. Among the Protestant Christians who denied the Communist-controlled Protestant churches in China, if one came from the worker class or peasant Christian families, she would be regarded as poisoned by religious and cultural imperialists.

If a Christian came from a bourgeoisie, educated, upper-class family, which had overseas relationships or relatives, she dropped to the bottom of the rank. I came from a bourgeoisie intellectual family and had overseas relationships in Taiwan, so I was on the very lowest rung. My cellmates gave me the nicknames: "a kitchen plate" and "a doormat." Everyone maligned and accused me of things in order to gain merits from the government. I was like "a kitchen plate" which meant that anyone could cut her food with a knife on me. As "a doormat," that meant that anyone could step on me. In the criticism meetings every day I was the easy target, being criticized and scolded for two hours.

My cellmates didn't really understand what Protestant and Catholic Christianity are. They hurled names and abused God using terms like "Cook Jesus" for "Lord Jesus" because the oral pronunciations of "lord" and "cook" in Chinese are the same. Hunger was always our companion, and uneven distribution of the food in any meal would cause quarrels. In order to solve this problem, the police decided that every day two persons would be on duty to take food from the kitchen and distribute it to us in the cell. The two prisoners who were on duty could get an extra small piece of sweet potato and the one who distributed the congee was allowed to scrape the congee pot clean, gaining half a bowl of extra congee to eat.

This tiny little reward became the privilege of the gold-teeth witch. She decided daily who would be on duty. Because she came from a poor peasant family, despite the fact that she was a murderer, the government trusted her. This witch was especially skillful in fawning to the police. She picked pretty women who had smooth tongues and skilful hands to serve the police, and clean their dormitories. Therefore, all the cellmates curried favor with her first and then got the privileges. There was a lot of jealousy and competition. All the female prisoners were afraid that I, a college student might grab the favor of the police, so they hated me despite the fact that I had already become an ugly looking black slave.

They often made things hard for me. For instance, if I were on duty distributing the food, I was not allowed to have that piece of sweet potato and the half bowl of congee scraped from the pot. I considered that since I am a Christian, how could I quarrel with them over such trifles? So, I often took the humiliation. They asked me to clean the women's toilet when we were scheduled for a half hour rest included in the mealtime. They wanted the praise of the police office that we had "the cleanest restroom." It was a good excuse to add an extra filthy job for me because "as an intellectual, I needed more reformation." Hence, every mealtime I had only ten minutes to eat.

One time it was my duty to distribute congee. I saw some cellmates put some sugar that their families sent them into the bowl for the gold-teeth witch to fawn after her. I thought in my heart I would never do that. After I distributed the congee, there was a little left over in the pot. It was the rule for me only that if I was on duty after I cleaned up the pot, the half bowl of congee should be handed to that procuress to decide to whom it should be granted. I ignored the rule and after I cleaned up the pot I gave the half bowl of congee to the young girl thief who slept beside me.

The witch suddenly sprang to her feet and shouted, "What are you up to? How dare you? You don't have the authority to grant that to anyone!"

"You don't either," I responded "your authority is not on the discipline rules of the prison. It is not my purpose to have this half a bowl of congee, but I want to break your evil rules and influence!" Everyone around me was shocked and stopped eating because no one ever dared to argue with the witch.

The witch stood up and aimed a finger at me. "You dare to make trouble when we are having meals. You are not allowed to eat anything today!" As she was speaking, she jumped at me and tried to grab my bowl.

I put down the congee pot, and my left hand quickly snatched her big hair bob, while my right hand was waving the big iron ladle high toward her head. I yelled, "Today I want you to know that I am not that easily bullied!" And I was about to strike her with the ladle.

I Realized My Sinful Nature

In a snap, two female prisoners threw themselves on me and forced me down on the ground. They beat my head and ears heavily with their fists. I could hear the witch shouting in a loud voice: "She is killing me!" Several police rushed in and used their clubs to beat my head several times. My head seemed to be cracked, my whole body got numb and I collapsed not having a bit of strength to resist anymore. The prisoners used very thin iron wires to tie my hands behind my back and took me to a single room in the police office and locked me up. My ears could not hear and I was deaf to what the police were saying. Then they drove all the prisoners back to the big cell room and resumed order.

Quite a long time later, the young military man came and untied me. My wrists were cut by the thin wires and were full of blood. He told me without any facial expression, "You can go back to the big cell now, but behave yourself!" The soldier escorted me back to the big cell.

My head was dizzy and heavy and I didn't pay any attention to the hostile and fearful looks given me. I lay down on my small square of floor and slept. But a little voice was telling me, "You could possibly be a killer just like that procuress, the gold-teethed witch!" I began to realize my own sinful nature, but I still didn't want to say "Sorry!" to anyone.

The unprecedented great famine all over China was increasingly severe. Therefore, among those who were in charge of the cooking and mess, some stole our food. Even the steamed black bread made of sunflower seed husk gradually got smaller and smaller. Many women in our cell suffered from gastric ulcers. I was one of them. Some suffered from hepatitis and tuberculosis. Whenever there were political drives going on in the society, a greater number of all kinds of criminal suspects were sent to our detention hard labor camp. Most of them were thieves, prostitutes and gangsters. Some sold their bodies for several meals and some stole some food to feed and support their families.

Criminals of conscience or criminals of reactionary ideology were sent here also in greater numbers. So, our cell room was jammed with people and the space for us to lie down became smaller and smaller. Newcomers brought us the news that many prisoners had already died of starvation in the hard labor prison camps in the northeast China wilderness, Gansu,

Ningxia and other provinces. We had been lucky. Only a few had died of starvation here.

Every time the police whistled for gathering, everyone trembled and feared that he or she would be escorted to faraway barren places and the risk of starvation. Therefore, everybody strived to remain in this hard labor camp in the suburb of Tianjin to survive. We all hoped that our cases could be resolved and we would be released to go home. All the cellmates worked hard and made positive contributions in all aspects to please the Communists. In the past, those who criticized me were a bunch of illiterate people. They abused and scolded me in a noisy, disorderly way. I didn't even pay attention or listen to them. I just bowed my head and waited until the meeting was over.

Now, however, some false Christians of intellectual background came. Because they were scared to pay the price for Christ Jesus, they gave up their Christian faith, even criticizing and rebuking God. They also condemned me profoundly and forcefully. The police used an ex-Christian who already betrayed the Lord to deal with me. She gave her own experience as an example, how she relinquished her faith to censure me and how incorrigibly stubborn I was. She used me as a stepping-stone in order to get an early release. She said that she used to be a puppy dog, fed and kept by the U.S. imperialists. Now she totally converted to believe Chairman Mao to be the great leader. She asked me, "Why are you so dumb to believe God who makes you suffer?" This kind of individual criticism toward me coupled with threats and promises was a hard test for me to endure.

The police also threatened me by demanding that I give up my Christian belief and make a clean break and a clear distinction from my father. They insisted I report him to be in collusion with the U.S. imperialist and organized reactionary regimes. Otherwise, I would be sent to the northeast China wilderness or detained here for hard labor for the rest of my life without parole. As expected, the ex-Christian who betrayed the Lord and condemned the faithful pastors and believers in her Christian church was soon released. The government considered her to have made her contributions.

I Could Not Endure Any Longer

One and a half years passed and no police interviewed me or talked to me about my release. When I asked them, I got the same answer from them, "You should self-examine why you haven't had improvement in the reformation of your ideology and thoughts." I witnessed with my own eyes those who had betrayed the Lord getting praise from the government and being released. One by one they left. I was deeply confused and desperate. However, God's words always reminded me: "Whosoever therefore shall confess me before men, him will I confess also before my Father which is in heaven." (Matthew 10:32)

Reviews of my case and others were made once a year and every one had to pass this test. I did go through successfully. The police asked me "Do you still believe in Christianity?"

I had no other answer but said to them, "I have believed in Jesus since my childhood and I have been a Christian since I was little. I cannot criticize Christianity. It is not possible for me to give up my Christian faith!"

One year after another, this went on. Spiritually I became weak and my faith was at a low ebb. I was so homesick, missing and worrying about my parents that my heart was broken. I began to argue with God. "Your great apostle Peter was put into jail for only a few days and you sent angels to unlock his shackles and lead him out. I am but an ordinary believer and I have already been tortured here for over two years. You should have mercy to send angels to rescue me. You forbid me to betray You and give up my faith, yet You don't rescue me. Does this prove that You still love me? Oh, God, please take me back to your home in heaven."

Spiritually I was depressed and I didn't have any hope that I could be released. I thought, why not try another way to live. When everybody was chatting and laughing, I did so too. When everybody was lazy, I was too. I just loafed and idled away my time day by day.

It was the Chinese lunar New Year's Day and the chef of the police dining room wanted to make dumplings for many policemen. Dumplings are the traditional food for the Chinese New Year and since there were so many policemen, thousands of dumplings had to be made. They picked five female prisoners who knew how to make dumplings to help in their kitchen. I was one of the five selected. We five divided our jobs. Another cellmate and I would roll out wheat flour dough for dumpling wrappers and the other three would put the meat fillings into the wrappers and seal them. We worked for several hours and from time to time the police came and took away the trays of raw dumplings we had made to boil them. We were so hungry our stomachs were rumbling hurtfully. Our eyes were flashing so that we could hardly stand to continue to work.

The delicious aroma of the dumplings being cooked was reaching us from time to time adding more pains to our empty stomachs. Sometimes I paused and lifted my head. I was startled to see that the other three who put fillings into the wrappers were covertly swallowing raw dumplings. "Are raw dumplings edible? How can they eat raw dumplings?" I was shocked. When they saw that I had noticed, they were very embarrassed and looked nervous. They knew this was a good chance for me to report to the police their wrongdoing, making contributions and gaining merit for myself. The three threw several raw dumplings to me and made gestures for me to swallow. I hesitated for quite awhile.

"Is it okay to eat raw meat?" I saw they had swallowed raw dumplings swiftly and did not vomit. I decided to try also. As soon as the raw dumpling entered my mouth, it tasted awful, so sticky and sour. I could not chew them, but quickly swallowed, not one, not two, but three dumplings. I felt sick but unable to vomit because the police came and went. Eventually my stomach pain ceased. With raw dumplings in my empty stomach, I felt physically strengthened a bit until we fulfilled our job. Of course, afterwards we didn't report each other's wrongdoing. My cellmates felt quite at ease and their attitude toward me became more relaxed, because I had more in common with them.

That night those four inmates all soundly slept. But, a dreadful voice in my mind kept clearly accusing me, "You are a thief, you are a sinner. Your Lord will not love you anymore."

I argued, "No, I am suffering for my father and the American missionaries. I am innocent."

The Holy Spirit's tender voice right away whispered in my ear: *"For we have not an high priest which cannot be touched with the feeling of our infirmities; but was in all points tempted like as we are, yet without sin."* (Hebrews 4:15)

The strong voice from the tempter accused me, "You are not suffering for the Lord. Now you are but a thief and you deserve your punishment. People hate you and now God does not want or care for you anymore. You will disgracefully and shamefully die here!"

The sins I committed and the disgrace I felt struck me down and I asked myself, "What sort of person have I become? Lord, I cannot endure any longer. I am only a piece of clay, which has failed many times to be made into a vessel. I am not qualified to be a vessel. Please take me home to heaven. Though I will not be qualified to attend the Feast of the Lamb, maybe I could hide somewhere under the table in heaven rather than to suffer here." During this dark period, there were no hymns or peace in my heart and no hope for me on this earth. I reached the lowest point in my spirit at this time.

Chapter 14

Damaged Voice and Painful Sores

During my imprisonment in the early 1960s, in addition to our political studies every evening, the police compelled us to praise the Communists and Mao Ze Dong with songs such as, "Sailing on the high seas, we need the navigator," "Heaven and earth are great, but not as great as the kindness of Communist Party, which is the greatest!" and "Without the Communist Party, there would be no new China," "Chairman Mao is the great savior of the Chinese people, the red sun that will never set", for example. This gave the gold-teeth witch and other cellmates who loved to sing ditties a good opportunity to shout and sing at the top of their voices. I was really reluctant to sing or to listen, but it was better than being criticized. I disliked those songs and disagreed that Mao is the savior. I have my Savior Jesus.

Instead of singing I was just shouting. Sometimes I even stopped shouting, but the witch discovered me. She then forced me to sing loudly. I simply used an off-key voice to disturb them, pretending I didn't know how to sing the melodies. They got tired of my lack of cooperation and stopped me. I thought my plan was working and that I could take some rest, but the witch immediately fixed her eyes on me and asked, "Why don't you sing with us?"

I said, "I have an off-key voice."

She answered in a strange tone: "Is that so?"

Several days later, the witch came back from the office and told me she had a way to cure my off-key voice and that I had to sing along with them. After that, whenever we sang and shouted all the praise songs, she forced me to drink something that she said was a Chinese herb medicine of folk prescription. It was half a cup of pure vinegar with a mixture of grayish and red pepper powder. Two of the witch's favorite cellmates would watch me drink. When I drank the liquid, its taste was both sour and spicy, burning hot. I vomited it out but two inmates pushed me down and opened my mouth with their hands, forcing me to swallow. They did this every night.

After one month my voice became very hoarse. I almost totally lost my ability to speak, let alone being able to sing. Hatred and fear welled up in my heart. I wanted to resist and I asked to report to the police office. Their response was, "No time to interview you." I made a written report and submitted it to them, but it disappeared forever without news and I had no place to bring suit.

At nights I said to the Lord, "Now I have nothing plus nothing. The only thing I had was my voice, which I dedicated to You since I was little, but now that has also been taken away by Satan. The procuress is an expert at killing the prostitutes. If she can destroy my voice today, how will she harm me tomorrow? How long will You hide from me? Can You hear my groaning? Lord, when shall I see Your righteousness, how long will You turn a deaf ear to my prayers?"

I had not a bit of love toward those who were persecuting me. I only cursed them and wanted them to be punished. Dark and miserable days came and went. The way for evil persons seemed to be smooth and those who fawned to the witch and the police were released one after another. But the insults to me did not decrease. I longed to go to my home in heaven.

For several months thereafter, they all concentrated on me during the political studies, criticizing me, still holding persistently to the reactionary stand. I had a wild fantasy that Jesus would bring Chairman Mao to trial. As I already mentioned, sleeping on my right side was a young thief, a girl only sixteen years old. She often cried out from homesickness. So I comforted her and shared Jesus with her. The cellmates found out this and threatened her to expose me. The young thief could not stand the non-stop trials against her so one night in the meeting she acknowledged that I led her to the "wicked" way, using sweet words to persuade her to participate in the reactionary superstitious sect, that she nearly believed 917's "cook" Jesus.

The gold-teeth witch stood up immediately and said to me, "How stubborn and dishonest you are! Now everybody stands up to denounce you. Those who trusted the party and criticized their reactionary religion were all released. You not only refuse to criticize, but even try to corrupt people to believe in your religion. We firmly ask the government to punish you severely, you reactionary religious believer!" She was just standing in front of me with her spittle all over her mouth: "Can your 'cook' Jesus slaughter me?"

I boiled with anger and grabbed her hair bob and told her, "It is just because I believe in Jesus that I have not killed you!"

At that time the witch cried out aloud, "She is killing me again!" All the others burst into shouts and came toward me, pressed me to the ground, kicked and beat me and then dragged me to the office. They accused me that I was swollen with reactionary arrogance and intended to kill people, so the police right away locked me up into a single dark cell. I collapsed on the floor unconscious.

I woke up some time later and discovered that I was in a dark muddy room and the space was barely enough for me to lie down and stand. I couldn't even fully stretch out my arms and the only light was dim as a failing flashlight. There was a small sliding window on the locked door. Straw was spread on the ground, very wet with a strong moldy smell.

My ears were still ringing and my head severely ached. A moment later, the guard brought in sheets, washing and brushing stuff and some clothing for me. It seemed that I was going to stay there. I put my stuff on a moldy chair. Thank God there was another chair that I could sit on day and night. Through the entire night I stared at the sky and the bright and twinkling stars through the tiny sliding window. This made me miss my parents afar. Until almost daybreak the morning star was still very bright. "Oh, Jesus, our morning star, please deliver me from evil!"

But there was another voice saying to me, "If the Lord Jesus really cares about you, you would not be here, would you?"

There were two laws and two powers fighting within my heart. The sound of sacred hymns was always within me prevailing above everything.

The hymns were those I loved to sing during my childhood, such as: *"Oh love that will not let me go, I rest my weary soul in thee. I give thee back the life I owe, that in thine ocean depths its flow may richer, fuller be."* Whenever I sang these songs with my hoarse voice, the voice of Satan was gone.

I was in solitary confinement day after day. Water and meals were sent to me through that small window. I was totally isolated from others. A female guard led me to the restroom three times a day, which was quite a distance from my cell. I could walk while breathing some fresh air and enjoyed some sunshine. The single cell was very small and wet. I chose not lie down on the dirty, wet straw. When I stepped on it, the dirty water would ooze out and bugs would emerge from the straw. My washed clothing had to be dried on lines in the tiny cell, which only increased the humidity.

Soon I began to feel itchy all over my body, beginning from my waist extending to my chest, my back and my arms. I scratched my skin so hard, the itchy parts were bleeding before the terrible itch stopped. One day when that young military man was sending food to me and saw blood was all over my arms, he opened the door and took me out to get some sunshine. He took some dry straw for me to exchange for the wet straw. That was the most comfortable day for me. However, I developed terribly painful sores and became worse.

I thought that they would interview or criticize me, but I was completely ignored. I didn't know how many days I had been locked up in solitary. When that young military man was on duty, he showed some compassion to me, and I dared to ask him, "What date is today?" I drew a line on the wall as a mark of passing days. The itch all over my body was increasingly severe and I wished I could have a piece of small tile with which to scrape myself. I used the dry straw stalks for scraping, but they didn't last long and became wet.

I thought of Job and cried out aloud to the Lord. Since I was the only one in the cell, I often talked to myself in a loud voice. "Lord, when Job suffered from sore boils You gave him a piece of potsherd and dried ashes, so he could repent in dust and ashes. Now I need dried ashes. I know that I was fierce and angry to those who insulted me and attacked them by my own flesh and blood, and I was wrong! There is no difference between their flesh and my flesh. I have sinned against You. Please forgive me. I beg You to help me forgive them though I know I am unable to do so."

One day I asked for paper to self-examine and confess. I wrote sheet after sheet of how my cellmates imposed all kinds of limitations on me in addition to the discipline rules of the prison. I wrote about how they forced me to drink the strong pure vinegar with grayish powder that destroyed my voice completely. I also admitted that I shouldn't quarrel with them. After I completed my report, from my blood-stained arms, I gave it to the young military guard, who read it repeatedly. He took my report and walked away.

Our wonderful Lord did not forsake me and He comforted me with His words, *"Yea, though I walk through the valley of the shadow of death, I will fear no evil: for thou art with me; thy rod and thy staff they comfort me."* (Psalm 23: 4) Counting the lines I made on the mud walls, I was locked up in the solitary cell for over three weeks. My heart didn't feel lonely, as all the hymns were my companions. I dared not think of tomorrow. I only prayed to the Lord that He would grant me greater faith so that I could truly believe, *"Because He lives, I can face tomorrow, because He lives all fear is gone."*

The day after I submitted my report, the young military man took me to the hospital and I was diagnosed with a skin disease. I had to take cooked Chinese herb medicines. As it was impossible for them to cook herb medicines for me in the single cell, the police office permitted me especially to return to the big cell. It seemed to me that this young military man was a side door to enable me to get out of temptation.

Upon my return to the big cell, I thought the gold-teeth witch and her triumphant gang would mock me. I never thought that after I entered the cell, all the female prisoners would be friendly and nice to me. They even helped me get some hot water to wash off the bloody stains on my body and clothing. They didn't say anything, but I quickly found out that the gold-teeth witch and two prisoners who bound me up had disappeared. Several days earlier, the police whistled, ordering a big crowd to gather and had sent them away and nobody knew their destination. The three who bullied me most were all gone.

Of course, a new head of the cell would be appointed right away by the police. No matter who she was, she would be more reasonable than the witch. My cellmates murmured that I was the only one who dared to resist the witch, so I received some kind of compassion from them. On the day I returned, it was the young thief sleeping beside me whose duty was to distribute our supper. Because I gave her an extra half of a bowl of congee the first time that I had quarreled with the witch, she returned a piece of sweet potato to me that she had received for being on duty. I knew that she felt guilty in front of me for her false accusation that gave me heavy suffering. But, praise the Lord, I had forgiven her and still felt pity for her.

Chapter 15

Suicide Attempt and Second Vision Revealed

Good days didn't last very long. When I was locked up in solitary, though it was humid, dark, cold, and I was suffering from severe skin disease, I still had some privacy and quietness. I was able to pray aloud and sing hymns with my hoarse voice. After I returned to the big cell, I was surrounded again by cursing, scolding and the noise of humming ditties. Every evening we had political studies and had to hunt "class enemies". We had to criticize ourselves or criticize others, but all the accusations were fabricated nonsense. Everybody was lying and shameless so as to appear harmless and blameless and win credit from the government. All kinds of nonsense and rubbish against one's conscience were spoken and done.

Communism became a religion and their rulers were as gods, especially Stalin and Mao Ze-Dong. So every night everyone had to worship and praise Mao Ze-Dong, for example, "Look at the Plough, which points us the direction, only our savior Mao can give us hope." "Dad is close and dear, mom is close and dear, but Chairman Mao is the closest and dearest." "Arise, ye sinners of all nations, there never has been any savior, and we do not depend on any god or emperor." To me these words were so annoying.

How pitiful are we Chinese and how long are we going to continue to worship idols?

O Lord, Take Me Home!

No matter who was being criticized, counter-revolutionaries and prisoners of conscience were always the targets of criticism and accusation. I was especially singled out to be ferociously cursed because starting with my grandfather on my mother's side, my family had been Christians for three generations. All those who fawned to the police and flattered the head of the cell were released one after another. After every round of accusations, the conclusion of the police for me was always: "Effective in reformation through hard labor, but still stubbornly clinging to the stand of reactionary religion."

They also said frankly to me, "The reeducation through hard labor here has no limitation to terms and days. If one is reformed well, one could be released in one year. But, in the case of someone like you who resists the reformation, you could stay here for life. It is your own choice."

Large character print slogans were hung on the walls where we slept, saying, "Leniency to those who confess their crimes and severity to those who refuse, stubborn, die-hard, clinging to your wrong position, your destination is death." When we prisoners slept, our feet were close to the walls and our heads were toward the walking aisle in the middle of the room so the police could count the number of heads of the prisoners to guarantee that nobody was missing. My eyes had no choice but always to stare at these slogans, especially, "Your destination is death!"

Surrounded by those female criminals who were always smoking and humming dirty ditties, I had no peace. I suffered more and more from terrible headaches, tinnitus and fainting, because of many beatings with an electric stick and from being locked up in solitary confinement. Sometimes I talked aloud to myself and didn't even know what I was saying. I was totally absent-minded, unaware of what I was doing.

When we stopped working in the field and lined up to return to the prison, I subconsciously left the ranks and went back to the field or walked away to nowhere. Of course, I was found and brought back and accused of trying to escape. I believed that if I were locked up here indefinitely, I would surely go insane. *He that shall endure unto the end, the same shall be saved.*"(Matthew. 24:13) But what is *"unto the end"*? I had already been locked up here for many years and I saw no end. The police said I would stay here for my lifetime.

I was sleepless throughout the nights and always faced the word "Death!" on the slogan. I thought that we Christians were not afraid of death. Now I am of use to no one; I am not able to support my parents or help my younger sisters. I would rather go on to our heavenly home and wait for them. So every night I asked God to take me home and made my last word of prayer, as if on my deathbed.

Because I was sleepless, I kept asking the doctor to give me some sleeping pills, which I then stored up. If I went to the clinic to get medicine for my cellmates, I would grab more sleeping pills. I planned not to eat or drink for several days so that I would be terribly weak and feeble. Then I planned to take a large number of sleeping pills to commit suicide, ending my miserable life.

After I decided on my plan, I secretly gave away my dark and bitter bread to my cellmates. Several days later I was so weak that I couldn't even stand. The medical doctor measured my blood pressure and it was only 80/46. He suggested that I have an infusion of glucose but I told him that I was afraid of shots and would rather drink it. So the doctor laid me down and gave me a cup of glucose liquid to drink, but later I threw it away. Everything was going as I planned.

One night I brought a cup of water to my bedside and tried to swallow all the pills I had collected, after everybody went to sleep. I made my final prayer, but suddenly, on the slogan which read, "Your destination is death!" a beautiful picture appeared of a big tree. Under the tree there was a well made of stone. The Lord Jesus wore a white robe while sitting at the well and beside Him was a woman kneeling, staring at Jesus. Next to her was an over-turned water pot with water flowing out. The Lord Jesus, with head lowered, was talking kindly to the woman. Full of surprise, she then lifted her head to Him.

This picture immediately reminded me of the story in the Bible where Jesus talked to the Samaritan woman by the well about the truth that He is the Living Water! Seeing this picture, I completely forgot what I was planning to do and immediately sat up, trying to get close to this picture. My heart was suddenly enlightened. This Samaritan woman was a sinner, but Jesus loved her greatly. The Samaritan woman received the Living Water of

Jesus Himself! She was but a walking corpse, a shameful, degraded woman even among the Samaritans. But after she heard the teaching of Jesus, she went back to the town and told everybody that she had found the Messiah and shared her personal testimony about Jesus.

The story of the Samaritan woman was right before my eyes and I was stunned for quite a long period of time before this picture. My soul was totally released by the Holy Spirit. I understood right away that the story of the Samaritan woman was what God intended to tell me. Jesus is the Son of God, the Messiah, yet He was sharing the truth with a gentile Samaritan woman.

Drawn by the love of Jesus, a sinner would confess his or her sin and testify for Jesus. I was a sinner, too, but I didn't recognize this and make my own confession, so that I could freely enjoy His salvation. The Lord Jesus loved these sinners, the surrounding prison inmates, but I despised, detested and hated them without mercy. Was I testifying for Jesus? I was unable to continue my plan until I confessed to Jesus the hatred in my heart.

The old hymn began to sing in my heart, *"A bruised reed shall He not break, and the smoking flax shall He not quench: Jesus is merciful and He is the Lord of grace and He loves me to the end."* I understood that Jesus meant this message not only for me but also for all the criminals around me. In my own heart, self-reproach replaced self-righteousness and confession drove away my arrogance.

They Became Lovable

I raised my arms and cried out, full of tears: "Lord! Forgive me, I am a sinner, please, Lord, forgive me!"

Suddenly I was hit by a cold rifle butt and heard a very husky, rude voice shouting, "What are you doing?" It was the guard who was always patrolling outside the cells and monitoring the prisoners. A light was always turned on in each cell. When the guard saw me raise my hands he came in and shouted at me. He found all the sleeping pills beside my pillow and confiscated them. He ordered me to put on my clothes and took me to the office. I figured the police had already gotten a report from my fellow inmates that I was on a hunger strike.

To my surprise, the police officer did not punish me. He probably realized that I intended to commit suicide, so they wanted to calm me down first. They also found out that my cellmates had put too much pressure on me. The police sent me to the medical clinic to have some infusions and shots to keep me alive.

After I recovered the police shifted my hard labor to go out and collect animal manure alone, separating me from all the prisoners during labor time. At night, the police ordered me to help write confessions for female cellmates because most of them were illiterate. The Lord is always so amazing that in order to let me learn the lesson of "brokenness and restoration" He prepared special teachers for me, my cellmates, whom I despised and hated because they beat and bullied me often.

When I wrote down their confessions one after the other about how they committed their crimes, compassion and sadness for them welled up in my heart. I could not even imagine what they had gone through, making them also victims and sufferers. When the female criminals described their stories, there were no expressions on their faces and it seemed that their hearts were apathetic and dead. But I, as the recorder, had eyes brimming with tears. I had to stop many times because I couldn't write anymore.

Their miserable and tragic childhoods contrasted with my easy, comfortable and wealthy childhood. For some of the female cellmates their biological fathers, stepfathers or brothers had sexually abused them. In many cases, these women had been only five or six years old when their innocence was taken away. They knew nothing about self-respect, self-esteem or self-defense. The purpose of their living was simply survival by selling their bodies.

Some of the criminals were good girls, but simply very poor and uneducated. They entered society and met bad men and learned how to steal. During the nationwide famine in China from 1958 through 1962, because their whole families were starving to death, they began to steal food to survive. They began to steal by grabbing some bread on the streets to bring some food home for their family members. Then they were caught and sent into the detention houses. After they were released, they stole again, were caught again, and finally imprisoned. Some just could not endure the insults, brutality and cruelty of their husbands, so they killed them out of self-defense.

Some Communist officials abandoned their first wives after they moved to the cities. The officials had affairs with other women and remarried.

Their daughters, however, responded to the injustice of the treatment of their biological mothers who had served their husbands and suffered for so many years. The daughters argued with their fathers, hurting them, so that the daughters were put behind bars. Such miserable and bitter stories one after another were described to me. Not having had any of these kinds of experiences, I could not even imagine that such tragedies could happen in this world! If I were one of them, would I commit the same crimes as they did and become a desperate victim without facial expression and feeling in my heart?

These poor women had never been loved by someone or even understood what love was. What God graciously bestowed on me was His amazing grace, abundant gifts, a wealthy family, comfortable home and higher education. I had lived surrounded by love, but I had no grateful heart. Nor had I learned from Jesus to love sinners. When I read "Les Miserables" by Victor Hugo and "Great Expectations" by Charles Dickens, I cried a lot. Now around me were so many pitiful, miserable women, to whom I had turned a blind eye. They treated me badly, but they were not aware of their sins. My swelling pride made me esteem myself higher than I should, so I despised them. After several days of recording their confessions, it seemed that my circumstance changed and my cellmates were more lovable.

As a matter of fact, God did not change the circumstance, but He changed my heart and empowered me to love those "Samaritan women" with whom I stayed day and night. I realized later that God used those circumstances to crush my self-righteousness. I asked their forgiveness one by one. My bitterness disappeared. After that I did my best to help them.

They would murmur, "That '917' is crazy. Three days ago she tried to commit suicide, now she is really happy." I didn't care what they said. I just enjoyed the love the Lord God poured down on me.

Chapter 16

Joy of Collecting Manure and Born-Again

The job the police assigned to me was to go out of the labor camp alone to collect animal manure to be used as fertilizer. This hard labor was terribly filthy and tough, but God rewarded me with unexpected joy and benefits. After I finished drinking my "four-eye congee soup" every morning, I brought my portion of two dark and bitter sunflower-seed husk bread and dried radish with me, and went out of the labor camp all by myself with a manure basket on my back. I felt as if I had been delivered from the persecution and once again saw the bright light of heaven!

There were boundless stretches of rice fields, twists and turns of small paths, green trees and a variety of wild flowers. The air was so fresh and pure that I felt refreshed. Along the small muddy paths, I passed village after village as I searched for animal manure and human waste that were left along the roads, paths and ridges between the rice fields. Manure was hard to find and collect because it was considered precious fertilizer that all farmers used to nourish their grain fields. After being locked up in the cell of the labor camp for so long, now all of a sudden, I was alone. Able to breathe the fresh air in the vast expanse of wilderness, I felt at ease.

Looking at the blue sky and the white clouds, I was aware of how small I was. It seemed to me that the whole sky was God's arms reaching out and embracing me.

Hymns that my mother taught me since I was little, such as *"How Great Thou Art!"* and *"Precious Lord, Lead Me On"* welled up in my heart. I couldn't help but sing freely with all my might: "Precious Lord, take my hand and lead me on." I was completely baptized in total dependence on the Lord and enjoyed the pleasant sweetness of intimacy with Him alone. Out in the fields there were no harsh cries, shouts, curses and abuse, no decadent ditties to hear, or dense cigarette smoke. Only the Lord Jesus and the whole of nature were with me. How happy and joyful I was, praise and thanksgiving for Him came from the bottom of my heart!

When the sun began to set and it was beginning to get dark, I knew the manure I had collected hardly filled a half of my basket. If I went back and reported to the police officer, he would harshly rebuke me: "You lazy bone, I didn't send you out to idle your time away. You must bring back at least fifty pounds every day!" I now had a quota to complete each day. That day I had no luck finding manure. I only collected a little light dried horse manure, so I was afraid to return to the camp.

I sat down on the muddy road and prayed. I guessed no angel would likely come down to help me accomplish the filthy job of collecting manure. As I began slowly to walk back to the camp, I saw an old farmer approaching me in a horse cart. At first glance, I saw that at the back of the horsetail there was a full bag of fresh manure. I quickly ran to the farmer and asked politely: "Dear uncle, could you give me some of your horse manure?"

The old farmer examined me a while and then asked, "Where are you from?" I pointed to the huge red gate of the labor camp quite a distance away, and the old farmer realized right away. Around that area, everybody knew that behind that particular red gate was a hard labor camp where criminals were being reformed. Then the old farmer educated me, "I see you are still very young. How come you were put behind that 'red gate'? Have you forgotten how your parents brought you up with much painstaking care and effort? I can give you half of the horse manure I have, but you have to promise me that you will begin a new life from now on."

"Yes, uncle, yes sir," I quickly responded and promised him, but for me to accomplish the quota was more important, so I didn't care too much about what he thought of me. That day I returned to the labor camp with a full bag of fresh manure and fulfilled the quota. From then on I got used to meeting the old farmer on my way back to the camp everyday. I called him my "manure-providing angel." With his help, I was able to complete my quota each day. But day after day I was still criticized by the guard for I didn't finish the total task of manure collecting.

Several days later, while I was waiting for the old farmer, I noticed him walking slowly toward me without his horse cart. I was quite disappointed when I saw that he had no manure. I said to him: "Uncle, long time no see, do you still have some manure for me today?"

The old farmer didn't answer right away, and then he said, "Follow me." I followed him into his village and as we approached his house, the strong stink of ammonia irritated my nose and eyes. The farmer led me to his livestock barn and stable and pointed his finger to show me: "The roof of my stable collapsed, so this is the deal. You ask your responsible leaders to send some men to help me build a new stable, and I will let you take all the manure stored in this manure pit."

It seemed to me that I had really found a treasure, so I ran back to the camp and reported to the police. The police talked to the officials in the office and they all thought it was a worthy deal. We had a lot of manpower anyway. The police called on over ten male prisoners and ordered them to bring some tools, wood boards and other materials. They followed me to the old farmer's home. All those strong hands quickly built a brand new stable for him and I was the one to take the lead to clean the manure pit. The manure had accumulated in the pit for many years and was already fermented. The manure generated maggots and they were very sticky. We had to use small shovels to scrape, bit by bit, place it into small basins and then lift them into buckets. Then we loaded them into the carts. Several hours later, we finally finished the job and the manure pit was completely clean. When we finished, all of us were covered in manure from head to toe.

After we returned to the reeducation camp, all of us were praised by the police. We had fulfilled the task of collecting manure as fertilizers once and for all. Each of us also had a special treat. We were allowed to use the police bathrooms to take showers. Since I was the only female prisoner, I was allowed to use the female police bathroom and enjoy the warm shower alone and in peace. The joy was surging like the tide in my heart. All by myself in the shower room, I couldn't help but count all the blessings that God bestowed on me since my childhood. I kept thanking God for His grace and also confessing my sins and repenting.

A stream of warm current poured upon my whole body. It was not the hot water but a warm spiritual current cleansing and purifying my heart. I was unable to distinguish which drops were from the shower and which were my tears of repentance and joy. I felt empowered. If a Samaritan woman could become a witness for the Lord Jesus, could not the Lord also use me? If Jesus told all the disciples to remember and tell everyone that sinful woman's righteous act, when she broke the alabaster jar of very precious ointment and poured it on His feet, why couldn't I be changed? No more like an alabaster jar, beautiful and shining on the outside, I was still dirty and smelly inside. Now I determined to be willingly cleansed, broken by the Lord and let Him pour His fragrant ointment on my broken pieces so that I could send forth His fragrance.

I was set in my heart and cried out: "Lord, I don't know when I will be free again, but, I will not be ashamed of the gospel of Christ nor will I throw myself at the feet of the world to preserve an ignoble life and betray my Lord. Lord, I will not try to commit suicide to escape the lessons you want me to learn. Please break me totally and rebuild and renew my spirit!"

The Lord lighted a spiritual fire in me to confess my sins. I felt so warm and fervent in my heart that I was totally relieved. The wicked one was far away from me. Only my gracious Lord was with me! I felt I had completely recovered from a critical illness and it seemed that I was empowered and able to follow Jesus, to run a thousand miles.

From then on, I felt that all the female inmates around me were so lovable. How had this hard labor camp suddenly become a rose garden? The love welling up in my heart kept me incessantly thanking and praising God for His grace to a wretch like me. Abba Father, I didn't know that you love me so much! I wanted to call upon those pitiful criminals and shout, "Let us come to the throne of our gracious Lord and repent and confess! The Lord Jesus loves you and loves me!" I wanted to lift up my hoarse voice and sing. I sang because I now had freedom. I sang because I didn't have any worry. *His eye is on the sparrow and He watches and protects me*. I knew that I was experiencing my rebirth and being filled with the Holy Spirit. I didn't care to think more deeply but just kept enjoying the sweetness of the Lord.

Chapter 17

Praising the Lord in Surgery

The police used hard labor to force me to do all kinds of back breaking tough manual jobs: going out without food to collect filthy manure, cleaning toilets, insults, humiliation, criticism, denouncing, threats, fear, torture, torments and ruining me. They tried to take away my youth. But God protected me and prevented the wicked one from hurting my life.

In 1965, the medical clinic at the hard labor camp bought new X radiation equipment and required all cellmates who constantly had fevers or were coughing to check their lungs. This was because tuberculosis was prevalent among the cellmates. When they examined me, the X-ray showed a big shadow hole on my upper left lung.

The doctors diagnosed my illness as a large round-shaped tuberculosis tumor with a clear-cut margin. This diagnosis terribly frightened all the police and the prisoners because if tuberculosis spread, then all of them would be infected. Suddenly I became their disaster, and the police officers of higher rank gave the order to send me to the best and biggest hospital of Tianjin City right away. I was to have medical treatment to prevent anything else happening, since I had to be sent back to the labor camp.

However, when the doctor at the clinic read my medical record and realized that I was a prisoner transferred from the hard labor camp, he didn't pay any attention to me. He casually walked out of the room to care for other patients.

My X-ray picture was still visible on the screen. As I was waiting there alone and humiliated, a group of medical interns led by a doctor appeared. He accidentally noticed my X-ray picture. He was attracted immediately. Upon entering the room and seeing the X-ray more closely, he asked, "Whose picture is this?"

I said, "It's mine."

He asked, "How long you have suffered?"

I replied, "I have felt physically weak for a number of years, but only recently did I get the chance to have a check up and an X-ray."

Then this medical specialist turned to his interns telling them, "The X-ray picture is showing so clearly a very typical tuberculosis tumor, which could rarely be found." They didn't stay very long but walked out of the room. Finally, the doctor who ignored me came back and told me, "We will hospitalize you today and Dr. Zhang (a well-known medical specialist of thoracic surgery) will examine you."

It Seemed That I Was in a Palace

Amazingly, I was hospitalized and received as the patient of a famous medical specialist. After a thorough physical examination, the doctors found that I was low in red blood cells, blood pressure and blood sugar. I was not strong enough to have surgery right away, so the hospital treated me with special nutritious food to bring my physical condition to normal. More than two weeks later, all my results from the labs indicated normal. After so many years of sleeping without a bed and constantly being starved, suddenly I was sleeping on a soft bed with clean white sheets. Served milk, eggs and other nutritious food, I felt as though I had been transferred to the royal palace.

Dr. Zhang clearly told me when he came to my ward and examined me, "What you are suffering is a large tuberculosis tumor and the only way you can be healed is to remove it. During the surgery, two of your ribs will also be removed. Because of this, after the operation your whole body will be tilted to the left. During the surgery, the knife will cut from the back of your neck and shoulder all the way to your chest under your left breast. Your left mammary gland will also be cut, so if you are married, you will not be able to feed your baby with your own milk in the future."

Dr. Zhang thought I would be full of worry, since I was an unmarried young girl. The calmness I felt surprised him. That calm was possible because I knew that Jesus said, *"I am the resurrection, and the life."* Whether I die or live, I belong to Jesus and He will take all the responsibility. As a matter of fact, every day I was facing death or life, who would care about a tilting body? I had no opportunity to get married, so why should I worry about feeding a baby?

Several days later, I learned that Dr. Zhang's mother was a Chinese indigenous missionary.

I remember the day of the surgery that was set for six o'clock in the morning. Prior to being sent into the operating room, the patient usually has to take a sedative, but I refused. I wanted to see what a thoracic surgery room looked like. After I was sent into surgery, I found out that I was a patient chosen for medical interns to observe as part of their training. They were sitting in a surgery observation room outside the operation room separated by glass windows in order to watch Dr. Zhang operate.

When the anesthetists gave me the anesthetic, they asked me to count. I was quietly praying, "Lord, I give myself to You. Hold my life and soul in Your loving hands." Not counting even to twenty before losing consciousness, I felt very peaceful in my heart.

When I awoke from the operation, I found there was a big crowd of doctors, anesthetists and nurses and somebody was shouting, "She's awakening!" Later the anesthetist told me that the anesthetic they gave me was a routine dose, but they didn't know that I was so sensitive to anesthetic. Then he explained that usually for a patient after a four-hour surgery, he or she would awake one to two hours after the surgery was done. They didn't expect me to remain unconscious over twelve hours!

After the explanation, they left. I originally thought, "Oh, this hospital is really concerned and cares for me and the other patients." But, later my ward mate told me that lying in the next ward to us, there was an intensive care patient who lost consciousness for over fifteen years due to an overdose of anesthetic during an operation. It was malpractice and the patient had become a kind of "guinea pig." His body had shrunken to a meter long. That was the reason the whole surgical medical team was so nervous about me.

After the operation, I was sent to the intensive care ward for observation. The ward mates asked me who introduced me to cause the director and Dr. Tian-Hui Zhang, the well-known thoracic surgeon, to specially operate on me. It was not until then that I suddenly realized that this famous Dr. Zhang would only accept invitations from high-ranking Communist officials to do special surgeries for them. Yet, my awesome God used a careless clinical surgeon to introduce me to this Dr. Zhang. With a casual glance, he became so interested in the tumor that I suffered, that he made the arrangement for my admission and operation.

More amazing to me was that early the next morning Dr. Zhang came again to my ward. After he checked all the tubes and systems of exhausting water from the lung, urine, and infusions of my body, he said: "I have good news for you. First, your lung is pink in color that means it is very healthy and clean; second, your tumor was very big, but it wasn't tuberculosis. It wasn't my mistake in diagnosis, because on the X-ray picture it was shown as a typical tuberculosis tumor. During the surgery, it turned out to be a very typical complex-structure tumor. It was benign. The removal of this tumor was a correct decision that will be good for your health. Well, your symptom really pulled a big joke on me!"

After he said this, I could not, and dared not, laugh because my wounds were still badly hurting me. In my heart I was very pleased. My God made a small joke with this well-known medical specialist. If it hadn't been for the mistake in diagnosis of the medical doctor in the labor camp, how would I have been sent to this first class hospital to enjoy nutritious treatment for many days and the best surgery by the most capable doctor? If I had been sent to the prison hospital, I didn't dare to think of the result of the surgery. They would probably have cut me into pieces!

Therefore, sometimes, God permits Satan to ruin our body and soul to a certain extent, but He is always in sovereign control of all and preserves our lives. How wonderful it was! I wanted to glorify His name! By Dr. Zhang's order, I was hospitalized for another four weeks to recover. Then I was sent back to the original hard labor camp for more hard labor and collecting manure.

Chapter 18

A Night Parolee

From 1964 to 1965, the year Mao Ze Dong initiated the "socialist education movement," throughout China in all the society, the so-called "Four 'Clean-ups' Movement" started. The main goal of this movement was to fight against corruption, stealing, waste and diverting public funds and property of the Communist cadres and officials. It sounded good, but it was actually another of Mao's political plots which he always used to raid his political enemies.

At the beginning it was led by the former head of state, Chairman Shao-Qi Liu. When the political drive impacted the jail system, the Communists punished some of the bad police officials by putting them in prison. As for prisoners of conscience who opposed Mao Ze-Dong and Communism only in ideology, after hard labor reeducation, the cases of those prisoners who had obvious changes in ideology would be reevaluated. They would then be sent back to where they came from to face a new future.

One day in the spring of 1966, the police called me to the office. When I walked in I was aware right away of several visiting high-ranking officials sitting in the room. They talked to me very politely saying, "We've been working here for several days and have examined all the personal criminal files of the prisoners kept here. Today, the government intends to point out a way for you. Your labor credit has been consistently good, and if you completely change your ideology and mindset, give up your reactionary religious superstition and become 'both red and expert', which means both socialist-minded and vocationally proficient, we will immediately send you back to your original unit. We welcome you back to the people ranks to continue to serve the people."

The official added, "This is your last day here either way. If you obstinately stick to the wrong course and refuse to come to your senses, then we have no other choice but to severely punish you and send you to another jail. We believe that you will not be ignorant and stubborn to the end. What do you think? Do you understand and recognize now that the U.S. imperialists invaded China through the religion of Christianity? Do you accept that the espionage activities of your father David Chang involved working for the Americans as a spy, and that you yourself have been poisoned by the Christian religion and remained reactionary in ideology?"

At the beginning, I had hope because their attitude was kind and polite. Later I had different thoughts, so I prayed secretly to my Lord first: "Lord, I may have freedom immediately, but they haven't given up the intention to use me to insult and malign You, Your name and Your servant. Lord, if I have to deny You and my father to get the freedom, then it still means that I betray You. My loss of freedom for six years would be totally in vain. Then it is surely not Your will to release me." Hence, I replied to them, "For six years, all the officials in charge have said that I am a stubborn fool and today you tell me the same thing. May I ask you something?"

They said, "Of course!"

Then I said, "Six years ago, when the governmental officials raised and asked these questions, I gave my answers to them clearly. Today my answer to you is the same, with no change! Christianity is not opium, nor a reactionary superstition to poison the Chinese. Since I was little, I have believed in Jesus and the greatest influence of Him on me is His love. Jesus so loved the world, all people and nations. The influence of the American missionaries on me personally has two aspects: first, they introduced me to Jesus' life and Biblical knowledge; and second, I was trained by them in English and music. I would not say that they poisoned me. On the other hand, during these six years being reformed and educated in this labor camp, I recognized man's sinful human nature, weakness, unrighteousness and being without love and mercy. Therefore, during these six years, I was willing to do all the hard labor and my attitude has been correct and I have certain achievements. I understand that I should be reformed and educated."

I took a breath and continued, "My father is a patriot with national integrity and self-respect. He is an evangelical Christian. In the official circles of the old society, my father had been honest and upright and did people good turns. Yet, he was pushed out by the corrupt government officials. I respect my father very much. I don't have any new understanding. If you think that I am stubborn and a fool for believing in a God that we could not see, why don't you just leave me alone? I didn't do anything to harm the country or the community. If you think God does not exist, why do you care so much, and why do you need to stir up trouble and lock a fool like me away for six years?"

When I finished speaking these things, I saw the expression of the official become sterner and he made his face longer. I didn't know how I had the boldness to complete my statement in one breath. The official finally concluded, "Some people would give up only at the sight of the gallows. The policy of our government is always consistent. Since you are willing to resist continuously to the end, it is your choice and you have decided all by yourself. Go and pack your stuff and we will send you off early tomorrow morning."

I knew that my prospect was dark, but I couldn't figure out where they were going to send me. I wasn't scared and panicked like I was six years ago. I think people who are locked up in the bottom of the society for a long period of time are just like food stored in the deep freezer. They are already totally frozen stiff. Their hearts are dead toward the world and their reactions to any happiness, anger, sorrow or pleasure are slow. Not until I was sent home and met my family face to face, would I believe I was free. Before me there is only one way, "To trust and obey Jesus" is what I told myself.

Jail Factory

The next day police escorted me in a car and drove me all the way into the city of Tianjin. Since all the car windows were shaded and we drove a long time, I had no idea where we were heading. Finally, the car reached its destination and I got out. Looking around, I noticed it was "Tianjin Municipal Prison". In front there was a huge tall iron gate and surrounding the prison were high walls with electrified wire. When I saw this, my heart tightened, I figured this time I would be sentenced for sure.

In the vicinity of the prison there was boundless wilderness. However, the police officer did not take me into the prison, but instead took me to the compound across the street opposite the prison, also with a high wall and electric barbed wire. At the gate a big sign was hung indicating "New Life Union Factory." What was this? The policeman left after he escorted me to the office and after a little while another policeman stepped into the office and questioned me. "Do you know what kind of place is this?" he asked.

"No, I have no idea."

This official told me gently, "This is a hard labor factory affiliated with the prison under the proletarian dictatorship. You have a record of hard labor for six years in a hard labor camp, but you have no crimes committed or criminal sanction. You have civil rights but the authority has temporarily suspended them. Despite your good hard labor record, your ideological thoughts are reactionary. You are stubborn in resisting to be reformed, so we should deal with you severely."

The eyes of this man did not even give me one glance as he was continuously reading my thick file. It occurred to me since the Communists liberated China in 1949, when I was studying in the middle school and college, all the students had to submit a report to the authority checking our ideological thinking and political consciousness. But why was it that thick? Would these personal files, written and reported, irresponsibly, by someone whom I would never know determine my fate?

I firmly believe that God is sovereign and has put my name into His Book of Life. This official went on to say, "Considering the future of a young woman like you, we, the government, intend to save it the best we can. According to your case we can not sentence you."

I put my life in God's hands no matter how they were going to deal with me. I replied, "Since you are not able to sentence me, please release me."

"No, we can not release you either. We will send you to this reform-through-hard labor factory to do hard labor as a released political prisoner under governmental watch. After the required working hours, you can check out at night and go home, but each morning you have to check in to the factory. The officials will be responsible for your reformation of ideological thinking and you have to observe all the disciplines. When you are at home, your local police station and your neighborhood committee will watch all your behavior. You are not allowed to leave Tianjin City. Every morning at seven you check in to the factory and every evening at seven you check out. Now you can go home!"

I couldn't believe that the Lord miraculously rescued me partially first! Today, I am able to go home and see my parents! Coming out of that gate, I didn't know where I was or which direction I should head to go home. However, I was overwhelmed and cherished how precious this freedom was!

I kept asking people about directions and changed many buses. I didn't live in the society for six years. I used fully two hours to reach the home with which I had been so familiar, but now was so unfamiliar. As I was approaching home, I was really homesick and concerned about my parents and family members.

I knocked at the door. My mom opened it. I couldn't believe that standing in front of me the woman with all white hair and stooped body was my kind mother, who used to be so elegant and graceful with dark hair and pearl-like teeth, who loved to laugh and sing. My mom looked up at me, stunned, and then quickly hugged me tightly. She couldn't speak out for a while. Then she began to tremble and asked, "My child, how could you come back? You didn't betray our Lord, right?"

As we walked into the sitting room, I saw my dad sitting on the sofa. He was full of white hair, his face pale and swollen, and his body feeble. Smiling, he got up slowly and limped to me saying, "My child, how could you come home?" I quickly took him back to the sofa to sit down.

Six years had passed and we were telling each other stories with tears and kept thanking the Lord. My dad now suffered from serious heart disease, so he was paroled because of his health temporarily. My younger sister next to me had graduated from Shanxi Provincial Medical College and was assigned to a far away mountain region to work in a hospital. My youngest sister had always been the brightest among her classmates in middle school, but was not allowed to enter college because our father and I were counter-revolutionaries. She had been assigned to a factory as a worker.

My mom was very feeble due to the heavy burden of the family and the sorrow of thinking of and longing for me. However, we all were grateful to God that He amazingly preserved our lives. We talked and talked with tears and laughter until midnight. That night I slept on a sofa beside my parents. I didn't want to be a step away from them. Praise the Lord I was still alive to see that my parents still survived. But how could I shoulder the heavy responsibility to support my parents' and sister's daily living?

Five o'clock the next morning, I had to leave home because I needed two hours to get to the hard labor factory. I felt my legs dragged by tons of weight because I didn't want to leave home, and I wasn't sure that I could come back to this sweet home again. My mom got up very early to prepare me a delicious hot breakfast and said, "My child, go, God has already preserved you for six years and He will not abandon you now. The Lord is watching over you in heaven. Stand firm in the truth and let's endure and hold on together!"

I was greatly comforted and hugged my parents as I left home. It was still very dark and stars were twinkling over the sky. I had to change buses four times. Then I had to walk quite a long way to reach the hard labor factory since the prison and its factory were located in the suburb of Tianjin City. There my life began as a night parolee for fourteen years.

The life of a night parolee and the hardships and lessons facing me were different from my experience in the hard labor camp. There I was locked up, but now every night I had the freedom to stay with my family. I wasn't able to get home until nine at night and every morning I had to leave home at five o'clock. I checked out from the factory at seven in the evening and checked in at seven in the morning. It took me two hours for the trip each way. In wintertime I never had a chance to see the sun. Only the moon and stars accompanied me.

I had Sundays off, so our family members were able to get together for services and fellowship as a house church where I was fed graciously in spirit. After I became a night parolee, I was very hungry and thirsty to study the Bible and other teachings from my father. I learned about the revelation of the Biblical truth in the Chinese culture and characters that I learned a bit in childhood, but didn't pay too much attention to at that time. My dad and I began to have deep spiritual fellowship. I was no longer a little girl, who used to depend on him. While I grew up, my dad became more dependent and needed physically more of my care, consideration and service. He acted as a spiritual elder helping me.

Another reason that God allowed me to come home and stay with my parents, a reason which I didn't know until later was that we could depend on each other for survival during the crazy "Cultural Revolution" catastrophe. Initiated by Mao Ze-Dong, it came right after I was half-released from the hard labor camp prison in the spring of 1966.

In the hard labor camp, everybody except the police officials was a criminal to be reformed and reeducated. We were equal, but now as I went back home to the community, the people I faced were citizens and had already been informed by the local police station and the neighborhood committee that my father and I should be watched closely. They all knew the government had determined that the nature of our case was contradictions between people and the enemy. Therefore, what I saw from the neighbors were all hate-filled glances.

Despite the fact that my dad was already old and weak, he was ordered to clean up trash of the compound every day and sweep the snow in the winter. We both had to send written reports to the local police station frequently about our ideological thoughts. The local police appointed our neighbors the surveillance task to watch us, including what we ate, what we did and said and who our visitors were. Our daily life was in the public eye. I heard at my back women's gossip accusing me as a "night parolee, bad apple!"

Since our factory was affiliated with the prison, when there were big mass meetings, all the laborers had to line up in ranks like criminals. Led by the police, we were taken across the street into the prison. There were a lot of adults and kids who shouted at us, "prisoners crossing the street!" to dampen our self-respect. The hard labor in the factory was also different. It involved mainly industrial production. The requirements of the production technology and the quota were quite high and strict. Among the things we produced were all kinds and sizes of door and window hinges, military uniforms, and raincoats for miners.

I had to carry boxes of metal stuff for hours and every box weighed over 100 pounds. I had to pile up these boxes into stacks forty boxes wide and twenty high, so they could easily be counted when delivered. I also used electric knives to cut thick rubberized fabric of fifty layers for the material to make military men's raincoats. According to the design, I had to do it with great caution. Otherwise my left hand fingers would be cut off. However, God protected me. Also one wrong cut would cost the loss of the material for 500 raincoats. What we got was not only a tongue-lashing, but because we damaged the national economic income, we would suffer demerits and be punished. No penalties could be assessed because our living allowance was already the lowest in society, equivalent to four dollars per month per person.

Everyday we prisoners just worked and worked and became overtired and worried about making any mistake. Many clever and smart female prisoners were doing a great job but the Lord taught me, a clumsy person. Amazingly, I soon was able to catch up to those who were intelligent with skillful hands. Every day we had to move very heavy big wooden boxes and pile them up high. One had to hold the box and climb up to place them high properly. If one accidentally dropped the heavy box, it would break one's feet. God heard my prayers so that no accident occurred and no mistake was made. One time I was even singled out as an "advanced worker." Since we were overworked and worked overtime, I often felt sleepy. In order to avoid injury, I had to pinch my own thigh to keep myself awake at work. Late at night I often fell asleep on the bus and went past the stop where I should get off.

During the "Cultural Revolution" there were repeated crazy political drives in the society that impacted our factory and the criticism movements were even more overheated than those in the society. Of course, a Catholic nun, a member of the "St. Mary's Legion" and I were always the targets. Some of the Catholic Christians and I refused to give up our faith, so many times we were detained in the factory and forbidden to go home. We were escorted to the prison to be accused and criticized with the criminals. Chief officials threatened to sentence us and humiliated and defiled us again and again. The Apostle Paul said: *"Knowing that tribulation worketh patience; and patience, experience; and experience, hope: And hope maketh not ashamed…"* (Romans 5: 3-4) Whatever misfortune would befall me, maybe even death, I just wanted to trust and obey and wait for Him!

I praised the Lord that He not only gave me a trial for six years, but also let me see with my own eyes those among the Catholic nuns who overcame. I also saw the strong faith my parents had even though they were already old, sick and feeble. All these encouraged me to believe that *"He that endures to the end shall be saved."* (Matthew 10:22)

When I was little, I often laughed at those Catholic nuns with their expressionless faces. Now I understood that to them the world is dead. How precious it was that we could face the wicked world with no emotion or expression. But I still had too much emotion, expression, pain, grief and feelings of unfairness, which made my nerves break down. Satan found that my heart was willing to obey my Lord, so he attacked me where I was physically weak. Sometimes I didn't know what I was saying or what I was doing with my hands. I was out of my mind. Lord, please heal me!

Chapter 19

Home Ransacked by Red Guards

Several months after I began my work at the New Life Union Factory, Mao Ze-Dong initiated the so-called "Unprecedented Proletarian Great Cultural Revolution." First the news spread that students rose in rebellion and they defiled, humiliated, criticized, denounced, beat and killed their teachers. I had graduated from the Catholic Shenggong Girls' High School (now called Xinhua middle school) in Tianjin. I was told a gentleman whom we had called Teacher Xiao who taught physics and was a devoted Catholic Christian, had his home ransacked. He was tortured and persecuted. Teacher Yun-Xiang Lao, a well-known mathematics teacher and both of the Yang sisters who taught Chinese literature were brutally tortured. One of them was tortured to death by very pure and concentrated Lysol liquid poured on her from head to toe by Red Guards until her whole body decomposed.

Mao's plot was to use the teenage youths, because they were ignorant and fanatic, to condemn their teachers as class enemies. These were the same teachers who had taught the students all kinds of good courses and knowledge. The Red Guards' slogan as Mao commanded them was, "Strike down all the class enemies - monsters and demons, forces of evil to the dust and tread their feet on their bodies!" and "Revolution is a violent operation when one class turns over another class."

So in the schools, competitions were provoked how to quickly and efficiently torture their teachers to death without using any weapon. In the mass meetings of criticism and denouncing, all the teachers were forced to kneel down and to pay their own cremation fees to the Red Guards in advance so in case they were beaten to death, their bodies could be directly transported to the crematory. All of a sudden the Red Guards became the proletarian force under the personal leadership of Mao Ze-Dong. Even the police and military men completely submitted to all the violent actions by the Red Guards in order to avoid conflicts.

Therefore, this anarchist movement spread very quickly from schools to institutions of literature and art and even governmental organizations. On the streets, any time and everywhere, you could see those so-called "elements of landlord, rich peasants, counter-revolutionary, evil-doers, and the rightists" being escorted by the Red Guards to be accused and denounced. Their heads were shaved randomly and their hair tangled as a mark of being disgraced. The Red Terror spread quickly to every corner in Tianjin and to other cities.

Is That You?

One night, on my way back home from the hard labor factory as I was waiting for the bus, I saw a tall woman dressed in rags with disheveled hair and dirty face. Her appearance was even worse than mine, a night parolee. It was very dark so I did not recognize her at first. Then as I got closer and looked carefully, I found it was my high school math teacher, Miss Yun-Xiang Lao. How did she get so poor and ugly? I still remembered that when she taught math to us, she was so neat, tidy and serious. She was always full of energy, well educated and surpassing others in learning. She was an excellent teacher. Very strict and scrupulous about every detail, she taught with skill and patience. Everyone respected her.

Everything still remained fresh in my memory so I called her name and she caught my hands and cried out, "Oh, it is you!" She greeted me like her close relative and spoke to me in a low voice crying, "We don't have students like you anymore. My students almost beat us to death." Then we got on the bus together and she told me the details. I told her my situation, that I was not able to contact or help her. I was afraid my status could get her into more trouble.

I gave her two Chinese Yuan, which was all the money I had, and said goodbye as the bus arrived at the station. I encouraged her to stay alive and wait and see. After I learned about all the tragedies, I was so miserable for the suffering and torturing of teacher Xiao and the tragic death of teacher Yang. My Lord, now knowledge and learning have become crimes! How can human beings inflict on other people such torments? What behavior and morality of the world today are these?

Before long the special residential area of five streets where we lived, known for the many high-class intellectuals, capitalists and other middle class residents, became the target of house ransacking and property confiscation by the Red Guards. Almost no household and family could escape. Furthermore, the mass of people in all of the society was mobilized to initiate another crazy drive directed by Mao himself to "destroy and sweep away the 'four olds', which were old ideas, old culture, old customs and old habits" and to "promote the proletarian ideology and eliminate the bourgeois ideology."

Many so-called "bourgeois" things were exhibited in the front doors of many houses, which were ransacked. Chinese women's long evening dresses, silk stockings, old wedding garments, evening gowns torn and cut were displayed everywhere. Precious perfumes were sprinkled and sprayed on the streets. All those being rebuked, cursed and denounced were dragged out and paraded through the streets to expose them to the public. The Red Guards were loudly beating gongs to attract people to come and watch the show.

Everyday when I left home, I was worried that our home would be ransacked and our parents, old and feeble would not be able to stand it. I reminded them, "We probably will be the next to be ransacked by the Red Guards, but don't be afraid, I will pray for you during my many hours on the road." But actually I was in terrible fear, awaiting the disastrous catastrophe to arrive. Sure enough, as we expected, the catastrophe befell us. It was a Sunday and my youngest sister Grace and I were at home. A group of Red Guards led by the director of the neighborhood committee of the Heping district and the Communist Party branch secretary of the 90th middle school located near our house arrived. The Red Guards were not older than sixteen. They first shouted some slogans such as, "Down with the landlord, rich peasant, counter-revolutionary, evil-doer and rightist!" and "Long live the proletarian dictatorship!"

At that time Miss Cheng-Zhen Cao lived in the sitting room on the first floor of our house with us. Kun Cao, her father, was a warlord of north China and won the election as the president of China for a very short time by bribery. My father knew Mr. Cao, who was dying and looking for well-known personages to look after his daughter after he died. Mr. Cao allowed his daughter to accept my father as her nominal father. Miss Cao, single all her life, lived with us.

The Red Guards found two targets to attack that day. They ransacked two households and confiscated the properties of two families, that of Miss Cao and ours. The Red Guards began to smash our antiques, tear up precious Chinese calligraphies and paintings. They asked us to hand over our jewelry and ornaments to be confiscated. We had no experience with this kind of robbery, but Miss Cao had already sealed all her precious jewelry and ornaments into a waistband and given it to my mom to wear on her waist.

The Red Guards knew Miss Cao was the daughter of a warlord. They assumed that she was very rich and owned a lot of jewelry. After the Red Guards searched every corner, they found nothing. They were so mad they tortured her cruelly. They forced her to wear only shorts and kneel down on an uneven washboard. With her two hands she had to hold two big bowls of water. If she could not stand it anymore and spilled some water, they would right away lash her fiercely with whips. She was also forced to shout out unceasingly, "Warlord Kun Cao was a killer. I am a son of a bitch. Debts of blood must be paid in blood!" The noise of breaking and smashing filled the whole house. Suddenly, a bunch of wild street kids appeared and took advantage of the chaos to break, smash, rob and raid.

As a Sheep Was Led to the Slaughter

The Red Guards rummaged chests and cupboards, searching every corner but couldn't find any jewelry. They were very mad. When they saw some paintings of Biblical stories and the picture of Jesus praying in Gethsemane, Bibles, thousands of volumes of books written in Chinese and English and my father's written works in my father's study room, they were furious. They searched for our family pictures, especially those taken with foreigners. They let loose a torrent of abuse shouting, "What typical slaves of foreign masters are these sons of bitches!"

Fortunately, during the ransacking of our home in 1955, police had already searched and taken away all my father's diaries written in English when he was studying and working in the U. S. Gone were the diplomas of degrees he pursued overseas, and pictures taken with foreigners when he was a diplomat himself. Otherwise, my parents could have been beaten to death. So, the Red Guards expressed their violent wrath by smashing everything they hated and had never seen before, such as the coffee pots, exquisite dinner sets, silverware, carved glassware, valuable chinaware, antiques and famous calligraphies and paintings. The Red Guards continuously tortured Miss Cao, while they forced my father to wear a big red cotton quilt and put on a tall paper hat with the Chinese characters "archbishop" written on his head to humiliate him. A big placard was hung around my father's neck and on it was written "big counter-revolutionary, foreign spy."

The Red Guards were ready to parade my father to condemn him publicly. They demanded that the one being paraded should carry a gong and keep beating it to attract people to come and watch. The Red Guards could not find any gong in our home, so they looked for a metal washbasin to replace it. My father knew where our stuff was and he pointed at a thin metal washbasin telling the Red Guards, "This one makes a loud noise when beating it!" My father's hair was roughly shaved off first. Then he was dragged to the streets to be paraded and humiliated with a rope around his neck just like "a sheep was led to the slaughter."

Several other Red Guards wanted to check our I.D. cards. Because the Red Guards were ignorant, when they saw on our I.D. "worker," they thought Grace and I were okay. They became nicer to us. What they didn't understand was that I was working in the "New Life Union Factory," a place to detain criminals for forced hard labor. The Red Guards just demanded us to "to make a clean break with our reactionary family" and support their "revolutionary actions."

However, they still kept asking us where we hid our treasure. We explained to them that our family had no money. During the Japanese imperialist occupation of China for eight years, the whole family survived by selling my mother's ornaments and jewelry and we also donated money to the church. The Red Guards did not believe us. They asked Mrs. Li, the director of our local neighborhood committee of the street, because she was our old neighbor for twenty odd years and knew us well. She replied, "This family is quite honest and is under the spell of Christianity. They have sent all their money and treasure to the church." When the Red Guards heard this, they gave up searching.

Next, they ordered us to bring all of our books, family pictures, everything that had something written on it to our front yard. The Red Guards forced my mother to kneel down and burn all the piled up books and forty family photo albums. Since my mother suffered from deep vein thrombosis in her leg and had not been able to walk properly for twenty years, she escaped from being paraded. When carrying all the books to the yard, my mother took a second to hide a Bible in our trashcan and another pocket Bible in her brassiere. When my mother was ordered to burn all the books, many burned slowly because they had thick covers.

The Red Guards gave my mom a burning stick to keep poking the raging flames. They also shaved off her hair in a random shape until her scalp was bleeding. It was in the middle of the summer in the intense heat. All the Red Guards ran away to take a breath of cooler air and only one was left. He kept cursing and ordering my mom, "Damn it, burn it!" In the intense heat of the raging flames, the face and arms of my mom were full of blisters. When Grace and I saw this we had the quick wit to run to the kitchen, pour some sesame cooking oil on a towel and smeared my mom's face to ease the burns. We also brought cups of cold water for her to drink.

Our nearest neighbor was the son of another well-known warlord by the name of Chuan-Fang Sun. Jewelry and treasure were found in their house, so the Red Guards were satisfied, but the son was forced to parade. His wife was called by the Red Guards to come to the yard of our house to help burn our books as a torture for her, so the Red Guards could finish their job as quickly as possible. They gave my mom and Mrs. Sun each a wooden stick to beat each other while burning the books as a punishment for themselves as class enemies.

Mrs. Sun was really boiling with rage. Her home was ransacked and all the treasure taken and now she was forced to come over to our home and burn our books. To give vent to her anger, she beat my mom ruthlessly. But, my mom would not beat Mrs. Sun and was quietly burning the books while enduring the burning pains of the beatings from Mrs. Sun. Her heart was pierced as if by knives as she watched my father's works and family pictures of three generations vanish in flames. People were watching and asking each other, "How come they have so many volumes of books? Now, all is gone!"

Although there were many blisters raised on my mother's face, she remained quiet and calm because the Lord was with her. Otherwise she could not have stood that terrible torture. After quite a while, the Red Guard found that Mrs. Sun was really beating my mom too hard, but my mom did not beat Mrs. Sun at all, so he cried loudly to Mrs. Sun, "You are bad, old bitch, keep burning the books!" Then he turned to my mom, "You can go in!"

I quickly took my mom to the bathroom and locked the door. I filled the bathtub with cold water and let her put her face and the burned wounds of her body into the cold water to ease her pain. By this time my father was back after the parade. His face was pale and his whole body was sweating. Someone had stolen the red quilt he had worn. The Red Guards took my father to the bathroom and bound his two hands at his back and hung his body up in the air by the water tank.

It was getting dark and two Communist officials came to invite the Red Guards for supper at another official's house. After the Red Guards who smashed and broke everything for a whole day were gone, these two Communist officials entered our bedrooms to search for leftover valuables. They filled their pockets even taking away our leopard leather mattress and my mom's fur overcoat. After they stole all these valuables, they sealed all the doors on the second floor of our house with strips of papers marked with their particular signs. They left only one room for Miss Cao to stay on the first floor. When they were about to leave, at this critical moment, I risked my life to beg them, "If you want my father to confess his crimes, could you just release him from hanging? I can see he is dying."

Maybe these two men noticed that we saw them stealing our valuable things, so they put on a fierce look, saying, "You can put him down to honestly confess his crimes. He should go nowhere except the bathroom. If he doesn't confess anything, you will be responsible."

Then they went to the third floor to search for other things to steal. I was so thankful to the Lord and quickly released my dad from the water tank. His breath was very feeble. I put him on the commode and helped him wash a bit. Grace brought his medicine for him to take. We fervently prayed that God would keep our parents from dying at that time.

A few moments later the two men walked down from the third floor and told us, "Now all the rooms of your house are sealed and nobody is allowed to open any door." We found that they left only one room for us to stay on the third floor. The only furniture that they permitted us to use was one double bed, one single bed and one small square dining table. They didn't permit my father to sleep on any bed and ordered him to sleep on the floor. Then the two men wrapped up a huge bundle of all our treasures and walked away.

After a whole day of being searched and robbed, we discovered that the young Red Guards were used by Mao Ze-Dong to destroy the "four olds," to beat people and ransack homes. The Communist officers, however, really envied and coveted many of the antiques, paintings and valuable clothing of the wealthier and well-educated classes. They robbed and grabbed as many of these household things that they could to use in their own homes. The hymn, *"Pray, my Lord, to steer our course"* was echoing in my heart for that whole day. *"Pray, my Lord, to steer our course to cross the bitter sea and the great waves. Huge storms blow on our faces and we worry about many reefs being hidden disasters to us. We only pray, dear Lord, that with your compass and map, please steer our course!"*

God Used "The New Life Evening Post" to Change Red Guards' Hearts

After those two men left, the Red Guards did not come back right away. We four family members were left alone and our home suddenly became so quiet. We hurriedly took dad to sit on the floor of the bathroom and fed him some water with sugar. My mom came out from the bathroom and comforted us, "I am better now. I have soaked myself in cold water and I changed the water all the time, so I don't feel much pain now." But, I still spread some more cooking oil on her wounds. We saw mom's hair was shaved randomly by the Red Guards and there were bleeding wounds on her head.

We asked her, "Are you in pain?"

She answered, "No, no, not at all. I have never felt so pleasant and cool in the summer time in all my life!" Amazingly, we saw mom's reddish face that was burned by the flames had cleared up gradually. Although there were some blisters on her body, she didn't feel any pain and there was no smell of fire left on her. I was reminded of Daniel's three friends in the Bible who came out from the fiery furnace.

At that time my father took a long breath and said in a feeble voice, "Don't worry, your dad will not die and now I feel very comfortable." Grace went downstairs to keep an eye out for the Red Guards to see if they were coming back. I placed my dad's head on my bosom and let him take a rest. We kept praising the Lord. The hours of terror had not yet passed, yet God had already preserved the lives of all our family.

Before long, Grace ran upstairs and told us the Red Guards were coming back, so we quickly placed dad back in the bathroom. Grace asked the Red Guards for a change of clothes because we were workers and had to go back to work. So they showed a little compassion and took off the sealed paper slip of our bedroom and let Grace enter. She grabbed beddings and clothes for the four of us using her quick wits.

It began to rain and the flames of the burning books were going out. For the whole day we didn't eat anything, so mom cooked some congee soup and with some leftover food, we ate it all and thought it very delicious. Despite having all of our original property stolen, we didn't have the end time feeling. I was so sorrowful that our family pictures of three generations and dozens of years would now be gone forever.

That night, under the watch of the Red Guards, my father slept on the floor with his body half in and half out of the bathroom and his head pillowed on his cloth shoes. We three, mom, Grace and I slept in the only bedroom we had available to us. The Red Guards would still not give up searching for treasure in our house and they went to our attic.

Suddenly they were shouting, "Look, what's this, hey, you come over!" They pointed at over twenty big boxes. I took a look and realized that those were my paper dolls, stage designs, and costumes. We four sisters had played with them as toys when we were little. They were so precious to me that I was reluctant to throw them away. I had stored them carefully. After they heard my explanation, the Red Guards said, "Burn all this feudalistic, capitalistic and revisionist stuff right away!"

In addition they also found the bound volume of "Tianjin New Life Evening Post" from the first issued newspaper all the way through the last one in 1954, when the Chinese Communists took over the press. The Red Guards who came on the night shift and were supposed to watch us were reading the "Tianjin New Life Evening Post" with great interest. The newspaper not only had the daily news but also had Christian articles, and many cultural and informative special columns and serials of good novels.

At five o'clock in the morning I got up as usual to go to work. The Red Guards who were still reading the newspapers told us, "Don't burn these newspapers, we will deal with them." I prayed that the articles in the newspapers would somehow awaken their consciences. I quietly went to the bathroom to see my dad and saw him sleeping soundly, peacefully like a child. It seemed to him that nothing had happened. I left our quiet and peaceful home, which was preserved by the Lord after the violent storm yesterday. Only the ashes testified to the terrorist catastrophe. Quietly I dug out several picture remnants that were not fully burned. I have put them in this book.

On my way to work, God's words kept echoing: *"Peace I leave with you, my peace I give unto you: not as the world giveth, give I unto you. Let not your heart be troubled, neither let it be afraid."* (John 14: 27) *"Who shall separate us from the love of Christ? Shall tribulation, or distress, or persecution, or famine, or nakedness, or peril, or sword? As it is written, For thy sake we killed all the day long; we are accounted as sheep for the slaughter. Nay, in all these things we are more than conquerors through Him that loved us."* (Romans 8: 35-37) Oh, Lord, today I felt the peace in the storm you granted to us. You were on board the boat. You didn't go to sleep or take a nap. You were testing the disciples' faith and You rebuked the storm and the storm calmed down.

For two or three days after our home ransacking, the Red Guards did not order us to clean up all the ashes. So when I went in and out of the yard of our home, as I looked at the ashes piled up, I felt deep sorrow. As for our family, we lost the photos of all the relatives and close friends for many generations. Family pictures of many years including pictures of my parents' ministries, my father's works including his precious records of church history and the rise and decline of gospel evangelism were all burned to ashes. They would never be recovered. However, our heavenly Father will remember always those who suffer for Him. It seemed that the flames of hatred could temporarily abuse power, but then it began to drizzle and the rain gradually dampened the wanton persecution.

Although we had a heavy loss of personal records, yet God's Word was kept in our bosoms and carved on our hearts. During such a catastrophe that seemed to be blotting out the sky and covering the earth as the Red Guards broke, smashed and robbed, we were still able to preserve a Bible and a few leftover family pictures. I remembered an old Chinese poem written around 220 B.C. in the Qin dynasty. Its first emperor was very ferocious and ruthless and burned thousands of volumes of books written by famous authors and buried hundreds of magnificent intellectuals while they were still alive. However, many valuable books were secretly hidden and preserved including a well-known book of military strategy and tactics written by warlord Sun at that time.

Not long after, the Red Guards came and ordered us to clean up all the ashes. Then they didn't show up often because Mao had another great calling for the Red Guards. They were to travel to the four corners of China to rebel against the old world. They were sent to clean up the "four olds" and establish revolutionary ties and exchange revolutionary experience. However, they were so interested in the "Tianjin New Life Evening Post", they took away the bound volume of the newspaper.

My father said, "These kids have read almost all of the 'Tianjin New Life Evening Post' in the bound volume, hopefully that God's Word would sow the gospel seeds into their hearts through the Christian articles." Nevertheless, at the beginning of the ransacking, the Red Guards used white paint to mark slogans and comments. In big Chinese characters at the front door of our house they wrote: "A small temple, but evil wind strong, the pond shallow, yet bastards many!" As a matter of fact the slogans should have read, "A small temple of God, but spiritual wind is strong, a few family members, yet His grace is abundant!" All the slogans and characters written on our door to humiliate and insult us could become the precious stones and pearls in the city of New Jerusalem someday!

Maybe the newspapers of the "Tianjin New Life Evening Post" that my father started and ran had somehow some influence on the Red Guards because they eventually allowed my father to sleep with us in our only bedroom instead of sleeping in the bath room. As they claimed that my father was a counter-revolutionary, he was not allowed to sleep on the bed but only on the floor. We were really sorry that dad had to sleep on the floor without a mattress and pillow and worried that this might cause his heart disease and high blood pressure problem to be more serious, possibly becoming a threat to his life. What we had never thought of was that after my dad slept on the floor for a few weeks, we measured his blood pressure and it was normal. Though his heartbeats were still like a "fast running horse," he felt quite comfortable.

The blisters on my mom's body disappeared. Because my parents' hair was still growing unevenly, we made cloth caps for them. But, she said, "I have never felt so cool in summer time, maybe that's why the baldheaded monks don't feel hot." Since all our furniture was locked up in other rooms and we had nothing but the bare walls in our room, every night when my father, with a long goatee beard, was praying with his head up, his shadow was reflected on the wall. He looked exactly like one of the three wise men in the Bible. We could not help but laugh. Yes, even during the tribulation we still had a sense of humor. My father added, "I want to introduce the newest and best treatment for patients who suffer from high blood pressure, which is 'to sleep on the floor!'" My father's joy and humor swept away all our worries and blues.

An Incident Similar to the Story of Mordecai

God also led my mother through many risks that sometimes we could not help but laugh at through tears. One Sunday, several fiend-like investigators came to our house asking for "Miriam Nieh." Grace was at work but I was at home. It was dreadful because we expected that our mother would not escape the fate of being cursed and denounced, but we only worried about when it would happen. My mother had been devoted to the Lord and served the community for many years. Of course, she naturally had many close relationships with American missionaries and missionary-planted schools.

With sidelong glances, never making eye contact, these chain-smoking investigators, their crossed legs swinging, questioned my mother. They asked nothing more than information about my mother's relationships with many Chinese and Americans, those who also worked with YWCA, churches and missionary-planted schools before the Communists took over China in 1949.

My mother looked very gentle in appearance but firmly resolute in her heart. At that time after much suffering, she was a badly frightened woman. The investigators asked for more than ten Chinese names of her former schoolmates. My mother racked her brain and tried to remember their names, but failed. This, of course, immediately offended the investigators.

They were so mad that they smote the table and cursed, "You are really dishonest. If you stubbornly refuse to speak and confess, you will be dragged out, beaten and denounced!" Sitting beside our mom, we were so anxious but actually unable to help her recover her memory. Then, shouting at my mom in a great rage, the investigators took out some pictures and put them on the table. "These people have already confessed and told us everything about you. How dare you say you don't know them?"

When my mom looked at the pictures of her friends, she suddenly understood what they were talking about and said, "Oh, yes, yes, I know them. Among these foreigners, this is Miss Francis, Miss Beadle, Miss Dickson, Miss Lawrence, and those Chinese are my classmates, Gertrude, Myrtle, Nancy..." and my mom continuously spoke out a whole bunch of English names and explained, "We only used English names at school."

When they heard this they were more furious. "We condemn you that you are truly the slave of the foreigners, which is not wrong. Tell us what kind of crime they committed."

My mother could not remember a thing and said, "Oh, we just studied together for a couple of years and then they all went to the United States and we lost contact."

One of the investigators stood up and said, "I didn't expect that you, an old biddy would be so crafty!"

Then my mother slowly pointed at a picture of one of her classmates and said, "I remember that she and I and other schoolmates had a demonstration and hunger strike in front of the old Tianjin police bureau. The purpose of this demonstration was to rescue En-Lai Zhou who was detained in the police bureau at that time. (Mr. En-Lai Zhou was the premier in China from 1949 to 1976 after the Communists took over China in 1949). The commander-in chief-and key organizer of this demonstration was Miss Ying-Cao Deng (later she became Mrs. En-Lai Zhou). Oh, yes, this tall lady and I were carrying the big flags. Miss Francis and other American missionaries sent food to us, the students."

When the investigator heard these stories he mocked my mother, "Oh yeah? This means that you are a veteran revolutionary. Who can testify for you?"

My mother replied in a low voice, "Nobody and there is no evidence." I trembled with fear that disaster would surely befall my mother, but God is present to be our refuge and help us for all times. At this critical moment, the Red Guards of the 90th middle school came to our house to borrow Grace's bicycle. As she wasn't back from work yet, the Red Guards, while waiting for Grace, entered our room and listened to our conversation.

When the Red Guards heard my mother's story, one of them interrupted, "What she said was true. When we examined the bound volume of all the 'Tianjin New Life Evening Post', one of the issues in 1949 when the people celebrated the 30th anniversary of the 'May 4th Democratic Movement' in Tianjin, there were several articles written about revolutionary history. One of them especially mentioned the victory of the demonstration of rescuing En-Lai Zhou. Among the students who participated in the demonstration were students from Keen Girls' School and the leader of the student demonstration was Miriam Nieh. Here is the bound volume of the newspaper, so you can read and check for yourself!"

The whole situation suddenly changed and the stormy atmosphere turned calm. We didn't even know that there was a news report about this demonstration so many years ago. Who could imagine that the Red Guards had read and still remembered this? At this critical moment they came and jumped up to witness for my mother.

All the investigators' tones turned mild at once and they said, "We guess you cannot think of anything more today. You still have to confess and make a clean breast of your crimes and we will come back sometime later." My mother was so alarmed and nervous that no matter who knocked at the door she would tremble for days. But, for her, it was over, at least temporarily and these men never came back again.

This incident reminded me about the story of Esther and Mordecai in the Old Testament. The wicked man, Haman, intended to kill all the Jews, but that night the king could not sleep. He commanded his men to bring him the book of records of the chronicles and they were read before the king. The king learned that Mordecai had made an outstanding contribution for saving the king's life, but he forgot to give Mordecai honor and recognition. At the critical moment the king promoted and honored Mordecai. The book of Esther also tells us that the king put the wicked Haman to death. The whole nation of Jews was saved and preserved. Oh, my God, You are an omniscient, most merciful and almighty God!

Chapter 20

Good People in Difficult Times

Even in those darkest hours of chaos, there were still kind-hearted people with consciences. Several days after we were ransacked, one night somebody was knocking at our door. It was Mr. Li, our coal-ball man who had sold coal-balls to us for many years. We got along well and treated him nicely. Every time when he sent the coal-balls, my mother always thanked him and served him snacks treating him with ice water melons in the summer and boiled stuffed dumplings in the winter. She gave him clothing, because no tip was allowed after the Communists came.

That night when he came upstairs and saw that all the rooms were sealed and my mother had an unevenly shaved head, he said in a low voice with compassion, "Is everything gone? You should have no problem anymore since they took everything away. Here, I have some money for you. It will be helpful." Then he took out forty Yuan (about twenty U.S. dollars) and put them into my mother's hand.

My mom, so touched with tears, said, "I don't deserve this, besides, your life is not that easy."

He sincerely insisted, "You have treated me so nicely for so long, don't worry. If you need me, let me know." He left the money and departed. After that we never saw him again. Anyone who even paid a visit to us was at a risk at that time.

Another morning, the old mailman came to us and gave my mom several letters and package pickup slips mailed from my sister Margaret and friends from elsewhere. He told us that several days ago when he was going to deliver mail to us he saw there were flames in our yard. He knew it wasn't the right time to come. Several days later when he came again and saw the Red Guards were still around and there were slogans maligning us hanging at our doors, he withdrew.

Today he saw everything seemed to be back to normal, so he came in and quickly handed over all the mail. He said, "There is nothing I can really do to help, but I can personally deliver this mail to you today. I feel relieved." He was very cautious and left immediately and we were so thankful to him. He did this many times. When the Red Guards were not around, he cleverly delivered our mail. We had no chance to see the old mailman after a year or so.

Mrs. Tang, a widow with two children, did washing, sewing, mending and housekeeping to make a living. Sometimes my mom asked her help with the housekeeping. Besides paying her, my mother always cooked some goodies for her children and gave Mrs. Tang her own clothes and dresses. She treated her as an affectionate friend. After our home was ransacked, one early morning she came to our house quietly and her tears flowed as she met my mom and said, "I was told everything." Then she opened a bag and gave my mom twenty Yuan (about ten U.S. dollars) and several items of clothing that my mother had given her in the past. She said, "I didn't bring the luxury silk clothes you gave me. I guess you dare not to wear them. These are some shirts for summer time and this black thick flannel jacket will be useful for when it gets cold. These were all your own clothes."

My mom hugged her. "How can I take back the gifts I gave you, and it is hard for you to make a living, how can I take your money?"

Mrs. Tang said, "My kids all encouraged me to send these. Go ahead, why don't you just wear your own clothes?" She dared not stay long, nor did my mom dare to delay her, so they said farewell to each other with tears and she left. We were told later that Mrs. Tang remarried and left the city and we didn't know where she was.

Since my father came from a poor family, on his side he had many poor relatives visiting us. When I was a little child, I remembered many of his poor relatives staying at our house room and board free. My father even sent them to schools or found jobs for them. My parents even handled their marriages. Some had no learning or skill, but my father spent time and money to introduce them to Tianjin New Life Evening Post as apprentices and trainees. Then they were promoted to official workers and clerks.

After the Communists took over the ownership of the newspaper, two ungrateful relatives became leaders to criticize and denounce my father when he was persecuted in 1955. These two relatives fabricated accusations and made many unfounded and malicious attacks on my father. They took the opportunity when the Communists encouraged, "Those who expose are innocent, and reporters and informers make contributions." To be trusted by the Communists, they condemned my father in order to diminish their kinfolk relationship with him. They went back to work or were even promoted.

Only one of my distant cousins, Yuan-Xu Chang, did not forget my parents' blessings to him. He resigned from the Tianjin New Life Evening Post office and worked in a factory. During and after the Red Guard's storm, he secretly visited us, putting his shirt on our back, even though he was poor. This comforted my parents very much. After I was rehabilitated, I visited him often with a grateful heart. I tried my best to support his family. He died from stomach cancer later.

Mrs. Li was the director of our local neighborhood committee and she came from a poor worker's family of two generations. Her husband was a retired military officer from the Korean War. Even the Red Guards feared him. One day when Mrs. Li was checking the sanitation condition of every house, she met Grace and me and spoke to us in a low voice, "We have been neighbors for over twenty years. The neighbors and I all know that you are honest and decent people. If you have any trouble, come and tell me, I will back you up. Shut your door tightly, since you are unmarried grown up girls."

We answered, "Thank you so much for your consideration and advice of caution in earnest. Since our home was ransacked, we never take off our clothes to sleep." Mrs. Li, as the director of our neighborhood committee, had no power to forbid the Red Guards to ransack our house. However, it wasn't easy for her to have this attitude and perspective toward us. We were very thankful to her. Later, there were several happenings when we were actually protected by her.

Under His Wing

Since 1955 when my father was unjustly put into jail, the pastor of our church had knelt down before Baal. "The Self-Governing, Self-Supporting and Self-Propagating Million Pound Foundation" founded by my father which had an office in our Methodist Wesleyan Church was immediately confiscated by the Communists. They changed the signboard and the leadership of the church to: "Three-Self Patriotic Movement Association" controlled by the Communists.

After that, nobody in our church dared to communicate or visit us. Only a few brothers and sisters in Christ with whom we grew up together visited us secretly. However, Brother Ding-Ze Lu, a bass singer in our choir, was a bold spiritual older brother in Christ with wisdom. He often visited us and every time he brought us something we needed. He was an engineer with good pay so he was able to help us. After the ransacking incident, the government predicted an earthquake occurrence and notified every household to evacuate to near by Minyuan stadium for safety reasons. However, nobody notified us. When Brother Lu did not find us in the stadium, he ran to our house to take us there in the early morning. Praise the Lord, this brother in Christ still cared for our lives. The metal door of our front yard was already dismantled and removed by the Red Guards, but every night for safety reasons, we put the door back without fastening it. When he pushed the door, it fell making a huge noise. We were so terrified and thought that some Red Guards were coming again. Later we explained this to him, not knowing whether to laugh or to cry.

Before 1949, Brother Lu married the younger sister of Madam Guang-Mei Wang, who became China's first lady, the wife of Chairman Shao-Qi Liu, the head of state in China. After the Communists took over power of China, his wife, the sister-in-law of Chairman Shao-Qi Liu, could not bear it that Brother Lu still kept his Christian faith and did not sincerely follow the Communists. So, she despised and divorced him and abandoned four children of her own. She remarried another Communist high-ranking official. However, Mao Ze-Dong hated Chairman Shao-Qi Liu. When the "Cultural Revolution" began in 1966, Mao suddenly announced that Chairman Shao-Qi Liu was the number one enemy, the highest person in power to take the capitalist road and the commander-in-chief of the bourgeois headquarters. Madam Guang-Mei Wang, the first lady, was brutally tortured, denounced and beaten almost half dead. Fortunately, Brother Lu, no longer related to them, escaped the disaster.

My father always taught us, "For those who grant us drops of kindness and favor, we should return them with springs of gratitude and grace." All the benefactors mentioned above were ordinary and poor people of the working class and evangelical true Christians. When I think of them now, I am still very grateful to them. However, it's a pity I don't know how to find them anymore. I can only pray to God that He will remember their kindness to us and bless them with His grace.

During the terrifying and horrible days and nights of the "Cultural Revolution," there were many brutal and tragic mass meetings of criticism and denunciation. These happened in Zhongnanhai, Beijing, where the headquarters of the central committee of the Chinese Communist Party is located, but also in the colleges, universities and governmental organizations, as well as in the communities and on the streets. Whether nonbelievers and anti-Christian people, or high ranking, top level people, at the peak of their power and career, no one could escape Mao's unprecedented calamity and misfortune of "Cultural Revolution."

During the miseries, numerous people suffered, were in despair and sorrow, desperate and sad, full of hatred and hostility. Some sold their souls, betrayed their family members, close friends and comrades in arms. Some went mad. Some committed suicide. Many Communist leaders and old Communists along with their families, loyal to the lofty ideal of Communism, were ruined and persecuted to death.

However, those who believed in God, their fates were in the hands of the Almighty and Sovereign God. Dr. Guo-Ping Nieh, my uncle on my mother's side was an example. He was the head of the English language department of Jingu University in Tianjin. As a Catholic Christian, he was cursed, humiliated and denounced by the Red Guards countless times. Later he said to us, "The hardest thing for me was that during all the meetings of scolding and denouncing, I was desperately sleepy." Those who tortured him could take turns to rest, but they never stopped afflicting him by "bombardment of rounds of long criticisms, denunciations and insults until the enemy is fatigued and weary." The Red Guards didn't allow him to take a nap or even close his eyes between meetings. They kept shouting at him and maligning him as the commander-in-chief of the underground Catholic Virgin Mary Legion.

"Thank God, they gave me food to eat," he said, "but, after I had my meals I felt more sleepy during the meetings. No matter how they cursed, insulted or interrogated me, I had only one answer, 'Yes, yes'. "

After two or three days, posters and slogans with big Chinese characters were put up everywhere inside and outside of the campus of Jingu University, "We firmly demand that the government suppress the Catholic spy Guo-Ping Nieh!" One day the Red Guards were tired of denouncing him so they determined to adjourn the meetings temporarily and allow him to go home to write his confessions.

Uncle Nieh's wife, my aunt, had been waiting for him every evening at the gate of the university to take him home after those crazy meetings. That day his wife came and waited as usual, but could not find him. She was worried that my uncle had been beaten to death. But the doorman told her that there was no meeting that afternoon. Very late that night, Uncle Nieh came home. "Where have you been? Do you know how much I worried about you?" my aunt asked.

Uncle Nieh calmed her down and gently answered, "They didn't allow me to shower for days and today they released me for half a day, so I went to the movie house first to watch a movie and relax my brains. Then I went to the public bathhouse to take a refreshing hot bath. Praise God, I am not smelly dear and I will get a good, sound sleep tonight." Then he went to bed and within three minutes, he was snoring.

Yes, all the worldly fame and wealth and all the capital and property can be taken away by force, but nobody can take away the peace and joy bestowed by our Lord! A true believer despises worldly suffering, yet the anti-Christ, Mao Ze-Dong, who used the sinful nature of human beings misled the Red Guards to provoke this unprecedented ugly, bloody and ferocious catastrophe of so-called "Cultural Revolution." Many believers who loved the glory of man lost their faith and betrayed the Lord. But true Christians hungered and thirsted for God's glory and sang in their hearts often, *"I'd rather have Jesus!"*

Chapter 21

Trials Under His Wings

An Illegal Clandestine Tribunal

Day by day we were living with fear and trembling. One bedroom, which was my father's study room, a kitchen and a bathroom were left for Miss Cao on the first floor. The Red Guards sealed the sitting and dining rooms on the first floor and all the bedrooms on the second floor. We Chang family members were allowed to use only one bedroom, a bathroom and a kitchen, which used to be our servant's room on the third floor. There was an open-air balcony at the end of our third floor corridor, which the Red Guards were unable to seal and we could still use.

Grace and I decided to hang up a mop at the balcony as a signal when we went to work. If one of us hung up the mop, it meant the Red Guards were here again robbing and searching, so when we came back from work we could report first to Mrs. Li. In charge of our neighborhood committee, sometimes she could think of some solution and help.

At that time Grace frequently took the night shifts and she was at home in the daytime. I worked in the daytime and came home around nine in the evening. God arranged for one of us to be at home always to accompany our parents. One day when I came home I saw from a distance the mop was hanging high at the balcony. I was so afraid of our parents' safety, so I

161

ran home and forgot to tell Mrs. Li. When I got to the second floor of our house, I found that all the sealed paper slips on the doors of the second-floor rooms were torn and my dad and mom, looking frightened, were staying in our bedroom on the third floor. "What happened?" I asked.

My dad was praying and my mom told me in a low voice, "Several men with fierce and malicious looks came to our house and said they wanted to use the rooms on the second floor and told us to keep away from the second floor, stay in our room and not come down." My mother told them that the Red Guards had already sealed up all the rooms on the second floor.

Those people said, "This is none of your business."

My mother said to them, "I have two daughters at work and they have to pass the second floor when they get back from work.

"You are allowed to pass, but don't stop and stay."

My mom said, "Red Guards are all teenagers, but these men are all adults of thirty and forty years of age. They are not that simple." We all withdrew and hid on the third floor and dared not venture downstairs to the second floor. In the middle of the night we heard a car stop at our house and several people came up to the second floor. Later, we heard loud conversations and beatings. We were awakened by sudden bursts of terrified and miserable crying and howling and other noise of striking, beating and interrogating. None of us got any sleep the whole night.

The next morning I left home at five o'clock, returning home at night. My mother told me, "Someone from the second floor came up to our kitchen on the third floor to cook. During the daytime nothing was stirring on the second floor. But after dark, there was a hubbub of voices and noises, which sounded like people being beaten and their miserable howls. I went to Mrs. Li to report the happenings. Mrs. Li asked me to report to the military men stationed at another street. Since I had to go to work and was unable to report to the military men in the daytime and nobody knew what would happen after reporting to the military authority, I didn't want Grace to do that. I had to wait for several days under extreme fear until Sunday.

Early Sunday morning, I ran to the military station building two blocks away. I waited for a while and a man who looked like an officer came out. I came to him and reported, "Your honor, officer, my home was ransacked weeks ago, but, recent days odd things happen in our house that I have to report to the military." Then I reported all the details of what had been happening in our house.

"Do they stay at your house everyday?" he asked.

"At least every night," I replied.

"O.K., go home and don't lock the front door of your house and don't tell anybody." So, I went home and told my folks and we prayed together to God to rescue us from this terrifying situation.

In the middle of the night the next day, we peeped from the window and saw a whole group of liberation army men coming to our house. They climbed over the yard wall and sneaked into our house without the slightest sound. The army men went straight to the rooms on the second floor. We heard some low questioning and conversation for about ten minutes, and some noise of moving stuff. Half an hour later, we saw the army men leaving, escorting several men and carrying several people on stretchers out to the military jeep.

Early morning of the next day I reported to Mrs. Li and told her that we are worried that those wicked men might come back to retaliate. Mrs. Li said, "Don't be afraid, you can report to the army men again and besides, my husband can also report to the military." So the neighborhood committee members came to our house to reseal our rooms on the second floor. Later Mrs. Li told us that when she went into those rooms on the second floor, she found on the sofas and floors a lot of blood stains and human hair, iron sticks, hooks and ropes.

We asked Mr. Li, "What was this all about?"

He said, "This was the revolutionary rebels setting up an illegal clandestine tribunal to punish those they hate." After we went through these terrifying happenings we experienced what Psalm 23: 4 tells us: *"Yea, though I walk through the valley of the shadow of death, I will fear no evil: for thou art with me; thy rod and thy staff they comfort me."* God's Word also gave us the strength: *"Behold, the eye of the Lord is upon them that fear Him, upon them that hope in His mercy"* (Psalm 33:18). God, how powerful are Your arms, whom else shall we depend on?

Violent Gang Fights

The Cultural Revolution in the society progressed from the stage of "breaking the 'four olds'" to the stage of what Qing Jiang (Mao Ze-Dong's wife) called "to act with verbal offense and defense with force." This was a stage of fighting with violent force starting between the rebels who were loyal to Mao and the conservatives who were loyal to Shao Qi Liu and high-ranking Communist officials, and among the Red Guards rebels themselves.

Classes were suspended in middle schools and colleges. On the campus homemade weapons and hand grenades were used and campuses became battlefields. As the chaos continued, propaganda teams of army men took over the schools, colleges and even government departments, which meant that Mao actually put everything under his weapon, the military control. Tanks intruded into the campus where conflicts with force and chaos spread extensively. Not only the Red Guards and the rebels cursed, denounced and tortured teachers, even many professors were condemned as reactionary bourgeois academic authorities.

All sorts of "reactionaries" including many Communist officials in power were condemned as taking the capitalist road. There was no more social order or security. Nobody's life was safe. Originally the Red Guards came from the student ranks. Now they came from the proletarian workers who were also involved in the conflicts. The worst was that no matter who you were, including many adults and wicked people, if you put on a military uniform with a red armband indicating that you were a Red Guard, you had the right to ransack and rob any home and beat up anybody.

Anarchism prevailed. On the armbands of some of the Red Guards slogans such as "tough, tough, tough," "iron pole" and "die-hard corps" were marked. There were two conflicting parties. One party was composed of ordinary students, the original Red Guards. The other party was the "Committee of Joint Actions" organized by the children of high-ranking officials. They protected their parents who were targeted and attacked as enemies by Mao and the Red Guards.

People who were labeled as reactionaries and we Christians were the targets of both sides. The movement of the "Joint Action" Red Guards was initiated from Beijing and then quickly extended to Tianjin. These special Red Guards wore red armbands made of velvet. They began to have competitions of how to kill people in various ways, such as pouring nitric acid on their bodies, using red hot iron bars to stab people, lashing people to death with leather belts, and even turning people head over heels and inserting them into chimneys to choke to death.

Therefore, many unexpected Red Guards of unknown groups often came to our house. They used to scold us first and ordered my parents to recite the three most well known articles of Chairman Mao's works. Since we had no more valuable stuff, these Red Guards robbed us of some food and oil coupons, fresh steamed bread just cooked from the pot and even sesame paste we just bought. As the saying goes, "thieves never leave empty-handed." Since they could not find any money, they broke the stairs and walls to give vent to their anger. If they could not grab anything, they would begin to beat people. So, everyday we prepared some dumplings, steamed bread, and some pocket money to treat these unexpected visitors. Otherwise, anything could happen that would endanger our lives.

One night around nine, I just got back when a bunch of unusual Red Guards came. Grace was not back yet, so I hung the mop at our balcony to give her warning. These Red Guards wearing red velvet armbands with softball bats in their hands walked to the third floor where we stayed. They seemed to come for checking up and the leader questioned my mom first: "What was the unit of the Red Guards who ransacked your house and when? What did they take away?" Then they went down to the second floor and tore away all the sealed slips and searched for valuables. After they found nothing, they were so frustrated they came back to the third floor to question me, "What is your job?"

"I am a worker," I answered.

The leader pushed me aside and asked my mother again: "You ought to remember this is class struggle. Chairman Mao teaches us that toward you bad guys, we should not show kindness or be mild, gentle, temperate or modest. When did Chairman Mao receive us, the Red Guards at Tiananmen Square in Beijing?"

My mom replied, "I don't know."

He asked again, "When was your home ransacked?"

"August 20th," My mom answered.

"Oh, so you remember this clearly, but you don't know the time of Chairman Mao's reception of the Red Guards? Apparently, you are planning to bide your time to get revenge!" All of a sudden they dragged my mom to stand against the wall and the leader shouted, "Hong, aim at her!" A husky strong female Red Guard took a bottle of vinegar from the table and threw it toward my mom with all her might. I dashed to the place where my mom was standing and thought her head must be burst. Unexpectedly, the vinegar bottle brushed past my mom's ear and hit the wall and splashed like bloodstains.

I immediately threw myself in front of the female Red Guard and said, "Revolutionary soldier, this old man and old woman are dying, why don't you just educate me."

The leader pushed the female guard away and laughed grimly, "I didn't expect that you are the true bourgeois progeny. How dare you to resist the revolutionary action!" At that time, my mother was scared to death and collapsed. The leader winked at a tall guy and that guy grabbed a softball bat and struck my head. I immediately felt burning pain and warm, sticky blood seeped into my eyes. He swung the second time and the bat hit my neck. My ears were buzzing, my head cracked, and I lost consciousness.

Later my mom told me that when I was falling unconscious, someone intruded into our room. He was the elder grandson of the warlord Chuan-Fang Sun, our next-door neighbor. Before the Cultural Revolution he ran away from class, went bad and spent without restraint, until he entered Tianjin Steel and Iron Plant as a worker. I didn't know how he had also become a revolutionary rebel. When he heard there was noise of smashing and beating next door, he strode over the balcony and took a look at what was happening in our house.

The Red Guards who were beating me saw him wearing a worker's uniform with a red armband and didn't know who he was or his background. They stopped beating me and claimed that we did not behave well. Our neighbor Sun said that he could take care of this, so the Red Guards left. He accidentally saved my life.

After I woke up I saw my mom was washing my wounds with cold salt water. I thought I was suffering from cerebral concussion. I kept vomiting and felt dizzy and went to sleep. During the stormy period, those who were home-ransacked and sick or injured dared not go to the hospital for treatment because the medical doctors would also like to show that if class enemies like us were beaten and injured, we deserved the punishment. They would not treat us.

So I went to work as usual with my wounds. I often felt dizzy and threw up and suffered from terrible headaches. This kind of symptom lasted for a long time and the reason probably was that my head had been severely hit three times (twice in the hard labor camp and now once again). I had severe memory loss. Whenever I felt my head ache, I would be unconscious or all of a sudden I would not know what I was talking about or doing. Yet, God did not permit demons to take my life.

We praised the Lord that God saved my life and mom's and His word always comforted us: *"The Lord is my rock, and my fortress, and my deliverer; my God, my strength, in whom I will trust; my buckler, and the horn of my salvation, and my high tower. I will call upon the Lord, who is worthy to be praised: so shall I be saved from mine enemies. The sorrows of death compassed me, and the floods of ungodly men made me afraid. The sorrows of hell compassed me about: the snares of death prevented me. In my distress I called upon the Lord, and cried unto my God:" (Psalm 18: 2-6) "He sent from above, He took me, He drew me out of many waters. He delivered me from my strong enemy, and from them which hated me: for they were too strong for me. They prevented me in the day of my calamity: but the Lord was my stay."* (Psalm 18: 16-18)

Taking and Giving Beatings

Margaret, my younger sister next to me was working in Anhui hospital at Hefei, the provincial capital of Anhui province since she graduated from Shanxi Provincial Medical College. She was really worried about the whole family. It was Chinese Lunar New Year in early February, 1967, the holiday season which she had long been expecting so she could come home and bring us many goodies.

Since her graduation she had been suffering separation from home as a single girl. This time as she took the risk to come home, seeing the tragic condition of our family, she felt very sad. However, our dad encouraged her, "By grace we believe in Jesus and we should also suffer for Him. Those who follow Jesus have to walk the narrow path. Now is the time for Christians to be persecuted. If you want to have the glory of man, you have to betray our Lord. Those who deny our Lord on this earth, our Lord will not recognize them in Heaven. Let's obey Him and endure to the end and we shall be saved."

Margaret hid all the meat and food she brought in a box stored on the balcony, which was like a refrigerator, because in winter, the outdoor temperature dropped to ten to fifteen degrees below zero Celsius in North China. On Chinese Lunar New Year's Eve after she arrived home, we were about to have the traditional Chinese family reunion dinner being grateful to the Lord. Two Red Guards suddenly burst into our house searching for any left over valuables that they could rob.

When they noticed the good food on our table they began to curse, "Where have you hidden your money? Hand it over to us! Behave yourselves, otherwise, you are risking your lives!" When we heard their threat, Grace and I instinctively stood up and protected our parents.

Margaret had no experience at all of being home ransacked, so she stood up and asked them boldly, "What are you doing? We are state cadres, enjoying the New Year's Eve dinner. What authority do you have to interfere with us?"

The Red Guards did not expect anybody would dare speak to them like this, so they grabbed at Margaret and asked, "Who are you and where do you come from?"

"It is none of your business!" Margaret answered.

One Red Guard took out a leather belt with an iron buckle to whip Margaret.

I jumped at Margaret and explained to the Red Guards, "Don't be angry, my sister suffers from mental disorder, she just came home on a sick leave." But the belt with an iron buckle already hit my face. I didn't care for the pain but begged them, "See, let me punish her for you!" After saying this I slapped Margaret's face on both sides with all my might. My poor Margaret was frightened and she was so frustrated that her face turned pale. She had never thought that her older sister with whom she grew up and never had a quarrel with would beat her like that. Then we quickly wrapped the stewed pork, dumplings and other delicious food and gave them to the Red Guards to calm their anger. They were still cursing but left.

I took Margaret's hand and hugged her and explained to her that if we fought back recklessly, they would beat us to death. There would be no way we could enjoy a happy New Year and family reunion. I also told her that our daily life was on the edge of a knife. Margaret was still angry about so much good and delicious food that she had brought home from a thousand miles away being looted by the Red Guards. But our dad was laughing and reminded us, *"Don't forget that 'the Lord gave, and the Lord has taken away; blessed be the name of the Lord.'"* (Job 1:21) Then he continued, "Every meal, even a bowl of porridge or rice, is predestinated and provided by God." His comments made us all smile through tears and our blues were wiped away.

We continued enjoying the leftover food after the disaster. Despite my father being a feeble old man suffering from a heart attack who could collapse at the first blow, he also was the main target of all the criticism and denouncing. However, God gave him faith and joy and a mature and healthy spiritual life. God's words engraved on his mind often became our help and comfort. His optimism and humor gave us much joy and unquenchable expectation in our tribulation.

Chapter 22

A Spectacle on Stage

The violent storms of the Cultural Revolution were hitting our home from every side. As the interference of Red Guards from miscellaneous groups just began to abate, Mao Ze-Dong and his "gang of four" instigated another new mass movement. This was to mobilize once again the hatred toward the people who were labeled as landlords, rich peasants, counter-revolutionaries, evildoers and rightists, forces of evil and all enemies. There were orders from the central government that every district of Tianjin City should organize large mass meetings for striking and denouncing such enemies. They were ordered to put up open challenge arenas on the streets or rent movie houses to organize large mass meetings for over one thousand people. Their aim was to rebuke, denounce, humiliate and torture outstanding intellectuals, well-known professors, specialists and academic authorities in public.

Dr. Ji-Shi Yang being a famous urological medical specialist in Tianjin did not escape the miserable fate and was escorted to the open challenge arena to be persecuted. His brother Dr. Bao-Ling Yang was a returned student from the U.S. and a successful businessman who had four children in America. When his home was ransacked, a rusty hunting rifle used for hunting a long time ago was found. He was condemned for privately hiding a murder weapon and planning to resist the proletarian dictatorship. So Dr. Bao-Ling Yang was condemned as a "hidden American spy". He was ferociously beaten to the verge of death. When he became unconscious, the Red Guards poured cold water on him to wake him up. They then hung him on a pole to keep beating him. All those enemies who were beaten to death or became disabled at the scene of mass meetings were condemned as "those who go down in history as a byword of infamy because debts of blood must be paid by blood!" The Red Guards who called themselves "Revolutionary Soldiers" were taking charge of all the crazy mass meetings. As their consciences vanished, they were inhumanly brutal.

All the people mobilized knew nothing because they were brainwashed and kindled with flames of hatred as they kept shouting in an uproar. Dr. Bao-Ying Yang was hung on a tree for another whole day and Mrs. Yang was also punished with her guilty husband at the same time in their very own back yard. Dr. Yang was buried alive before he breathed his last. When Mrs. Yang saw her husband was beaten and buried alive, she collapsed and had a heart attack. A few days later she also passed away.

Dr. Bao-Ling Yang was a learned social celebrity, and a kind, composed person, the closest friend of my father. When my father was arrested and locked behind the bars, Dr. Yang often came and visited my mom and our family. Since his children were all abroad, after his tragic death, nobody appealed for redress of an injustice. So many similar tragic incidents happened in our district. We knew some of the victims and some we didn't know. During that catastrophe I had no tears to cry anymore, not only the overwhelming pressure suppressing me, but also from worries and indignations. Every day I lived in constant fear, waiting for this kind of calamity to happen to our family. It was inevitable.

One day as expected, the bloody terror arrived. The Heping district where we lived convened a mass meeting to strike and denounce my father. The authority of my hard labor factory notified me that they would take me to attend the meeting to be educated. I thought it was another meeting against me. Then I was pushed into a jeep, but there was no order for me to wear a high paper hat or hang a big board on my neck.

The jeep ran speedily to the Zhenguang movie house in nearby Huangjia Park, just a short distance away from my home. In front of the movie house, I saw huge slogans: "Firmly destroy the hidden counter-revolutionary, David Chang!" and "One must not be soft on class struggle!" The jeep stopped and I was pushed into the movie house, as I prayed, "Shall we survive today? Can my father stand this persecution? Oh God, Father, please rescue us!"

As soon as I entered the movie house I saw my father, kneeling down on the stage, his hands bound tightly behind his back. Two adult Red Guards pressed and forced my father's head down. My father wore a high paper hat on which all his "crimes" were enumerated. On his clothes "counter-revolutionary" was written in big characters and with a huge big red X. My heart was trembling with fear and I realized this was not an ordinary mass meeting of criticism and denouncement. The victims with a big red X on them would most likely be shot after the meeting.

The Red Guards used very thin steel iron wire to hang a water bucket on my father's neck. One was declaring the facts of his crimes. Every time he declared one of my father's crimes, he added one dipper of water into the bucket. He kept adding water and the weight of the bucket increased, the thin wire imbedding itself into the flesh of my father's neck. The people in the hall were cursing, scolding and shouting slogans insanely.

The police who escorted me pushed me and said, "See, do you want to behave and accept the education or not? If you change your mind and support the Cultural Revolution, we give you a chance to expose and denounce your father, a counter-revolutionary and draw a clear-cut line from him. Our government is always lenient and welcomes you to come over to our side. If you firmly oppose the people and refuse to confess the crime how you collaborated with the U.S. imperialists to use the reactionary religious superstition, Christianity, to continuously poison the people just like your father David Chang does, you will come to no good end!" Then they escorted me to the stage to stand beside my father and watch my father being tortured.

My head numbed as if I were wearing a heavy hat weighing a thousand pounds. The Red Guards ordered me to face the crazy mob as they were shouting madly. They were like roaring lions and we were waiting to be devoured. I felt that my father and I were personally on the scene right in the middle of the arena during the ancient Roman Empire's persecution of early Christians. One Red Guard kept using his rifle butt to hit my father and the other kept adding water to the bucket that hung on his neck. My father lowered his head, streaming with sweat.

No matter how he was being humiliated, cursed, tortured and maligned, his face was always serene. I knew the strength in his heart, but I saw his face was so pale like white wax. He had already collapsed and could not endure any longer. I felt such wrath I even choked. I could no longer hear the surrounding noise of the mob. My prayer was to God, "Lord, I am not Samson, I don't have the strength to push down this movie house, but You are the almighty God, how can You let these fanatic beasts devour Your faithful servant? My God! I have believed in You since I was a baby. Please manifest Your power to send an earthquake. My father won't live very long and I don't want to live anymore either. Let my father and me perish together with these beasts!"

Nevertheless, nothing happened. I forgot that it was the moment when the Apostle Paul and Silas were praying and singing hymns to God when they were locked up in the prison that the earthquake occurred. If my heart was filled with anger, how could God listen to me? But, I really still could not stand anymore watching my father being tortured, and the great anger swept away my fear. I rushed to my father and turned over the whole water bucket. This act enraged and aroused the wrath of all the people and they shouted slogans louder and some even jumped to the stage to beat me. My father had already collapsed on the stage and I was unable to protect him to rest in my embrace.

Two Red Guards on the stage grabbed my father's collar and forced him to raise his head, so everybody could look at him. My father was so pitiful, his face deathly pale. His hair and clothes, streaming sweat, were drenched. Then somebody on the platform declared, "Let the counter-revolutionary, stubborn and stupid, David Chang see God and escort the unworthy progeny of the counter-revolutionary back to her hard labor factory to reform!" The angry mob threw out many coarse epithets demeaning my father.

The Red Guards kicked my father who lay on the stage. He made no response. Some people off the stage began to shout, "He is dead, he is dead!" So, all the people were dismissed because it was getting dark and they were tired, too.

The leaders of the Red Guards had a little private talk. They gave me a bicycle and ordered, "Take him home and solve your problem yourself!" At that time, no hospital dared to accept any injured or dying enemy from this kind of mass meeting. They gave me a hand to enable father to sit on the bicycle seat and let the upper part of his body lean against my shoulders. Their original plan probably was to execute my father, but seeing that he was already half-dead, they left him alone.

I didn't know what to do or what to think. My heart was filled with pain, sorrow and anger. Hope was gone as I pushed the bicycle carrying my dad and went out from an exit of the movie house. My two shoulders were sustaining my father's heavy body. I was exhausted and I proceeded with difficulty. My tears were dried upon my swollen face, eyes and broken lips.

I kept calling my father, "Dad, dad, are you still alive?" My father had no response. I cried, "No, daddy, don't leave me, daddy!" After a little while, he used his hand to pinch my arm, "Oh, he is still alive!" I right away murmured, "Daddy, God had seen how we were being tortured, and you were almost dead. I prayed, "If You are the sovereign God, send a big earthquake so we can perish together." "Daddy, have you heard what I said?"

My dad had no strength to talk but he still murmured disjointedly in a low voice, "You shouldn't say that, child. Today is a glorious day for both of us. We were made a spectacle on the stage to the world and to angels and to men. That is in the Bible: 1 Corinthians 4: 9, and Hebrews 10:32-36." I kept my mouth shut. But God's Word began to come back to my heart. Paul's and Silas' hands and feet were all chained up, but they sang hymns praising God. God sent the earthquake and they didn't run away, on the contrary, they tried to prevent the keeper of the prison from killing himself.

During the time of the Roman Empire, Christians were sent to arenas to be slaughtered, torn to pieces and eaten by the beasts. Believers were singing hymns even at the moment when they were bound at the stake being burned to death and they cried out to the Roman spectators, "Come down and join us, let's go to Heaven together!" Some Romans were touched and they jumped down to the arenas and were martyred with Christians. All these eventually became Caesars', especially Nero's, nightmares and glorified God. When Peter was martyred he asked to be crucified upside down.

The thoughts of these saints were totally different from mine when I was standing on the stage. Where did their strength come from? On the verge of his death, my father still had strength, joy and expectation. From where did they come? My hatred and anger asking to perish with the enemies were nothing but flesh and blood, which cannot achieve God's righteousness or glorify the name of the Lord. I was speechless. "Lord, forgive me, I was wrong again!"

The Communists intended to use a bloody terror mass meeting to give me a lesson of "class education". Instead, God gave me some discipleship training through a vivid lesson. In the critical moment of life and death, Christians have to love only God's glory. *"Except a corn of wheat fall into the ground and die, it abideth alone: but if it die, it bringeth forth much fruit."* (John 12:24) *"And I, if I be lifted up from the earth, will draw all men unto me"* (John 12: 32). God wants His children always to bear the death of the Lord Jesus that the life also of Jesus might be made manifest in our body.

The people who presided at the mass meeting reported to the officials of my hard labor factory that I behaved badly. So after I came back to work, they criticized and denounced me one hour every day, alternated with time for my personal confessions. I began to learn obedience and did not pray for an earthquake any more. However, what I could never have imagined was that ten years later, a devastating real earthquake indeed severely shook Tianjin.

Despite my father being physically very weak and his heart condition getting worse, he was still grateful to the Lord to have the privilege to suffer for Him. He often encouraged us, "Children, our family will be greatly blessed by God." I saw the life of our Lord manifested clearly in my father day by day and he became a strong staff on which we weak ones could lean. I began to believe that God amazingly changed my status from a prisoner to a night parolee so that I could come home for eight hours everyday. Was it actually God's plan that He wanted me to serve my father, His servant, so that I would grow up spiritually and become more and mature in my spiritual life?

Chapter 23

Love in the Violent Storm

The love of Christ shall not depart from us, but be manifest to us very beautifully. He knows when the pressure of the tribulation becomes too heavy for His children, and His rod and staff will comfort them. The violent storm of home ransacking was barely past, when one evening on my way home on the bus suddenly Ms. P, my bosom friend who had suffered with me in the hard labor camp, got on the bus. She looked wan, sallow, nervous and extremely worried. We were so pleasantly surprised at our reunion that tears flowed from both of us. I held her hands tightly and said, "Where on earth have you come from? You must come home with me right now." But, she said that she had to rush back to the school, where she worked as a teacher. We quickly exchanged our mutual condition and I learned that she had married a Christian man. I was unspeakably happy for her.

Several days later, Ms. P brought her husband and her son to visit us and she understood that I was still praying for my marriage. She said, "How do you pray?"

I answered, "If God wishes me to get married, I pray God to prepare for me a faithful brother in Christ who is willing to suffer for the Lord."

"What? What did you say? Say it again!"

So, I repeated it. However, we had a lot of topics to talk about, so I forgot what I had said to her. Ms. P was also criticized and tortured by the Red Guards, red revolutionaries and her students. Her husband came from Hong Kong and later in 1957 he was condemned as a rightist, which was categorized as one of the enemies. During the Cultural Revolution, her husband was also labeled as a counter-revolutionary and beaten by the Red Guards. However, he was a Christian, full of faith, and my parents really loved them. We were chatting and laughing.

Ms. P asked me, "Do you Christians all pray for your marriage as you said? Maybe I can help." Ms P liked to share jokes a lot and I didn't take very seriously what she said. Since our reunion, we tried to get together whenever we had the chance. Despite our home having nothing but bare walls, having no money to buy meat, we made dumplings with vegetables and enjoyed our fellowship, sharing our testimonies with joy.

One Sunday in April in 1967, in high spirits, Ms. P came to see me. "Do you want to come with me to meet a friend?" she asked. I was about to go out shopping, so I followed her and entered a café. I saw her husband talking with a strange man. Then I realized that Ms. P had the intention of introducing their friend, Brother Freddie Sun, as a boyfriend for me. We felt like old friends even at the first sight and talked very congenially. Both of us had similar family backgrounds. Both of his parents were returned students from the United States, and his mother was the president of the National YWCA of China. This brother had a southern Chinese accent and he looked serious, not tall in height, with sharp eyes and high eyebrows. He seemed to have a kind of heroic spirit and was honest, upright and reasonable. Although we talked in a low voice I found out that he loved the Lord and our fellowship sharing in the Lord was very warm and earnest.

Later, Ms. P told me that this Brother Sun had been the fiancé of her younger sister-in law. During the political catastrophe, her younger sister-in law was terrified and denied the Lord so they broke their relationship. Ms. P and her husband stood completely on Brother Sun's side with compassion. When they asked him, "How do you consider your marriage in the future? What kind of girlfriend would you like?"

His answer was exactly like mine, "I am waiting for a sister in Christ who is willing to suffer for the Lord." So, Ms. P and her husband had a great desire to be our matchmaker. Later, they found out that both of us had the same faith and many characteristics in common and they would like to help and promote our friendship. After Brother Sun returned to Beijing, he immediately wrote me a letter to thank God that he could make my acquaintance.

It seemed that we both regretted that we had not met each other earlier, as we found each other congenial. God apparently planned all of these circumstances and it was His will. I had read many love stories and novels and watched many romantic movies both from China or foreign countries but none of them could compare with ours.

We didn't have a chance to meet each other often, because it was a five-hour round trip between Beijing and Tianjin, so we just wrote love letters. And our love letters were composed of being grateful and faithful to the Lord with one heart and sharing the same vision of church and encouraging each other in tribulation. The love songs we sang were praise hymns pouring from our hearts about the amazing love of an almighty God, even though my voice was still hoarse and his off-key. Therefore, our love talk was similar to those music lyric arias of symphony poems praising God.

Whether we were in the park or taking walks on the boulevards, we had endless words and boundless passions to share. It wasn't only two of us, but also the Lord was in our midst. I believed that the small love arrow of Jupiter would be touched by the graceful melody of our love. He used affectionate rope and a lovelock to bind us together. We were like lovers on an isolated island almost submerged by the waves of the hurricane of a stormy sea. However, the Lord Jesus prepared a huge tree with a mass of branches and leaves to shade and hide us as we waited for Him to calm all the violence and let us enjoy unexpected peace and romance.

Freddie worked with the Institute of Geology in the Chinese Academy of Sciences in Beijing. In order to come to Tianjin to see me to extend his love, he spent a lot of money on traveling and mail. His love letters were fantastic and would be considered first class all over the world. He was timid to express orally his deep love, yet he could use easy smooth words in his letters to express his profound feelings vividly and thoroughly. His letters showed not a bit of the conventional pattern of bill and coo, but were poems of a blend of loving God and loving me. This touched me deeply in my spirit.

Freddie was earnest and serious, spoke little, but seemed hard and stiff.

How did he attract me and make me fall in love with him? I must admit that it was his faithfulness to the Lord and his love letters that touched me until my tears flowed. I would read his letters over and over again and carefully stored them in a box like a treasure until 1974, when our home was ransacked. The police confiscated all of our written materials, our love letters among them. They were lost forever, which became my lifelong regret.

I took seriously my parents' opinions to seek their consent as a confirmation. I originally thought we could date for at least a year and then talk about being married. I probably still had little faith. Sometimes I doubted how this man who was always so tough and rigid in speech and dealing with people without any tenderness could write me so many letters full of affection. "Is there somebody helping him?" I asked God for confirmation.

However, Freddie said, "There are fifty-two weeks in a year. Could we speed things up a bit, otherwise I will have to take the train from Beijing to Tianjin to see you for fifty-two round trips."

Two months after we began dating I brought Freddie home to meet my parents. What I didn't realize was that his visit to my home and his conversation with my parents would win such favorable comments from them. Both of our families had many things in common, and mutual friends, which shortened the distance between us. Freddie was also very excited and said, "I have never seen and could rarely find such a couple of spiritually mature elders and kind-hearted seniors, let alone being survivors of such terrible persecution." When Freddie talked with my dad, they shared a variety of topics of common interest, such as the future and vision of the church, the current political situation of China and others. Freddie was a little nervous. He often pushed back his glasses, which easily slid down his flat nose, to their normal position.

My dad said, "This young man has high aspirations and ideals and is faithful to the Lord. He is like my own son!" My mom knew Freddie's mother, since my mom was the president of the trustee board of the YWCA in Tianjin and Freddie's mom, Kuo Hsieu Wang, worked as the president of the National YWCA of China in Shanghai. They had many mutual friends. All the members of our family agreed and gave us the green light to proceed, which was the first confirmation.

Wedding in the Midst of Disaster

The night after my parents consented and gave us the green light, I accompanied Freddie to the railway station. We were locked up in each other's arms hugging and kissing. However, I still remained a little worried about this man. While the love letters he wrote me were so touching and his love toward me both sincere and earnest, yet I sensed that he was an extremely rational man, a man with reason prevailing over emotion. He never showed any humor or made a joke nor said any sweet words and honey phrases.

When he had conversations with my dad, he could non-stop discuss the future and vision of the church. He enjoyed talking about national and international political affairs, many topics and historical events from ancient to modern times and from China to the foreign countries. His face looked like an "iron-faced man." Could a husband of this kind know how to love his wife? As time went on, would I feel that he might make me dull and sick? I was an emotional person and a sensitive woman, who loved to talk, to laugh, and cry. Would he someday find it hard to get along with me? Therefore, I prayed God to give me another sign to confirm to me that there was a soft and gentle part of him.

Indeed, some interesting thing happened. One weekend Freddie came to see me again. I opened the door and he gave me a scare. I saw him holding in his left hand one single rose that wasn't in a bottle with water. The poor drooping rose was already wilting from the long train ride from Beijing. In his right hand he was holding a paper bag with strawberries. His white shirt was stained red with strawberry juice. When Freddie saw me, he smiled with an embarrassed expression and said, "I remembered you love strawberries. Strawberries are just on the market in Beijing, so I bought some before I caught the train. All the way it was fine until I entered this lane a moment ago. A boy was running and hit me, so the strawberry juice splashed on my shirt. And, this rose looked good when I bought it. I don't know why it looks so unhappy now." I could not help but laugh.

Some spiritual wind must have blown to him from God to touch Freddie's heart to be a little bit romantic and caring of me. And this red strawberry mark really made it abundantly clear that his pure heart was toward me. All my misgiving and worries were dispelled. I thanked God for giving me the second confirmation and I completely accepted that Freddie was the other half that God granted me for a lifelong companion.

Our wedding date was set for October 24, 1967, which we later discovered was also the birthday of the United Nations founded on the same date in 1945. At that time the Red Guards made known to us that the ransacked families should not celebrate any happy events. We were not allowed to dress up to wear red and green elegant clothing. But I secretly bought a piece of greenish thin wool and handmade a jacket as my wedding dress. For the Chinese, the color green represents life.

We had no wedding gowns, no rings, no fresh flowers, no church, no pastor, no sacred music nor a crowd of guests. It was a world far different, as far apart as heaven from earth, from what I dreamed of when I was a young girl. As a bridesmaid often at those grand wedding ceremonies with which I was so familiar, the contrast of what I actually could have was enormous.

However, God provided our wedding banquet party, so it was perfect and full of blessing even in the midst of disaster. As Freddie and I were ready to go to the city hall to have our marriage registration and certificates, several Red Guards intruded into our house again and took away some of our food and coupons. So we newlyweds never had the experience of walking through a cheering crowd of guests with showers of colorful flowers. Instead, we walked through Red Guards under their angry glares.

That evening, my brothers and sisters who lived in Tianjin, Miss Cao and a few relatives and friends gathered together in the only bedroom we had. My sister-in-law did her best to prepare a banquet of two tables. We were afraid of the Red Guards discovering that we had a celebration that evening, so my sister-in-law racked her brains to hide all the food and goodies on the balcony one day in advance. After the Red Guards left and the guests arrived, she began to cook the dishes, but she couldn't find green onions, ginger, spices and this and that, so she called up everybody to look for them. What fun it was!

The wedding ceremony was simple, but perfect and holy. My father did the Scripture reading and then he prayed and blessed us, the newlyweds. At first, the hosts and guests were all cautiously talking and laughing in low voices. We were afraid of disturbing our neighbors and attracting the Red Guards. We didn't have enough chairs, so each guest was asked to bring something to sit on. One chair we borrowed had only three legs but was also used by a guest who was apparently sitting on it. When I found out I apologized to him, but he smiled and replied, "Don't worry, I wasn't actually sitting on it, I know how to practice Chinese martial arts!" His remark, of course, evoked the whole room to rock with laughter.

Neither the hosts nor the guests had elegant clothing. My mom wore the wool jacket that Mrs. Tang sent back to her. She looked nice. Before we set our wedding date, my mom said that if we waited until winter to get married, she wouldn't even have a nice cotton-padded jacket to wear. But nothing could take away our joy and happiness. Just as the Apostle Paul said, *"I know both how to be abased, and I know how to abound: every where and in all things I am instructed both to be full and to be hungry, both to abound and to suffer need."* (Philippians 4:12)

Since there was only one room for our whole family, there was no room for us newlyweds. So right after the banquet, we cleaned the kitchen and put up a temporary bed of wooden boards with new pillows, new sheets and blankets, which were gifts from the guests. We lighted a pair of candles for our wedding chamber. People may have their wedding festivities, yet we had candlelight worship in the kitchen singing the hymn, *"His Perfect Love."* Freddie said that tonight we not only had become a married couple, but, as we kept our faith and God with us, we would be a small church on this earth, and were like the two small golden candlesticks in the church shining in a dark world.

Early next morning, we caught the first train to Beijing. Because Freddie was still a free man at that time, the authority of the Institute of Geology, Chinese Academy of Sciences, assigned a small room for our use. It was a three-room apartment house, which was shared by three families including us and we shared the only kitchen. I was very thankful to the Lord.

For our newlywed's room, my aunt gave us two pieces of her old furniture and Freddie's aunt gave us some old thick mattresses which she had used in her wedding some forty-five years ago. We made some new cotton wadded quilts. Relatives and friends sent us some gifts that were also their leftovers after the catastrophe. All these were so precious to us. The little room was quite comfortable. I was sorry for my dad still sleeping on the floor and my mom having only poor clothes to wear. It made me weep.

Chinese often say that, "Before a person is thirty years old as a grown up adult, people look upon the wealthy father and respect the son. Thirty years later, people look upon the successful son and respect the father." The

Bible tells us, *"Children's children are the crown of old men; and the glory of children are their fathers."* (Proverb 17: 6). I, indeed, enjoyed a well-to-do life, the best Christian education and circumstances for me to grow up all provided by my parents. Today I had absolutely nothing to return to them. All I could do was to follow Jesus and depend on each other with them for survival during the catastrophe. Praise the Lord, though we had no crown nor glory to give them, my parents were fully contented with our little faith for the Lord and a little filial obedience to them.

Freddie and I had no honeymoon, because I had only three days plus a Sunday for my wedding leave. So after we arrived in Beijing, we visited the "Fragrant Hill," a well-known sightseeing place in the western suburb of Beijing. The whole mountain was full of red maple leaves and colorful trees. There was a beautiful "glass lake" and the reflections of the red maple leaves turned the whole environment into a reddish color. It seemed to us that all of nature was adorned for our happy event, just as the poem reads, *"half of the river is misty and half of the river is red."*

We sang many hymns together up in the mountains and I had never been so happy for many years. In the love letters Freddie wrote me he said that he had visited and climbed to the top of the "Fragrant Hill" alone and shouted out to the mountains in a loud voice, "Dorothy, I love you!" And the mountains echoed back his voice. That day we both shouted out to each other, "I love you!" and our voices also echoed back wave after wave in the midst of the mountains higher up. All the ugly tribulations of terror, hatred, killing and beating in the world were under our feet and vanished to the winds at the foot of this mountain. Only love echoed and reverberated in a world without love.

The three sweet, honey days in Beijing soon passed, and I was sitting in a train going back to Tianjin. Outside the windows, the scenery sped by and I sighed with many thoughts and feelings. I treasured the thought that my God is really doing great things. *"You are the almighty Counselor and Your name is Wonderful. In You there is nothing impossible, but Your ways are higher than my ways and Your thoughts are higher than my thoughts."* My heart was singing with the marching beats of the train, "Joyful, Joyful…."

Chapter 24

Banished from Our House

As the Cultural Revolution extended, tribulation after tribulation befell our family. We praised the Lord that He protected us from the danger of those who secretly set up a clandestine tribunal in our house and their possible revenge after we reported them to the military. The next revolutionary action the Red Guards wanted to pursue was to throw out from their original residences all the ransacked families. They regarded them as enemies. I saw, under escort of the Red Guards, many ransacked families in our community were moving out to other places. They used their bikes for transportation to carry some necessary belongings.

One Saturday afternoon, we were notified that we should pack immediately to move out from our house and the Red Guards would escort us to a worker's home. When I came home from work I saw my parents were sitting on the street like beggars. Grace had a cart loaded with some of our leftover furniture, kitchen stuff and some bundles and bags with our clothing. My parents and Grace had already moved out of our house and were waiting on the street for the whole afternoon. Because that worker and his family were not willing to share a house with us, we were waiting for the notice for where we should go.

My parents were very calm. They didn't feel that another great disaster was coming. While we were waiting, we met some of our old neighbors who were also ousted from their houses. I asked them, "Where are you moving to?"

They shook their heads and said, "Very far." The fates of all the ransacked families were similar, so we just nodded our heads and gave a smile to each other as a gesture of compassion and good-bye.

Very late that night, the Red Guards and the representative of the neighborhood community came and led us to a first-floor flat of an apartment compound just around the corner. We were assigned to live in two small rooms. High walls outside of the windows of both rooms blocked all the sunshine. It was very dark and damp. A small business owner lived in the other two bigger rooms in the same flat with a lot of sunshine. This owner was very active in the Cultural Revolution, so he was appointed as an agent by the authority and we were under his surveillance.

It was the first time in our lives that we shared an apartment flat with somebody else. We shared also one small kitchen and one small toilet with only a squat pit with flushing. There was no bathroom or a shower. My parents were not used to this and we were ordered to clean the kitchen and the toilet everyday. My mother was often cunningly mistreated, allowed to use the kitchen only after the neighbors had finished their cooking. My mom always got blamed and was pushed aside. She could not adjust to the sudden change and inconvenience of her daily life. As she lived in constant fear and insult, always in low-spirits, she began to suffer psoriasis, which was hard to cure. She had also long been suffering deep vein thrombosis. I was so sorry to see her dragging her heavy, painful legs to do all the strenuous housework. Who was able to rescue and help us?

We prayed to God everyday for His healing. Even after the catastrophe, when we had only one room in our old house, at least we still could enjoy some privacy. We could use our own kitchen, washroom, bathroom, the balcony and the corridor and the space added together was not small. Now we had two little rooms, but the space added together was smaller than that of our original big bedroom. Also, our rooms were so close to neighbors that all our chatting could be heard.

However, praise the Lord, one year later, an old lady who lived in another flat in the same apartment compound came to us and asked my mom whether we would like to exchange our flat with theirs. Of course, we would, so after the approval of the neighborhood committee, we quickly moved from the first floor to their second-floor flat. The space of the two rooms was the same but we enjoyed sunshine again and my mother's skin disease was cured without any medical treatment.

Nevertheless, there were new tribulations for us to endure. Mr. and Mrs. Yang, our new neighbors, were assigned as the agent and we were under their surveillance. So we went from the frying pan right into the fire. Mrs. Yang bragged that she and Qing Jiang, Mao Ze-Dong's wife, were old revolutionary comrades back in the 1930s in Shanghai. She often boasted that they were in the same movie theatrical company. She claimed that she and other comrades did the disguise makeup for Qing Jiang, so Qing Jiang could escape from Shanghai to Yanan, where the Chinese Communists were based at that time. Later Mao married her.

What we didn't expect was that this family overdid their surveillance and even reported to the local police station what we ate daily and what they overheard from us. At the same time they spread rumors maligning our family in the neighborhood. My parents were often the targets of criticism in the neighborhood group when everyone had to learn Mao's teaching. Mrs. Yang's criticism toward my parents was utterly absurd. Mrs. Yang condemned my mom as being so feudalistic to my dad that she even called her husband, a counter-revolutionary, "Papa". When she heard my parents speak some English words in their conversations, she condemned my parents as "slaves of foreigners!" My mother might hum a few phrases of hymns unconsciously in the kitchen, causing Mrs. Yang say, "You worship America, pro-Americans, singing western songs and dreaming of America all day long!"

No matter how feeble my dad was because of his heart attack, and my mom being half-handicapped on her lower legs, they were compelled to clean the public trash, sweep the leaves and snow of the whole compound in winter for several hours. Sometimes when Grace returned from work, she saw our dad and mom sitting on the stairs of the first floor. Too weak and exhausted, they weren't able to climb to the second floor where we lived. So Grace had to help them home.

After the Yang family knew that I was working in a hard labor factory, they showed more contempt for me. At times when we met in the corridor, I was cursed and shoved by them. They called me "cheap wretch!" Mrs.

Yang always complained that she lost something in the kitchen. We had to endure all the wrongs and injustice. The Yang's family kept telling people that all the members of our family were counter-revolutionaries. My husband was a counter-revolutionary detained in a hard labor camp in Beijing My father was a counter-revolutionary being paroled because of illness. I was a night parolee of the hard labor factory.

Grace was an unmarried young girl and she had no way to resist. She was so sorry to see that we were maltreated, maligned, and beaten. The only contribution she could give was to work harder to support the family. In our compound, those families who were of true worker origins or who had good class background did not bully and humiliate us. Those who stepped on us and intended to climb higher were those who had problems themselves, small businessmen and intellectuals with bad class backgrounds. They bullied and threatened us under the power of the authority.

Since we moved to this big compound occupied by many households, we were always the target of rebuke and attack. I constantly prayed to God to remove our wicked neighbors, because the sting tortured us daily. But God told us that, *"My grace is sufficient for thee."* (2 Corinthians 12: 9). What happened later proved that God's amazing grace is more than sufficient for us. In 1976, the severe Tangshan earthquake occurred and seriously affected Tianjin. The apartment building where we lived was unharmed, but our original house was seriously damaged. If we hadn't moved out, we could have lost our lives when the old house collapsed.

Chapter 25

Miscarriage and Then Double Blessing

Most newlyweds would extend their honeymoons for months and years to begin their new life as a married couple and build a love nest together. For me nothing had changed, because I was a night parolee and not permitted to leave Tianjin City and I still lived with my parents. Freddie had a small apartment room in Beijing, which was not really a home for us. He still lived as a single person.

He came to Tianjin to visit me on weekends every three to four weeks and rushed back to Beijing in the early morning on Mondays by train. My husband to me was still a guest. We still wrote love letters to encourage each other spiritually. However, even this kind of romantic reunion once a month did not last long. Around nine months after our wedding in August, 1968, suddenly Freddie's letters, which I had regularly received weekly, stopped. On the weekends when he was supposed to be back, he wasn't. My parents and I were anxious and worried, because another political drive of "purifying the class ranks" initiated in the society and the movement became more and more fierce. Since we had long been persecuted politically, we were very sensitive and cautious.

Soon Sister Fu-Ran Zheng, who grew up with us and worked in Beijing, came and told us that Freddie was being investigated in the current political movement in the Institute of Geology. He was not allowed to come home. We went through suffering again and kept praying day after day. Soon the authority of the hard labor factory where I worked notified me that "Freddie Sun is a hidden counter-revolutionary." They forbade us to write to each other. Neither was I allowed to go to Beijing to visit him.

I worried that my parents could have another round of cursing and denouncement and I was also seriously concerned about Freddie's suffering and being beaten. Would he just disappear like this and be gone forever? Lord, did you give Freddie to me as my husband just for a couple of months? I would not cry at home to make my parents' hearts feel heavier. Nor did I dare to cry for him in the hard labor factory because they already criticized me that all the members of our family were enemies of the state. They said, "The pond is shallow but bastards are many." I often prayed for Freddie on the bus. I just finished a six-year separation from my parents and now I began to suffer separation from my husband. Many times I cried out to my Lord, "Why, why is it always me?" But, there was no answer.

Nine months passed. One night suddenly somebody was knocking at our door. I opened it and it was Freddie! Smiling, walking with two crutches, he entered our home. He had been put under investigation for being a Christian and was locked up in the detention house of "monsters and demons – forces of evil" and forced to do hard labor. Freddie told us what happened to him as if he were telling jokes to wipe away all our worries. He said that "he had been promoted." After he was criticized and denounced in a mass meeting, he was paraded and escorted to the detention house where he found out all his inmates were either Communist party secretaries or his professors in the Institute of Geology, Chinese Academy of Sciences. Communist party secretaries were condemned as "persons in power taking the capitalist road" and the professors were accused as "reactionary academic authorities."

None of the detainees were allowed to call each other by names or titles, such as: "Secretary XX," "Mr. XX," "Sir," "Professor XX" or even "Comrade XX." The only title they could call each other was "Classmate XX," because this detention house of hard labor for all the enemies was supposed to be an "ideological reeducation class". The disaster was that during the hard labor one morning, a huge cement block fell on Freddie's right foot and he suffered a smashed bone fracture. He used the other foot to ride a bicycle to the hospital and had a plaster cast made. Since he was unable to take care of himself or to do any hard labor anymore, he got permission from his authority to come home to recover.

We had two rooms, so one room was spared for us and especially for Freddie to recover. My mom looked after Freddie with great care, and my dad enjoyed talking with Freddie with fervor from morning to evening. Freddie was eagerly learning a lot from my father. My dad spoke approvingly of Freddie, "He is truly my son who knows me well!" Hence, we had an unexpected happy family reunion.

Every evening when I came home, I found my husband like a wounded soldier waiting for me. We had only simple food, but our chatting and laughing in the warmth of our family swept away all my bad feelings during my daily toil. Three months later I found myself pregnant. Freddie and I were extremely happy, which was a joyful blessing from God in the midst of tribulation and injury. Despite my pregnancy, I did not get any special care or mercy from the authorities to lighten my hard labor. I had to fulfill my hard labor as usual. The effect on my pregnancy was serious. I could not eat, but just kept throwing up and felt very sleepy all day.

At that time our hard labor factory manufactured iron door and window hinges. Annealing hinges were sent to us one after another on the conveyer belt speedily. We female prisoners had to pick by hand these hinges of different sizes to sort and put them into different boxes. Feeling sleepy, I often didn't act quickly enough, resulting in my hands and fingers being hit by the speedily passing iron hinges. My fingers soon became swollen like sausages. Many inmates' fingers were broken. In order to escape the reproach of our overseers, I had to pinch my thigh from time to time to wake myself up.

Another tough working procedure for us was to wrap up all the boxes of hinges with iron sheet belts. Each box, weighing as much as 100 to 120 pounds, had to be lifted, and then placed into piles cubically of twenty boxes in each dimension. Everyday when I made these piles, I had to use all my might to hold these heavy boxes in my arms and climb the stairs of boxes one after another. Whenever I carried one box I cried out, "Lord, help me not to fall down from these piles to hurt the baby in my womb." Sometimes I had to lift the box onto my thigh, and then straighten my waist to stand up and use my belly and arms to place them. My thighs were full of blue swollen lumps and I was totally exhausted at night when we finished our daily jobs.

One night on my way home, I felt a terrible pain in my belly and when I reached home, I found myself bleeding. I had a miscarriage that night. My heart dropped to the bottom as my three-month baby was lost from my womb. The Lord knew that for Freddie and me, it was impossible for us to stay together as other married couples did. How precious was the baby He bestowed on us, but Satan took the baby's life away through this tyranny, which brought us great agony.

Only my dad said, "Jesus Christ is the Lord of life. He will bestow again." Freddie was also very calm, but I knew he was hurting. I prayed with tears, "If this is Your will, we will fall silent and speechless. You are the Lord of resurrection. We pray that You will seize back the baby from Satan and give us another child, because You are the greatest God!"

When Freddie's foot was finally recovered from the injury, he went back to the Chinese Academy of Sciences for forced hard labor. I had lost a lot of blood but the authority gave me only a very short time to recover before I had to go back to my hard labor factory work. However, I kept praying to God to fight for us and give us His grace and mercy to let us have another baby. We prayed to be able to pass on the Christian faith from generation to generation.

Freddie was doing hard labor in the Institute of Geology more than 100 miles away from me. He was forbidden to visit me monthly. He was only allowed to come back on special festival holidays.

Since 1970, the year following my miscarriage, Freddie was assigned to lay bricks. He became a bricklayer mason for building houses. His supervisor, an experienced mason, liked him very much and took him to build houses and pave the roads everywhere. After the working hours actually there was nobody watching over him. So Freddie often rode his bicycle to the railway station and sneaked back to Tianjin to see me. Under the hot sun, his job was to boil the tar to repair the roofs of office buildings. It was very hot in the summer, so he stripped off his clothes to the waist when he worked. He was so sunburned that his skin peeled.

From 1969, the year I had my miscarriage, to 1971, I found Freddie kept increasing his appetite so that he could eat fifty meat dumplings when he got home and became physically stronger. He seemed to love his manual labor as a builder. Freddie was also growing spiritually. He encouraged me to pray frequently and have faith constantly and consistently. Freddie and I believed the Lord would give us children. We did not ask for children as our property as the Chinese saying, "To raise a child is for him to take care of you when you retire at old age."

In this era when atheism prevailed, if we didn't have a child, the grace and blessing from God to us would be stopped with our generation. My prayers were more consistent and I said to Satan, "Don't be proud of yourself, my parents' God and Freddie's and my God will surely fight for us and preserve the salvation for His children from generation to generation." We prayed for two years that God would give us a child.

Despite our suffering, we kept praying and our faith was strength- ened. How could Sarah give birth to Isaac after her menstruation stopped? Shall we see the same miracle? In the spring of 1971, I found myself vomiting again. I was unable to eat properly, but I didn't feel sleepy this time. On the contrary, I felt vigorous. Yes, I was pregnant again! The Lord had heard our prayers and He is God, true and living. I was so happy and realized my God is amazing! During the two years, God taught us how to pray as our faith and obedience were tested. During my pregnancy this time, the one in charge of us in the hard labor factory was a new director, a female. Suffering from habitual abortions, she had no children.

My belly became larger and larger and after three to four months of my pregnancy I could hardly walk. This female director oversaw us in the workshop and she saw that I was using all my strength to pile up the heavy boxes. She noticed I was pregnant and my body was heavy, so she talked to the leader to switch my job to a workshop for sick and handicapped prisoners. The job was much lighter. Praise the Lord for her kindness. But very soon I couldn't even sit and work. The leader thought that I loafed intentionally on my job, so she ordered me to go to the hospital for a checkup. If everything were normal, I would be criticized and denounced.

The doctors checked me and I had an X ray. To my great surprise, the doctor found that I had conceived twin babies! I cried joyfully with tears to praise the Lord. But, I worried again under my current condition, how could I afford to feed two babies? That night my father assured me, "When heaven graciously sends the rain, God puts on every wheat ear a drop of water. If God gives us twins, He will prepare their food."

After six months of pregnancy, my belly was extraordinarily big and I walked more slowly, coming home very late. However, nothing could stop our joy and gratitude to God and this was evidently His double blessing. Freddie and I began to think of the names for the twins with a grateful heart. We agreed that their Chinese names must carry the Chinese character for "heaven," and then follow by another Chinese character of "morning star," "joy," "love," or "kindness."

On January 23, 1972, it was heavily snowing. After twenty-six hours of labor, God blessed us with lovable twin boys, each weighing a little over five pounds. Joseph was six minutes older than Daniel. We gave Joseph and Daniel Christian names, God's servants' names in the Bible who lived under the rule of Gentile kings. We were Christians who lived in an atheist country. In Chinese, Joseph was named after the star of the Plough, the Big Dipper, for God gave us the light, direction, hope and expectation in the darkness. Daniel was named after the joy that God had bestowed on us. Fraternal twins, their countenances and their personalities are completely different.

Suppressed at the bottom of society, yet we became the most joyful family in this world. All the people around us saw and said, "Double blessings have descended upon you." Praise the Lord, He overcame death and not only returned back the child we lost, but bestowed on us an extra one. When Joseph and Daniel were four years old, not only did they not look alike, with different personalities and characters, but also the difference of their height had become noticeable. Joseph became so much taller than Daniel that they looked like brothers of two years difference in age. The twins were convincing evidence that God answered our prayers and granted us a double blessing. We thanked God that after two years of testing our faith, He taught us lessons that our joy could be fulfilled.

Chapter 26

Twins' Baby Dedication and Husband Arrested

Little Joseph and Daniel were a great comfort and joy in our tribulation. They never cried aloud to make trouble for us. Since we had no money, we never bought any juice for them to drink. My milk was not enough to feed them both and also there was no baby food, so they needed to be fed with extra milk. According to the government, the ration was one pound of milk per day for a baby under one year old. The milk was diluted with water, so Freddie was looking for milk powder everywhere.

However, God fed them miraculously and I added some vitamin B and C for them. They had great appetites and digested well. The only problem we had was a shortage of cloth diapers. There were no paper diapers in China at that time so, we had to use old used bed sheets as cloth diapers. We washed and hung them everywhere in the room like flags of all nations. It was a tiny room of eight square meters, where Freddie, the twin babies and I jammed in. We put up a big bed for us two and a small bed for the babies to sleep at each end and we had a small stove and a desk. Freddie asked for and was granted leave in Beijing to serve and help me in my maternity leave. He had to prepare the milk, feed the babies, change and wash diapers for them especially at nights.

Freddie didn't get any sleep for fifty days since he took the night shifts to take care of the babies. In daytime, he couldn't get any rest either. This was continuous bombardment of fatigue, and made him so overtired he claimed this kind of "hard labor" was tougher than he had in Beijing. So after fifty days and nights of "twin babies sitting," he "escaped" and returned to Beijing.

After my maternity leave, I had to go back to work and I had no time to feed the twin babies. My mom and Grace took care of these two babies. These two little cute boys swept away our worries and tiredness. Little Daniel loved to laugh and make sounds. We didn't know what was he thinking. He didn't care about eating or sleeping, just wanted to sing "Yi, Yi...Ya, Ya..." making some noise to attract our attention.

After Daniel knew how to stand, he held the rails of his little bed and sang in his own way incessantly, while using his little feet to tap the beats. Little Joseph was serious and rarely smiled. He paid all his attention to eating and sleeping and he was quiet all the time and very patient. While learning how to stand, he consistently used his head against the wall for balance. He always concentrated so intently on what he was doing, he looked like a scientist.

Every night when I put them to bed, they pillowed on each of my arms and I sang hymns and lullabies. They closed their eyes and seemed to enjoy the songs. Praise the Lord, the twins grew up healthy and grandpa and grandma were happy for and proud of them. The Yangs, our neighbors, also came over to look at these two babies who never cried aloud or disturbed them. All the neighbors said that it seemed there were no babies in our apartment flats.

Just as my dad expected, "God will provide and feed them." Just a few months after Joseph and Daniel were born, Freddie's father, their grandfather in Shanghai, received the benefits of putting into effect the Communist party's policy and regained part of his original salary. Of course, every grandfather loves his grandchildren, so their grandpa in Shanghai wired money regularly to us. This guaranteed we could buy enough milk powder to feed them.

My parents and I thought that Joseph and Daniel should have their baby dedication, so their names can be remembered in Heaven. However, at that time, there was no church and no faithful servants of God who could officiate at this ceremony for them. I lifted up our need in prayer. One evening on my way home, I met Sister Guo-Hua Liu, a Catholic nun with whom I had been in jail. She was a close friend of my cousin Yong-Xin Xiao, who was the leader of Catholic St. Mary's Legion in Tianjin and had also been imprisoned. Sister Liu and I had many secret contacts and fellowship when we were in hard labor and closely watched by the police, who forbade Protestant and Catholic Christians to mingle.

Under the circumstance of persecution, the relationship between born-again Christians whether they were Protestant or Catholic was always heart to heart close. Accompanying Sister Liu was Sister Zhang, another Catholic nun, who also had been escorted back to her native town to do hard labor for many years. As they were trained midwives in the Catholic hospital for gynecology and obstetrics in Tainjin, in their native village in the countryside where no medical doctor could be found, farmers came to them for treatment and delivering babies. Their love and medical techniques cured and helped many village people. Even the wives of Communist officials were healed. So the local Communists of their village had favorable comments about them and gave them the special privilege that they didn't need to work in the farm fields. The local Communist cadres helped them to establish clinics for medical treatment and delivery of babies for the local villagers and paid them.

They were terribly busy and on this trip they came to Tianjin to purchase some medicines. They were looking for the cheapest hotel to stay overnight. I invited them right away to stay with us and we all slept in our big bed. We exchanged endless stories and gracious testimonies. I asked them whether they could baptize my twins. Praise the Lord, they said they were officially ordained Catholic nuns and frequently baptized babies in the past.

The next day, Sisters Liu and Zhang went to the streets to buy medicines and in the evening I bathed Joseph and Daniel and cleaned our small room. Our whole family had prayers first and these two Catholic nuns prayed and blessed Joseph and Daniel first and then had immersion baptisms for them. The twins seemed to be very pleased and didn't cry or make noise. I was moved to tears. I thanked God that He loved them and they could be baptized when they were little and be remembered in heaven.

After I delivered the twins, I suffered serious nephritis and lumbago and felt so much pain in my waist that I was unable to carry my babies in my arms. When the twins were learning to sit and walk, they gave me a lot of joy and fun, but also it was very hard for me to bend my waist to help them. So I often knelt down and walked with them on my knees.

When the twins were two years old, the pain in my mother's legs got so bad that she had no way of caring for my babies anymore. So, Freddie brought the babies to Beijing and put them into Mrs. Jin's home, a boarding nursery. Every evening after work, Freddie went to see the kids and played with them a while. On Sundays, Freddie took them to the parks and visited the zoo, the most favorite sightseeing place of the boys.

I was longing for my kids but as a night parolee I was not allowed to visit Beijing, the capital, without permission. Ignoring the rules and the possibility of punishment, I sneaked into Beijing on Saturday nights and spent Sunday with my babies, returning back by train on Sunday nights. Sometimes I enjoyed being with my kids until very late Sunday night. By the time we brought them back to Mrs. Jin's home, they had already fallen asleep. I put them on the bed and lay beside them. They would suddenly wake up and look to see whether their mom was still around. When they saw me still there, they looked very pleased and grabbed my arms and closed their eyes to listen to my songs. I quietly left when they deeply slept.

Both of them became aware that their mom would leave them when I visited them again, so they grabbed me tightly and wouldn't let me go. But I had to leave. When I had barely walked out of Mrs. Jin's yard I heard Joseph and Daniel begin to cry for mom and saw their little shadows through the windows. My heart was really bleeding and broken. I had to rush to the railway station to catch the last train back to Tianjin. I kept asking the Lord with tears, "When can we have a normal life and a home of our own where my husband, two babies and I can live together daily?" I talked to my babies' photos with tears calling their names, "Mama is not stonehearted, mama loves you so much, but I have to do hard labor. Mama will be back. Oh, Lord, what sins do the kids have to deserve this? I pray You would let them return to their mama's bosom!"

This kind of life of separation from my babies lasted several months. Freddie and the twin babies were in Beijing and I was in Tianjin. I was longing for my husband and kids daily. The babies' daily foods were only milk powder, rice flour and vegetable congee. We could not afford to buy meat, fruit and juices for them. Sometimes when they shared a piece of cucumber or could have a boiled egg, they were very happy. Occasionally, we put some ground pork to mix with their vegetable rice porridge. Daniel would point his little finger right to it and say, "Mama, I want meat, meat."

In May 1974 I didn't receive Freddie's normal letter which he wrote me regularly telling me about our babies' condition and their lives. I began to worry. Three weeks later, the office of the hard labor factory notified me that, "Freddie Sun is a counter-revolutionary and he has been arrested. You have to draw a clear line of demarcation from him. Your family is the den and shelter of counter-revolutionaries. It seems that your family is not that simple, you are a counter-revolutionary clique. You are under surveillance, yet you are still very active in counter-revolutionary activities and are really swollen with counter-revolutionary arrogance! Now we will isolate you in an education class for confession starting tomorrow!"

When I heard this, my head ached and grew numb and my two legs were so heavy. Oh, Lord, me again! How could I go back home to tell this bad news to my parents and where was Freddie being detained? As soon as I arrived home my parents showed me Mrs. Jin's letter telling us that Freddie did not show up for three weeks. The money for my babies' room and board ran out, please come to Beijing.

I was terribly grieved and confused. I didn't know Freddie's situation, but I was sure that the government would be severely strict on him. How were my babies doing since they hadn't seen their dad or mom for weeks? But tomorrow I still needed to attend the education class, and I had no way to go to Beijing. My heart was filled with tears of blood.

In the midst of the tribulation, God inspired Grace, my youngest sister, who had been so courageous and kind to speak up, "Let me ask for leave so I can go to Beijing and bring the boys back home." The next day Grace went to Beijing. But, I was compelled to stop my daily work and write confessions.

The police officers said to me, "Confess or not is your problem. Freddie Sun has already proved himself guilty. Tons of evidence of crimes he committed are waiting for him." Actually they were deceiving and threatening me.

Several days later, officers of Tianjin public security bureau interrogated and threatened me, "You are a counter-revolutionary gang. Many people in Tianjin, Beijing and Shanghai have exposed and denounced Freddie Sun and the crimes he committed." All the threats did not take away my longing for my babies. Mrs. Jin could not continue to care for my kids since baby-sitting was her only job.

During the interrogation, I suddenly had a terrible headache and fainted in the office of the hard labor factory. At first the police thought that I was pretending to be dead, so they poured cold water on me to wake me up. I woke up for a little while then fainted again, so the police rushed me to the emergency ward of the hospital for criminals to have treatment.

When I regained consciousness, they asked me, "Can you stand?" I stood up slowly but was very weak. They escorted me back to the isolation room again for more confession.

The female police officer who was kind to me and lightened my heavy hard labor when I was pregnant, instructed me, "You can go home, but every day you have to come back to the factory to work and write your confession. The government deals with your case leniently because you have young children to take care of."

Dizzy, I walked back home with heavy steps to see that Grace had already brought back home Joseph and Daniel from Beijing. The twins looked like little muddy monkeys with dirty clothes and long hair. They probably hadn't had a bath for a long time. Grandma was feeding dumplings to them and they ate the food with pleasure. When they saw me they were so happy and both tried to be the first to talk to me and kiss me. How could they understand that their parents were having another round of tribulation? They only knew that they had returned to the company of their grandpa, grandma, mummy and Auntie Grace, who loved them so much.

We decided not to tell the kids anything about Freddie's situation, but Joseph and Daniel wanted their father. I told them, "Daddy is sick and hospitalized."

"We want to see Papa!"

"Papa suffers from an infectious disease and the hospital does not allow us to visit him."

The two kids blinked their eyes not understanding my explanation. Even though they enjoyed the warmth of the family very much, they asked me several times a day, "Where is daddy?"

Chapter 27

Father Arrested Again

I lost my memory a lot after this incident. I felt dizzy and was unable to write anything. Since I didn't submit any "confession", I was cursed by the police and I fainted again. This time the doctor gave me a lot of sleeping pills. They found from my medical record that I had suffered before from mental disorientation. The police decided to end my confession with nothing definite and granted me several days sick leave. Joseph and Daniel were so happy when I could stay home for a few days. Usually I came home very late and I thought they were already asleep. Actually, they just closed their twinkling eyes and were waiting for their mom to return. They had to hug each of my arms and then went to sleep soundly in peace.

Peaceful days for our whole family did not last very long. One day when I almost reached home I saw two police jeeps with red police flags parked in the big yard of our apartment compound. Surrounding our apartment was a crowd of residents of the area. I immediately sensed that something must have happened to my family. I hurried home to find that Grace wasn't home yet.

Two policemen were searching our drawers. The two kids were so frightened that they hid themselves behind the quilt stacks. Everything in my home was in a mess and my mom was scared to death. A uniformed policeman declared to my dad, "You are under arrest!"

I walked into the room and boldly asked them, "Why do you arrest him? He suffers from heart failure and stays at home all the time. Aside from labor hours in the yard, he never even walks out the door." The police totally ignored me. They handcuffed my father and escorted him downstairs to the police jeep. I ran up to him and put on him a heavy jacket and a waistcoat. People were shouting in confusion, scolding and cursing as the police jeeps left.

As I returned to our flat, my mom spoke to me in a low voice, "Go and check the trash can!" I walked to the trash can and found it hadn't been searched. When my hand reached to the bottom, I found a Bible wrapped in a plastic bag.

Then I walked into the tiny room. Two little heads appeared behind the quilts. They cried out, "Mama, mama!" and buried their heads into my bosom holding me tightly. I hugged them and then discovered that all our family letters including Freddie's love letters, which were stored in a silk covered box, were all gone. The police even took away our love letters! Did our love letters offend the law? Oh Lord, how long will we have to wait to see your righteous judgment?

Since my father was arrested, Grace's and my responsibilities were heavier. Not only had we to worry about our father, but also the condition of our mom's legs had deteriorated. She could hardly walk. So in the daytime we had to find a baby sitter for the children. Thankfully, near our house a worker's family by the name of Zhang lived in a big house that originally belonged to a ransacked family who had moved out. Mrs. Zhang would like to baby sit Joseph and Daniel to earn some money and she could also cook for the kids. And praise the Lord, Freddie's father was happy to pay all the expenses. So Joseph and Daniel were put into daycare. Although they had no toys, the kids could run and play in a quite spacious room, so they were happy. Since I had to leave home early and come home late, it was Grace's job to deliver and pick up Joseph and Daniel to the daycare daily.

Grace worried also about our parents' physical conditions, so she was stressed and overtired. One day at the factory, her finger was jammed in a running machine and bled seriously. She was quickly sent to the hospital.

After the surgery she was in such bad pain that she couldn't sleep. I felt sorry for her since it was on my account she was in this predicament with my kids becoming her extra burden.

I was under heavy pressure daily with the worsening condition of my mom's legs, my 78-year-old father in jail again, our twins being two and a half years old, while I had to do back breaking hard labor with my dizzy head. In addition, when I returned home I had to help my mom to take care of housekeeping and laundry. We were really a group of old, weak, sick and disabled people who could not withstand one more blow from Satan. But, God preserved us and nobody could take away the wonderful peace in our hearts. We did not always feel happy but we were definitely not desperate.

Everyday I was comforted when I saw my babies chattering and laughing. Jesus says, *"In the world ye shall have tribulation: but be of good cheer; I have overcome the world."* (John 16: 33). When the Israelites were freed from Egypt, in front of them it was the Red Sea and behind them pursued the Egyptian soldiers. Millions of Israelites, men, women and children were facing a situation of life and death. But Moses said to them, *"Fear ye not, stand still, and see the salvation of the LORD, which He will show to you today."* (Exodus 14:13). So, day in and day out we lived in His peace that passes all understanding.

We were not allowed to visit my father for a year. Then one day in 1975, one year after his re-arrest, the police notified me, "Go to the local police station and take David Chang home." Praise the Lord, I was so happy, but worried about my dad's health. I knew my father must have had another heart attack and I didn't know how bad his condition was. At least he was permitted and able to come home. I ran back home to tell my mom and also the director of the neighborhood committee, Mrs. Yue.

I borrowed a bicycle and went to Mrs. Zhang's daycare telling the kids that we were going to bring grandpa home. The twins also pushed their child cart and we three as a team went to the local police station. My dad was sitting on a bench looking very weak and pale but smiling, "Oh, my darling babies, you also come to take grandpa home!"

Joseph and Daniel cried out, "Grandpa, grandpa, come home!"

The police declared, "David Chang had another heart attack, so the government deals with his case leniently. He is declared as a counter-revolutionary and will be watched and reformed by the local people of the neighborhood. He is not to be sentenced, but he has to submit a confession every week. Anyone who communicates or visits you and vice versa, you have to report to us, the local police station. Now go home!"

I didn't know what impression these policemen had when they looked at us: an old dying man, a weak woman and two little kids. Are we the "enemies" in their eyes? If so, then they were too feeble themselves. My father suffered from heart failure and anemia. He looked very pale and was totally unable to walk. So I helped him sit on the seat of the bicycle and the upper part of his body leaned on my shoulders as I pushed the bicycle home. All his personal belongings were placed in the child cart pushed by the twins who loved to help mama and grandpa. We walked slowly for one hour to reach home and we didn't care about people's attention.

However, one old man, our former neighbor, Mr. Yan who was sweeping the street, came over and congratulated us, "Oh, Mr. Chang is coming home, it's so good!" He was condemned as a landlord and sentenced to do labor around the community. Just like the Chinese saying, "We are those bare-footed, who are not afraid of those who wear shoes." We ransacked families were compassionate to each other. Mr. Yan helped my father the rest of the way home and put him on the bed. The kids were so happy that they thought they had accomplished a great job. They could see grandpa again.

My father slept lethargically for many days and when he woke up he told us, "Don't be worried. Nothing happened to me, praise the Lord! I was sick most of the time in jail. When they asked me about Freddie Sun, my son-in-law, and how he had organized the underground church, I answered how do I know? They accused Freddie and me as instigators who set up illegal religious activities. I said, 'Freddie Sun was being reformed through hard labor in his Institute in Beijing. He only comes back several times a year. I don't even see him much.' " Of course, we knew who was the one who falsely accused Freddie and dad. However, the Lord says, "*Vengeance is mine; I will repay.*" (Romans 12: 19). We had nothing but His wonderful peace.

Chapter 28

Husband's Illness and Third Vision Revealed

After Freddie was arrested, Sister Zheng, who grew up with us, came secretly to see us. She told us that her husband, Dr. An-Xi Yang, the son of a well-known evangelist, Pastor Shao-Tang Yang, was arrested at the same time. We could only pray together and comfort each other. I knew that Freddie was a tough guy who would rather die than submit to Satan, so he must be severely tortured and beaten. I prayed for him daily with a broken heart and soul, "Lord, when are you going to rescue Freddie from imprisonment? What is his current situation and how do the police treat him?" My faith weakened and I was very worried. I looked at the twins who slept soundly beside me and prayed that God would preserve Freddie's life so that these two boys would not be orphans.

My Little Rat

One night, while I was praying in tears, I fell asleep. In a dream it seemed that I was with a tourist group visiting the "Forbidden City," the royal palace of emperors in Beijing. I got lost and was alone. I walked into a small, dark courtyard of a small palace and a sign was hanging on the back of the front door, "No Entrance!" Then the door was creakily shut and I could not get out. I proceeded, but it was very scary.

Surrounding the yard were bleak and desolate palaces and all the doors were tightly locked. Small bells hung at the eaves of all the houses. However, at the eave of the house above my head there was no bell. A small wooden board suspended by wires had a rat sitting on it. The rat was only a short distance from me, but I couldn't reach him. This little rat was fat and covered with golden hair. Its eyes were closed but blinking, sometimes even smiling. It knew that I was there but did not respond to me, and it seemed that the rat was quite comfortable and at ease.

I cried out, "Hi, little rat!" It didn't pay any attention to me but its ears moved. I hate rats and mice, so they really scare me. When I was in the medical college practicing in the anatomy lab to do autopsies, I was not afraid of dead human bodies. But when I had to operate on rats in the lab, they made me sick and absolutely horrified. But, this little rat didn't frighten me at all and it was so lovely. I woke up in peace and it was barely dawn. I got up and immediately told mom my dream. What did it mean? Was God answering my prayers and wanted to talk to me?

After work when I came home, my mom told me probably she had the answer to my dream. God must be telling us that Freddie was all right, because Freddie was born in 1936. According to the Chinese lunar calendar, it was the year of the rat. He was in prison but wasn't beaten to death, since this rat was alive and fat. I also had thought of this dream for a whole day and felt peace. It seemed that God rekindled the flame of my faith by giving me this dream and teasing me, "Don't worry, your little rat is fine." After Freddie was released four and a half years later, I told him about the dream and when it occurred.

It was truly amazing. Freddie said at that time he was locked up behind bars in the detention house in the Tianjin jail. This was located right across the street from the hard labor factory where I worked. We were very close but could not see each other. After dozens of strict interrogations and some of his trifling written confessions were made, the police were busy in many cities for investigation, so his case was temporarily suspended.

During the first several months after he was arrested, he was locked up in a cell and the only other inmate was a medical doctor. This doctor was sent and instructed by the police to watch Freddie closely and report everything to the police. However, as they became good friends and kept no secrets from each other, Freddie was not under any strict surveillance. Since there were only two of them in the cell, the prison food sent in was much more than they could eat. Both of them gained a lot of weight.

Freddie said, "We had nothing to do and the only way for us to kill time was sitting on the benches idly reading Chairman Mao's works, chatting and a little napping. I had the faith, so I had the golden hair. I wasn't starved to death or beaten, I was just fine!" Freddie's story fit perfectly the vision that I dreamed. Our Lord was really telling me that my little rat is in peace, well and safe. God is amazing. He comforted me in some humorous way and I comprehended more deeply the verses in Psalm 73:25, "*Whom have I in heaven but thee? And there is none upon earth that I desire beside thee.*" Lord, we need only You and we just have to be patient and wait.

Mom, Where Is the Window?

One year later, I was suddenly called to the office at the factory and the police notified me that "Counter-revolutionary Freddie Sun is critically ill. We give you a special permit to send some nutritious food to him." I was filled with anxiety and fear and I knew the news would be a blow to my parents. I broke the coin bottle in which we saved money to buy some beef, candies, peanuts, and milk powder. When I was wrapping it up, Joseph and Daniel saw so many goodies that they ran over to me. Daniel quickly picked up a piece of meat and put it into his mouth. Joseph was about to grab too, but I said, "Daddy is very sick, this food is for him. Mama will buy some for you later. Now let's go and visit daddy."

When Joseph heard this, he put the meat back. He was only three years old, so I felt sad and let Joseph have it. Thinking a prisoner in critical condition would be allowed to meet family members, I dressed the two kids up with new clothes that Freddie bought for them. All along the way the kids kept asking me, "Where is daddy, will he buy some toys for us?"

All the family member visitors of the hospitalized prisoners waited in a long line in the prison hospital yard. The police searched carefully every item that visitors brought and there was one big yellow dog in the yard. I saw Freddie among many prisoner patients at a huge window of the ward on the second floor. His head was totally shaved and he looked very pale and thin.

I waved at him and pointed at the kids to him. I quickly told the twins, "Quick, look at papa up there!"

When the kids looked up they saw Freddie with a shaved head, dressed in a black prison uniform, so pale and thin that both Joseph and Daniel cried out, "No, that is not papa!" I failed to draw their attention to wave at Freddie. While I was waiting in the line I let the kids play with that yellow dog, so Freddie could see his sons a longer while.

Finally, it came to my turn to hand over the food to the police. They announced that no family member of a prisoner patient was allowed to see the patient, even if he were terminally ill. I surely didn't want Freddie to see me cry, so I held the boys up in front of the ward window and spoke loudly to the kids, "We will come again!" to let him hear and see us as long as we could. But the police noticed and shooed us away. We had to leave, moving away slowly.

I kept turning my head back and the kids disappointedly asked me, "Mama, how come there is no papa?" I explained to them the man I had pointed at was papa, but they just couldn't believe it. No matter what, Freddie was still alive and he smiled to us. Praise the Lord!

Two weeks later the police notified me again that Freddie was still in critical condition and I could send nutritious food to him. So I cooked some delicious food and brought the kids once again to the prison hospital. This time I urged them again and again to wave to daddy. I wanted to let Freddie see us a longer time even if the kids did not recognize him. What became apparent as soon as we entered the yard of the hospital, however, was a huge wooden board wall shielding all the windows of the wards.

The police had become aware that many prisoner patients were looking at and waving to their family members, so they put up the wall to block any communication by sight. Joseph and Daniel were expecting to see papa, but now the boards blocked their view. They cried out, "Mama, where is the window? I want to see papa, papa!"

I had no way to comfort my precious babies and all I could do was to shout loudly, "Be good boys darlings, you will see papa someday!" to let Freddie hear that we were there. The two boys blinked their eyes and didn't seem to understand but sighed at seeing the wall. The hope of many family members to see their dear ones by waving hands was shattered, and the only chance of possible communication was cut off. I gave each of them a big piece of candy and shouted at the wooden wall, "We will come again!"

The twins were extremely disappointed. All the way home, Joseph didn't utter a word.

Many days passed and I thought the boys had already forgotten the sad visit to Freddie. Joseph and Daniel had no toys to play with in their childhood. They had only some picture books for children such as "Dr. Bethune" and "The Childhood of Golgi," for example.

One day, Joseph suddenly said to me, "Mama, when I grow up I want to be a doctor and give medicine to papa so I can go to see him everyday!"

I hugged him with tears. "My precious, you are so thoughtful and your papa will be waiting for you." Joseph had already some serious thoughts: to be a doctor one is able to see papa.

Another day my mom was holding Joseph and singing songs. Joseph said to my mom, "Grandma, when I grow up, I will make a bronze statue for you." He knew the grandma of the reknown Russian writer, Golgi, raised him. When his grandma passed away, Golgi made a bronze statue to remember her. Sitting beside grandma, Daniel didn't use much of his creative brain.

He echoed, "Grandma, are you going to die? I will buy a big bronze statue for you." When my mom heard this, she didn't know whether to laugh or cry, but just love them more. Grandma's love made them feel safe and warm. However, why they couldn't see papa every day was always a puzzle on their minds.

Chapter 29

Ark of Safety and Death of a Tyrant

In January 1976, Haley's Comet appeared in the sky at nights. According to the Chinese astronomical records for thousands of years whenever comets appear, natural disasters and human catastrophes or war would happen in China. Because of their huge size, comets impact the earth. At around three o'clock early in the morning of July 26, 1976, it was very hot and I hadn't gone to sleep yet. Suddenly I saw a purple light flashing across the sky and thunderous noise followed as many tanks just passed by on the street in a couple of seconds.

I tried to get off the bed but the whole room was vibrating, rocking up and down and sideways. Within seconds I could hear buildings collapsing. People were running out with howling and yelling. I saw from the window that smoke and fire were everywhere and realized right away a severe earthquake had occurred. All the lights went off and we were in complete darkness.

I instinctively grabbed my boys one in each arm while Grace was helping our parents to get up. Not even able to stand, how could we six, two old half-handicapped people, two kids, Grace and I run out from the building? My dad said calmly, "If this is the end of the world, the Lord will come and take us home. Let's pray and ask God for His forgiveness of our sins." Finally the shaking and quivering gradually stopped when we were still praying and we looked at our small room and found only a mirror was broken.

Since there was no earthquake prediction, nor pre-warning, nobody had any preparation. The devastating earthquake suddenly occurred and many people died and were buried in the debris of the collapsed buildings. However, God protected us the weak and feeble ones and we praised the Lord and went to sleep with our clothes on. How horrible it will be when the *Great Tribulation and God's Judgment Day* come to this world, but the Lord will certainly rescue us just like He did from this disaster.

The next day when we went out to the streets we were sad to see that everywhere people were looking for their lost love ones. Later the official news reported that the epicenter of the earthquake was at Tangshan city, sixty miles northeast of our town Tianjin, and it was above eight on the Richter scale. The death toll in Tangshan was over 240,000 and in Tianjin over 200,000.

The third floor of our big house we used to live in no longer existed because the roof and ceiling collapsed and the balcony fell. If we had not been banished from our original house eight years ago we could have been buried in the debris and dead. But God prepared these two small rooms in the apartment building that suffered only minor damage as a Noah's Ark to save our lives.

Forty-five days after the Tangshan earthquake, on September 9, 1976, Chairman Mao Ze-Dong, the Chinese dictator died. Before Mao's death, two other Communist leaders, Premier En-Lai Zhou and Military Commander in Chief, Marshall De Zhu also died in 1976. As the Communists had exalted Mao as an immortal god, many were shocked and disillusioned at his death. For weeks, the entire country was forced to mourn for the tyrant. Radio stations played nothing but funeral music. Anyone who showed no signs of mourning for Mao would risk seeming to be unfaithful and be in trouble.

Hope arose in my heart that Mao's evil policies would die with him. I was wrong. The persecution continued. Several weeks after Mao's death, the officials of the factory notified me that my husband "counter-revolutionary Freddie Sun was sentenced to fifteen years." He would manufacture

T-joints from scraps of recycled metal at a steel plant hard labor prison. After fifteen years, the boys would be eighteen. Would they even recognize their father? Somehow my father remained calm and reassured me that the darkest hour comes before the dawn, and that God would fight for us. His words greatly encouraged me.

The Chinese Academy of Sciences officially fired Freddie, and I was given three days to clean out our little apartment room in Beijing. I was put under stricter surveillance and forced to attend two political "reeducation" classes - one before work each morning and one at lunch. I now had to leave my house even earlier than five o'clock each morning to get to the class on time.

I suffered from continual headaches due to extreme fatigue. In addition, I could barely see out of my right eye or hear from my right ear due to the three concussions I had previously endured. When my fellow inmates were instructed to criticize me, their criticisms sounded like a dull humming noise.

The next morning after I arrived at Beijing, my older brother, his friend and I pulled a wagon about ten miles through the heavy snow from the train stop in the inner city of Beijing to its northern suburb to empty Freddie's and my apartment. We arrived to a grim scene. Dirt covered the floor, and the wind was blowing snow through the opened windows. The light beside the bed was broken, and the comforter lay torn on the floor. All of the dresser drawers were opened, and clothing was strewn across the room, soaked and moldy. The suitcases that we kept under the bed were rotting in a puddle of muddy water.

It appeared that Freddie was arrested suddenly in the middle of the night. The few pieces of salvaged furniture we transported to my brother's home and I caught the next train back to Tianjin. The ride home offered me time to reflect on everything we had lost.

My little family of four was all I had left. I prayed that God would give me His heavenly perspective instead of a worldly one. The hymn *"I'd rather have Jesus"* echoed often in my heart. That year, in 1976, two weeks after Freddie was sentenced to fifteen years and less than one month after Mao's death, the "Gang of Four," a group of Communist Party leaders including Mao's widow and three of Mao's close associates, was arrested by new Communist Party leader, Guo-Feng Hua. A massive media campaign was launched to blame the extreme polices of the Cultural Revolution on the

"Gang of Four," which were said to be in opposition to Mao Ze-Dong. For the first time since the Communist take-over in 1949, people celebrated with great joy. Parades and carnivals marked the end of the Cultural Revolution. Members of various family backgrounds and classes joined together to rejoice. Liquor stores were sold out. Since it was crab season, every family bought three male crabs and one female crab, symbolizing the members of the "Gang of Four" composed of three men and one woman.

Even the poorest of families somehow managed to scrape together enough money for a bottle of wine and crab dinner to celebrate. All of the posters and banners plastered with Mao Ze-Dong's portraits were torn down. The shouting and laughter heard in every street proved that the hopes and dreams of the Chinese had not died out with the Communist take-over and rule.

The damage caused by the Cultural Revolution was monumental. Mao's policies bred a generation of ignorance. The youth forfeited their education for hard labor. The Red Guards, mostly young teenaged kids, were sent to remote regions to work in the countryside under Mao's orders to "reclaim the wasteland and learn from the poor peasants." Young girls were also sent to remote and desolate regions, where they were isolated from their parents and unable to marry and start families of their own. Through God's grace I was finally able to look upon the Red Guards with compassion, realizing that they were deceived by Mao and were also victims as well. God was teaching me to forgive our enemies.

Although the lives of many people in China improved, prisoners and hard labor factory workers received no special privileges. Family members of prisoners were permitted three visits to the prison per year on Chinese festivals. To reach Freddie's prison factory, I had to ride ten hours on a train from Tianjin to Hengshui county, Hebei province. I then walked an additional ten miles on a dirt road through desolate countryside where the prison was located. I remember my first visit. At four o'clock on a bitter cold winter morning, I arrived at the railway station of Hengshui along with other prison visitors.

After about an hour of trudging through the snow, we could see the tall chimneys of the steel plant: motivation to continue for another hour. When we finally reached the prison gate, several prison guards ordered us to line up. Our clothing and belongings were fastidiously searched. The basket I clutched was stuffed with treats for Freddie: meat topped with thick soybean sauce, deep-fried cakes, pickles and chocolate.

"This prison is for reform, yet you encourage hedonism by bringing these treats?" A guard shouted at me. I should have known that prisoners were not permitted anything but the most basic food. I watched the guards ruin the packages held by the weary travelers. They unwrapped each piece of candy, squeezed toothpaste from its container, tore apart cotton quilts and sliced open homemade cakes searching for any possible hidden messages.

Finally, the visitors were escorted, twenty at a time, to a room with a long cement table. We took our seats on one side of the table and waited for our beloved husbands, fathers, sons or brothers to emerge from the opposite door. We had thirty minutes. Freddie finally took his seat across from me. He looked so pale and thin! I wanted so much to embrace him, but the width of the table was about six feet, prohibiting physical contact between prisoners and family members. Guards sat at either end of the table and continually circled the group.

Forty people began to speak at once. Pure chaos! Women cried and children shouted. On each visit, Freddie and I were placed at the end of the table, right under the guards' noses. We could barely hear one another and had to ask the guard to relay our words to the other. Occasionally we were able to use our hands and eyes, as well as a few English words. I let Freddie know that my parents, the children and I were healthy, and that his father in Shanghai continued to send money for our support. Although he looked so physically weak and frail, Freddie's faith and joy was evident, and I knew that God was with him.

After what seemed more like thirty seconds than thirty minutes, a whistle sounded, ending the session. I left the building to embark upon my two-hour walk, followed by the ten-hour train ride back to Tianjin. The visitors who accompanied me back to the train station walked with slow, deliberate steps. Some kept their heads down to hide the tears, others looked straight ahead without expression and I was one of them. I steeled myself against the ache that threatened to eat me alive. I looked down at the food the prison guards prohibited me from giving to Freddie and then looked back at the tall chimneys of the steel plant until they disappeared in the mist.

When I reached the train, I was thoroughly exhausted. I thought about the boys who longed to accompany me. I tried to explain that I could not carry them in my arms on the extensive journey, but I knew they could not fully understand. Every visit to the steel plant prison was like ripping off a scab on a wound that took months to heal. I had to fight the depression that threatened to overwhelm me.

I had never imagined that my marriage would be like this. Those heartless men in their official uniforms had stolen it away. I saw my husband for a total of two hours per year. I wondered if I would be an old lady before we could share our lives together. I frequently took out Freddie's photographs, showing them to our sons and telling them stories about their father. My heart broke at the thought of Joseph and Daniel growing up without a father. I wondered if my boys would follow Jesus in this atheist country without a strong Christian father to guide them.

III. Rebuilding

31. I lost my eyesight, but the Lord healed me

32. My roommate in UNC Medical College

33. Some brothers and sisters of Raleigh Chinese Christian Church

34. My first used car

35. My beloved Christian host family in North Carolina, 1984 Mr. and Mrs. Sam and Francis Arbes and their family

36. I served the Lord at Good News For All Nations TV

37. The Lord revived my voice to praise Him; on my left is Mrs. Peacock, a soprano vocalist and on my right is a violinist, Miss Mary Francis Boys

38. The Medical College of University of North Carolina

39. The Lord gave me visions and ministries of "C"; the first "C" was "cook"

40. The second "C" was Chinese Bible study fellowship; these are the teachers of the fellowship at my kitchen

41. Sharing in the women prayer group at Cary, NC

42. Chinese Bible study fellowship at Chapel Hill, NC

43. The Chinese Bible study fellowship at our home

44. The third "C" was children ministry

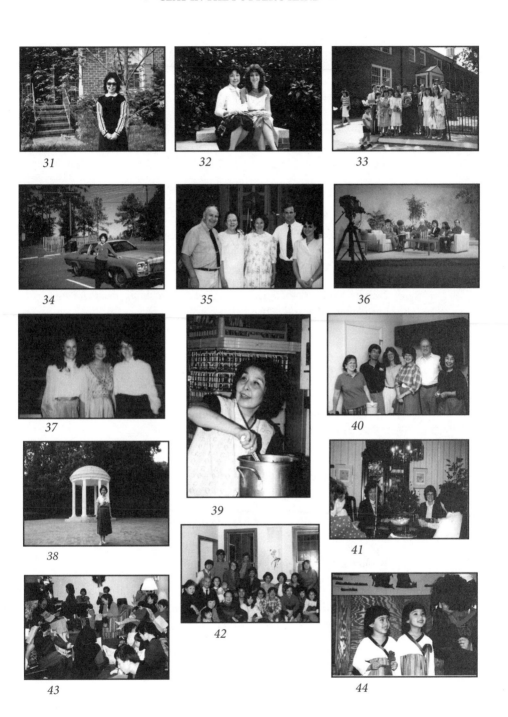

31

32

33

34

35

36

37

39

40

38

41

43

42

44

45. *Twin babies in our Chinese church*

46. *Even a one and a half year old girl can play keyboard to praise the Lord*

47. *A little girl plays the accordion in our church*

48. *The 1987 New Year celebration with the Chinese students studying at the University of Virginia at Charlottesville, VA*

49. *Despite losing the function of my right hand small finger during the hard labor, I can still play the piano in church services for the Lord*

50. *In our "Revival Chinese Christian Church", 99 people were baptized from 1989 – 1997; This was the fourth "C", church*

51. *The 1995 retreat conference at our Chinese church where the theme was "Life, Spiritual Life and His Great Commission"*

52. *I was preaching in our Chinese church*

53. *Sharing Jesus with Chinese scholars*

54. *Women Bible study fellowship*

55. *In 1987, Reedy Creek Baptist Church and Raleigh Chinese Christian Church in North Carolina celebrated our 20th wedding anniversary*

56. *Our whole family enjoyed our reunion in the U.S. in October, 1988*

45

46

47

48

49

50

51

52

53

54

55

56

57. As for me and my house, we will serve the Lord

58. The high school graduation day of our two sons (2 pictures, same caption)

59. Praise the Lord, our sons Joseph and Daniel served the Lord in our Chinese church while they were in Charlottesville and now they serve the Lord in Evangelical Formosan Church of Washington, D.C. (2 pictures, same caption)

60. Freddie and Dorothy joined Christian Aid and established the China Division and began to involve the Lord's Great Commission, the fifth "C" (2 pictures, same caption)

61a. Being ordained and sent to China by Dr. Bob Finley and Board of Christian Aid Mission in 1989

61b. Helping our Chinese coworkers to establish Bible schools to spread the gospel in China

62. I was teaching in a Bible school in China

63. Pioneer missionaries Mecca Zhao and his wife planted the "Macedonian Church" in Xinjiang; we are following their steps

64. We have a close partnership with the Chinese Christian Evangelical Association in Taiwan; the director, Pastor and Mrs. James Shia

65. Staff of CCEA and they used to be called "The Year of 2000 Gospel Movement in Taiwan" in 1990s.

57

58

58

59

60

59

61a

61b

62

63

64

65

66. We visit many prisons and share Jesus with prisoners in Taiwan

67. Pastor and Mrs. James Shia, Sister Grace Cheng, Mr. and Mrs. Shih-Liang Chang of CCEA who greatly supported the first printing of my autobiography in Chinese.

68. We had mission trips in Southeast Asia evangelizing in Singapore, Philippines, Indonesia, Malaysia; in Australia, Latin America, Canada, the U.S. and elsewhere

a) a mission trip to the Philippines;

b) a mission trip to Singapore;

c) a mission trip to Indonesia;

d) Ministries with U.S. missionaries;

e) Ministries with Taiwan Christians;

f) Sharing testimonies with Dr. David Jeremiah in San Diego, CA;

g) Being the major speaker at Women Aglow 25th Anniversary Retreat Conference;

h) Sharing testimonies at First Baptist Church in Atlanta, GA and meeting with Pastor Dr. Charles Stanley;

i) Sharing Chinese indigenous ministries as representatives of Christian Aid Mission at the World Mission Conference in Amsterdam, Holland in 2000;

j) Sharing and praising in Puerto Rico;

k) Preaching in Chinese churches in Canada;

l) 50th Anniversary Celebration of Christian Aid Mission;

66

67

68a

68b

68c

68d

68e

68f

68g

68h

68i

68j

68k

68l

68. Continued...

m) Praising God with indigenous missionaries of all nations at 50th Anniversary Celebration of Christian Aid Mission

69. The wedding ceremony of our son Daniel Sun and Julia Chang in 2002

70. Our family picture

68m

69

69

70

Chapter 30

God's Care and Fourth Vision Revealed

My sons were eager to attend school. They stood at the windows each morning to watch the older kids walking down the street with their school bags. When the day came to enroll them, I grabbed their hands in mine and off to the schoolhouse we went. The boys were ecstatic, skipping and giggling alongside of me. Our celebration ended when we arrived at the school building. I learned that because three people in my family were considered "counter-revolutionaries," no kindergarten or grade school would accept my sons.

I walked out of the office to the expectant eyes of my sons, who waited for me in the hall. I could not tell them the real reason why they were not allowed to go to school. I could only grab them in my arms and tell them that we would try again next year. I held my head high on the way back to stave off the tears that threatened to trickle down my face. I had to be strong and resourceful. My boys would not grow up ignorant.

I scraped together the paltry sum I had managed to save from pathetic factory wages and bought schoolbooks. I enlisted my mother's help to teach my sons to read and write while I worked at the factory during the day. The boys were quick learners and I was thrilled with their progress.

After several months of studies, Ms. Zhang, a teacher at the local school, unexpectedly visited our home. Although I had never met Ms. Zhang, she somehow knew our situation. She recommended that my sons take an intelligence test, because if they passed, the school would accept them as gifted children. This opportunity was remarkable! I started to worry that Joseph and Daniel were just average students. What kind of questions might appear on the test? Could I properly prepare them?

Examination day arrived sooner than I would have liked. I wished we had more time to prepare. I held my breath as I turned the knob to the testing room. Only eight other children sat inside. I squeezed Joseph's and Daniel's hands and told them I would be waiting outside, praying for them the entire time. "Be calm and only answer those questions that you are sure about," I told them behind my facade of confidence. "Then, if you have time, answer the rest."

I watched them walk inside and take their seats. The door closed behind them. I stood in the hall, anxiously fiddling with buttons on my blouse. The Lord reminded me in that moment that my sons' admittance to the school would not be determined by any teacher, but by Him. I took comfort in this fact as I waited. The door finally swung open and several children emerged. Joseph was wearing a huge smile and excitedly told me that he passed the test and would be admitted.

We waited for Daniel, who remained in the room after all of the other children had left. Ms. Zhang finally appeared, holding Daniel's hand. "Daniel failed the arithmetic test," she began, "But, he performed wonderfully on the political knowledge test. He perfectly recited Chairman Mao's three well-known articles, as well as many other quotations and we have decided to admit him." I was stunned. My boys would be going to school!

On our way home I learned that Daniel had memorized Chairman Mao's articles while listening to his grandpa recite them for the Red Guards. My father repeated them everyday in preparation for the Red Guards' interrogation. I smiled when I thought about how God had taken what our adversaries meant for evil and turned it to good. What a wonderful God who even sees to my sons' education. I praise Him!

**Rehabilitation of the Wrong and Unjust
Cases of My Father and Husband**

In the spring of 1978, those who had been unjustly accused were able to appeal. I prepared an appeal for my father, Freddie and myself and gave them to Ms. P, who submitted them to the authorities. For almost ten years already Freddie had been jailed, worked in a forced hard labor camp and then worked in the hard labor steel plant prison.

I remember one night I had a dream that Freddie came home, wearing a new fur jacket and new golden-framed glasses. He carried a new suitcase in one hand, and an overcoat in the other. He looked like an overseas Chinese just back from abroad. I was so happy that tears streamed down my face as I asked him over and over how he made it back home again, but he only smiled. I kept this dream as a promise that Freddie would be back soon.

Several days after my dream, a police official approached me at the factory. He told me that I needed to go to the Tianjin Municipal Court to pick up my husband. I was given two days off, with a warning not to inform anyone of this. Oh happy day! I remember that the sky was so blue and the sun was shining on that crisp morning in November.

I told my children, "Daddy's coming home!"

They were so happy, jumping up and down, and asking, "Daddy isn't sick anymore?

I told them, "Daddy is sick no more!" I took them with me.

I breathed in the air as I virtually flew to the court. A judge met us at the door and escorted us to a room where Freddie sat. He looked very weak and pale, and I noticed the big, blue circles around his eyes, but he was wearing fresh clothing and grinning from ear to ear. We shared a long, tearful embrace and left the court. My husband was actually coming home with me! The boys were a bit shy at first, but as soon as we were back home Freddie grabbed them up in his arms, kissing them and hoisted them up onto his shoulders. Then, their shyness disappeared and the boys talked incessantly, as if no time at all had passed. At school, the boys told everyone that their father had come back.

The next day after his homecoming, Freddie traveled to Beijing to the Chinese Academy of Sciences with the vice president of the Tianjin Municipal Court. In front of the entire staff of the Institute of Geology, the judge announced that Freddie had been wrongly accused. He was compensated for the wages of the last five years and given a vacation. After depositing in the bank three thousand Yuan, equivalent to about fifteen hundred U.S. dollars, he hurried back home to Tianjin. Autumn was drawing to a close and Freddie used some of his small fortune to buy a new blue jacket and golden-framed glasses – just like the well-to-do Freddie in my dream.

We took the boys to meet their grandfather in Shanghai for the first time. My father-in-law fell in love with his grandsons, and we had a wonderful family reunion. Little did we know that this would be our first and last reunion, as he suffered a fatal stroke a year later and passed away.

My mother-in-law had been condemned as an American spy and persecuted to death in the Cultural Revolution. She resigned from her teaching job at Wellesley College, in Wellesley, Massachusetts in the U.S. and returned to China in 1949. Most of Freddie's family, who were formerly loyal to the Communists began to recognize the malevolence of Mao Ze-Dong's policies.

One Sunday afternoon in the spring of 1979, the director of the neighborhood committee and the local police officers came to our apartment to inform us that my father had been wrongly accused, and all surveillance and "reformation" would immediately end. Several days later, representatives of the Tianjin Municipal Political Consultative Conference visited my father to invite him to serve on the board of the Research Institute of Culture and History in Tianjin.

Suddenly, we had many unexpected visitors. Our old friends, who dared not visit us while we were under surveillance, now came by to congratulate us. But through it all, my father's joy remained constant. Both honor and disgrace are insignificant to those whose eyes are set on Christ and the life to come. Freddie prepared elaborate banquets for those who remained loyal to us during our persecution.

As time went by, people began to understand the life-changing love of Christ as exemplified by my family, who held no animosity towards those who unjustly persecuted us for two generations. We soon moved from the tiny apartment into an old house with three bedrooms, lots of sunshine, laughter, old friends and new friends visiting, sharing and praising. After twelve years of marriage, we finally had our own place..

Chapter 31

My Rehabilitation and Father's Home Call

After Freddie's reputation was restored, he was quickly promoted and given many important tasks by the Chinese Academy of Sciences. However, we still didn't have a home in Beijing, so Freddie slept in the office. I was still working in the hard labor factory. I started to appeal my case and the police knew that sooner or later I would be rehabilitated, so they were very polite to me and permitted me to take leave for my appeals. But they often reminded me not to tell anybody that I was appealing my "wrongful" case because those who were allowed to appeal were considered prisoners of conscience, counter-revolutionaries, etc., not ordinary criminals. This was because every criminal wants to claim that they were unjustly sentenced, which creates a problem for the police.

My life was getting better, and I was allowed to visit Beijing with my boys to see Freddie. When he was working, I took my boys with me to the judicial department to present my appeal to the authorities in Beijing. It was snowing heavily and bitterly cold, and crowds of people were lined up for miles on the street to appeal their false charges. We had to wait an entire day. According to official statistics, millions of unjust cases existed all over

China and over 40,000 appealers came to Beijing each day to present their cases. They had no money for food or lodging so they slept on the streets.

One year after I appealed, the public security bureau told me that they could not find my file. My case had to be handled by the authorities of the police who arrested me in 1960. I consulted Tianjin Municipal Public Security Bureau and an officer there asked me if I knew who had arrested me. I was appalled at their seeming lack of information, but began my story.

I told them that the secret police interviewed me, and later claimed that I had behaved inappropriately. Without a warrant or even a reason for my arrest, the police escorted me to the detention house for two weeks. After that I was confined to a hard labor camp. Two weeks later I was given a notice that stated: "Being reactionary in ideology, reeducation through labor needed for one and a half years."

By now, I had been in detention and hard labor for twenty years. The police officer then asked me if I still remembered the appearance of those who had questioned me. I had not forgotten and described the overweight chain smoker of medium height with a round face, and the tall, thin man with the horse-like face covered in pimples. Recognition flashed in the officer's eyes as he laughed at my description.

He said, "The fat guy's last name is Zhang, and the tall guy with the horse face is called Ma (which means 'horse' in Chinese)." He proceeded to inform me that these two men were transferred to factories, and only after they are found could my case be resolved. During the Cultural Revolution, started in 1966, Mao Ze-Dong persecuted, imprisoned, tortured and even killed some of his own followers. These men were victims just as I was. My heart sank. The population of the city of Tianjin was over ten million. Like a stone thrown into the sea, my case would surely be lost forever. All I could do was to wait upon the Lord through faith.

Father's Home Call

I waited for months, and during this time, my father, the person I most respected, depended upon spiritually, and with whom I was the closest, unexpectedly went peacefully to be with the Lord. One week before his death, my father was extremely joyful, continually counting the blessings God had bestowed upon him. He said that a man who does not recognize the blessings in his life does not mature in faith.

Before he began to depend upon the Lord, he was a poor country boy with only himself on which to depend. However, after he submitted his life to the Lord, God used him in an amazing way. "An honor that I didn't deserve," he said, "God makes the weak one strong and exalts the lowly ones." He expressed his unparalleled gratitude for my mother, who sacrificed everything to love him and wholeheartedly co-labor with him to the end. He also named his nine children, as well as his grandchildren. Together, his family includes over sixty members. Turning to me, my father said, "God has entrusted you and me with special tasks. Don't look down upon yourself as a weak woman, but have constant faith. I will see the Lord soon."

He told me once my case was rehabilitated, I needed to share the gospel and continue his mission to support indigenous Chinese churches, making Christianity in China truly Self-Governing, Self-Supporting and Self-Propagating. He said that Jehovah is the God who loves us Chinese, and that while I will experience tribulation, if I seek the glory of God, not of man, I will not be disillusioned with the honor or disgrace of this world.

He was eighty-four years old, and due to the humiliation and torment he suffered throughout the years, he was physically weak, swollen and pale. However, over the past two days he had seemed unusually healthy and his spirit seemed more alive now than ever before. How could he leave us now? "I have fought a good fight, I have finished my course. I have kept the faith. I dare not believe there is a big crown waiting for me, nor dare I say I am a good and faithful servant, but I will enjoy the glory that God bestows on me, as He wipes all my tears away," my father continued. "Many people leave their children suitcases of gold, but I leave behind only the Bible," he said. "I have not even a single pin that I can leave for you, but this Bible is God's grace, which is inexhaustible: a most rich and generous deposit. You deposit your faith and obedience into it, and you can cash His eternal wealth."

Early the next morning as I was leaving for work at five o' clock, I heard my dad calling me in a faint voice. I hurried into my parents' room where my father was laying, straining to fill his lungs with air, his face was pale and hands cold. I immediately gave him his heart medicine and attempted to make him more comfortable by propping another pillow under his head. It was early and my mom was still asleep, but my father rested his head on my arm. I heard him murmur, "Okay, it is finished." I thought he had fallen back asleep. However, when I checked his pulse, I realized that in that instant, my father had left for heaven.

My mom and Grace held my father's body and cried. He had suffered so much for the Lord, never living comfortably on this earth. He would not even witness my rehabilitation. Our sorrows abated, though, as we thought of our father entering his beautiful home in heaven, where we would all meet someday. As we were making arrangements for a Christian memorial service, the color on my father's face surprisingly returned; he looked so peaceful and tranquil: a gift that strengthened our faith that he was indeed in paradise.

I realized, as we sang hymns at my father's service, that we are all awaiting our glorious Lord to return in righteous judgment of this world, and to enter into the holy city of the new heaven and earth. *"Jesus is coming again"* filled my heart with anticipation of Christ's coming for days afterward, and the book of Revelation has since become one of my favorite books.

The following day was my father's funeral. We invited relatives, friends and a few government officials to pay their last respects and express their condolences to my father. My siblings asked me to prepare and read the memorial speech in remembrance of our father's life. I was able to quickly complete it, beginning with his salvation in Christ at age fourteen. He loved the Lord and was faithful to serve Him throughout his entire life.

He not only served the Lord fervently in the church, but also founded the "Chinese Christian Self-Governing, Self-Supporting and Self-Propagating Million Pound Foundation" and the "Tianjin New Life Evening Post" in 1943. My father had been blessed by the Lord with the vision that Christianity should become firmly established in China, and he worked to fulfill this goal until 1955.

My father loved the Chinese people. During the eight years when the Japanese imperialists invaded and occupied China, he chose to be imprisoned and impoverished, rather than betray his nation for personal gain. He preserved the national integrity. In 1939 through his generous contributions, he established a relief and vocational training center in Tianjin for the victims of natural disasters, which rescued over 100,000 victims and those without ways to generate income.

A student to the end, he diligently studied in China and abroad, using the knowledge he acquired to help others. He suffered much during his life, but never became bitter or resentful toward his accusers. He recognized that to follow Jesus meant daily denying yourself and taking up your cross. His children have embraced his godly heritage.

The memorial speech was not intended to be boastful, but as a way of sharing his testimony in the presence of governmental officials, including the social security police bureau, the so-called Chinese Christian Self-Governing, Self-Supporting, Self-Propagating Patriotic Association and my family. The Lord gave me the courage to stand up in front of people who used to persecute my father and boldly defend his honor and the gospel in which we placed our faith and hope. After I finished my speech, the vice chairman of the Municipal Political Consultative Conference of Tianjin stood to acclaim the many good deeds and compassionate work among the community, in Tianjin and other cities, that my father had accomplished.

Soon after my father's death, Grace met a Christian man who had been condemned as a rightist and assigned to a labor camp in northeastern China. After his release, he came to Tianjin, where they met and married. To marry a Christian was the only choice of a true believer. Then he and Grace moved to Hong Kong, where he was born. My mother sent Grace, her youngest daughter, off to a land of freedom with her blessings and a tearful farewell. Only my mother, the boys and I were left in the empty house in Tianjin and I knew she desperately looked to me as a permanent caretaker.

I was currently in the process of rehabilitation, after which I would naturally bring my twins to Beijing to reunite with Freddie. Eventually, I too would leave, but I knew that God who takes care of tomorrow would certainly take care of my mother. But I still struggled with feelings of guilt about not taking good care of my mother and family.

God Picks Up a Stone from the Bottom of the Sea

Soon after my father's death, one evening I left the factory and was waiting at the bus stop in the twilight when I heard the sound of approaching footsteps. I turned my head to see a man who pushed a bicycle with a broken chain. I could barely see his face, but by the dim light of his cigarette I distinctly recognized the features of the overweight man who had secretly arrested me. I rushed to him and grasped tightly the handlebars of his bike and asked him, "You are Comrade Zhang, are you not?"

Stunned, he asked me who I was. "Look closer," I said.

His eyes widened. "Oh yes, I remember you. You haven't changed much. Where have you been for so many years?" he said.

I told him that I was in the same labor camp where he had detained me over twenty years prior, and have been doing hard labor ever since. A look of astonishment and remorse crossed his face. He began to tell me that he was ousted from the police bureau by the Red Guards to do manual labor in a factory. Before we parted, he left me his address and telephone number and agreed to reexamine my case once he was released.

I sighed, realizing I must first pray for Mr. Zhang's rehabilitation so that he might help me to rehabilitate. God, how wonderful You are, in a big city of Tianjin with over ten million people, You amazingly set Mr. Zhang right before me with his chain-broken bike in the twilight of an evening.

Several months passed. Eventually, both comrades Zhang and Ma regained their former positions in the police bureau. Although they were loyal followers of Mao Ze-Dong, they had also been treated unjustly. The Red Guards had evidently killed their supervisor, condemned as a person in power taking the capitalist road. I dropped my allegations and offered no complaint against them.

Some months later I received a notice stating that my arrest and punishment was unjustified and my case is now officially corrected. Corrected? Over the last twenty years my youth was stolen, my talent ruined, my reputation tarnished and my health jeopardized. But apparently this one small piece of paper corrected all of this. I received no financial compensation for those last twenty years because the resources had been simply drained off after millions of people who were officially sentenced, and whose cases were settled earlier, received payments. I was left with nothing plus nothing. However, in this humbling moment, the Lord comforted me. Through this tribulation, I learned obedience, submission and dependence upon God. The things I actually lost in those twenty years were self-righteousness, arrogance, and pride. God replenished my loss with His abundance of grace and eternal gains.

Chapter 32

A Table Prepared in the Presence of My Enemies

In 1980, after two generations of my family were rehabilitated, I was invited to participate in a Christian forum organized by the Communist United Front Department, the Religious Bureau and Tianjin Three-Self Patriotic Movement Association. The forum was organized to give those Christians who were wrongly accused the opportunity to state their grievances. Over three hundred delegates were invited to this grand conference. The Communist officials who sat on the platform repeatedly emphasized their supposed innocence in the persecution of Christians in the last twenty years, pointing to the members of "Three Self Churches" as the culprits.

I remained silent only listening to the precious testimonies of those who gathered together in small groups. I was seated at a table with several people, including Yun-Zheng Huang, the leader of "Tianjin Three-Self Patriotic Movement Association." I was suddenly jerked from my silent contemplation when a man from the platform announced my name as the next speaker.

Unprepared and a little daunted, I arose and walked toward the stage. I looked out at the audience: those faithful brothers and sisters in Christ who had been so willing to suffer for their faith, and the others who persecuted us for over twenty years. The story and word from Genesis 50:20 came to my mind: *"But as for you, ye thought evil against me; but God meant it unto good, to bring to pass, as it is this day, to save much people alive."* I began to talk about the new life that Christ had given me through the trials I endured, and the lessons I learned knowing myself a sinner. I know I didn't deserve Christ's salvation, but the Lord saved me. It is the love of Jesus that I learned to practice with others.

I talked about the priceless treasures I had gained and encouraged those in attendance to forget the past and look forward to the work God has prepared for us in the future. My closing words were Romans 8:28: *"And we know that all things work together for good to them that love God, to them who are the called according to His purpose."*

Applause erupted as I concluded my speech. I noticed several Communist leaders asking Xio-Peng Yang, the supposed Christian who falsely incriminated my father and me, about my identity. Yang's face blushed with shame. He had reported and betrayed many Christians. The Communist leaders of the United Front Department and Religious Bureau came down from the platform and shook my hand, saying they were touched by my gracious attitude in light of my wrongful case. I received a warm reception and much encouragement from Christians seated at my table, as well as others, who said "Halleluiah, dear sister, on behalf of us you spoke out what we would like to share in our hearts!" I recalled Psalm 23: 5 *"Thou preparest a table before me in the presence of mine enemies."*

A few days after the conference the boys and I prepared to move from Tianjin to Beijing to reunite with Freddie. We finally had our own home: a small two-bedroom apartment flat. We divided the two small rooms into corners for studying, sleeping and dining. The furnishings were simple, but the portrait of Jesus prominently displayed left no question about our faith, because *"As for me and my house, we will serve the LORD"*. (Joshua 24: 15) The Chinese saying, "Nest of gold and nest of silver cannot compare with our own little nest of love" became a reality for us. Our two boys were never so happy. During their school lunch breaks, they raced home to eat with me. Every night, before my boys went to bed I sang hymns to them.

Job-hunting, writing, parenting and housework kept me relatively busy. My attempt to find employment was discouraging. I questioned who might want to hire a medical student who had not graduated and who had left the field for twenty years? However, God opened a door for me through Daisy Li, my old friend and classmate at Beijing Medical College. Mr. Wang, her friend, was an officer in the public health sector. He told me that I could apply for a job as an editor in the People's Public Health Publishing House to translate English medical journals and books into Chinese publications for the World Health Organization of the United Nations. If my English is good enough, I wryly chuckled. I had almost forgotten all of my medical knowledge and hadn't spoken English for the last thirty years, but there was no other door open to me. So, I thought this must be the Lord's will and not mine. So go ahead, Lord Jesus. You will help me, right?

On the first day of the interview, I took a written test along with twenty other people. Our assignment was to translate: 1) an English report about public health in Africa into Chinese, and 2) a Chinese medical journal into English. I barely accomplished the first, and the latter proved almost impossible. The following day I stood in front of a group of doctors and professors to take the oral portion of the test. They all spoke to me in English, daunting at first, but surprisingly familiar. Amazingly, I recalled most of the English words I learned as a child, and was able to respond to their questions.

My American accent apparently aroused the attention of a westerner in their midst who asked about it. He also asked me why there were twenty years, 1960 to 1980, missing from my career resume. I hesitated to answer, knowing that my life's story, which included the unjust charge, might offend the Communist officials present. Gathering my courage, I proceeded to inform the group that this was my very first job interview after having been imprisoned for twenty years, and that I had learned English from American missionaries as a child. The blank stares I received in return convinced me that I would probably not be getting this job.

But a miracle happened two weeks later. To my absolute astonishment, I was hired as a translator/editor! I immediately began the arduous training process, which required many hours of observation and much research, learning from others and self-teaching. Eventually, I was able to excel in my work and was later promoted to be the editor of the World Health Forum and the World Health Quarterly Journals.

My new position required me to accompany UN officials to negotiations, meetings and to tour with foreign publishers. I occasionally attended banquets with foreign guests in the Great Hall of the People, the

Chinese "Capitol Hill." I was overwhelmed as I entered the Hall for the first time, remembering that God takes delight in honoring those who are lowly and who depend upon Him for all things. But, I prayed, "Dear Lord, when could you use me full-time to serve You as your servant? You are my only Master, my only King, my Lord."

Chapter 33

The Red Sea and the Wilderness

I was enjoying my job with the United Nations, but still carried the burden to share Christ with my Chinese countrymen. In 1979 the Chinese Communists began to pursue an "open- door" policy, so the government allowed a few Communist-controlled "Three-Self" churches to reopen. The Communists, however, strategically picked the men in charge of the "Three-Self" churches. They were fiercely loyal to them and enjoyed the monetary benefits that resulted.

Many Christians, however, still met in illegal underground house churches, home fellowships and Bible studies. I continually prayed that God would reveal my niche in His great plan for China. Our goal as Chinese Christians was not only to meet together for mutual encouragement, but also to evangelize our great country of over one billion souls. The older generation of believers looked to us to share Christ with the younger generations. The task was daunting, and I wondered how God would use me to accomplish this mission. It was at this time that the Lord opened a door for me in the United States.

To enter the United States, I needed either a student visa, which I was too old to obtain, or an invitation to a medical college as a visiting scholar. Coincidentally, my position as the responsible editor of the People's Public Health Publishing House in translating World Public Health Journals was equivalent to a university lecturer. I received an invitation from the University of North Carolina as a visiting scholar. I was approved by the Chinese government and granted a visa by the U.S. consulate. Freddie's cousin, who lived in Hawaii, generously provided my financial support.

After only four years together with Freddie and the twins, I made the heart-wrenching decision to travel across the ocean to American shores. The thought of leaving my family was agonizing. Tears filled my eyes as I touched the faces of my lovely young sons, fast asleep in their beds at night. I struggled to find the words to tell them that their mother would again be leaving them.

Before leaving China, I visited the Beijing cemetery where my father's ashes remained to say my goodbye. Holding the urn, I lifted my head and prayed that God would give me faith. Inside the decorative vessel, I placed a small piece of paper upon which was written my father's favorite Scriptures and my parting thoughts:

"Who shall separate us from the love of Christ? Shall tribulation, or distress, or persecution, or famine, or nakedness, or peril, or sword? As it is written, For thy sake we are killed all the day long; we are accounted as sheep for the slaughter. Nay, in all these things we are more than conquerors through him that loved us." (Romans 8: 35-37).

"I have fought a good fight, I have finished my course, I have kept the faith: Henceforth there is laid up for me a crown of righteousness, which the Lord, the righteous judge, shall give me at that day: and not to me only, but unto all them also that love his appearing." (2 Timothy 4:7-8)

"Dad, I am free. Jehovah God has rescued me from bondage. He will take me to cross the "Red Sea" to Canaan. I firmly believe the Truth that you fervently kept, and will honor the God Who kept you strong. ~ Dorothy."

That day, I also reserved a place at the cemetery for my mom, who was over eighty years old with her health deteriorating. I was often tormented with guilt over the fact that I was leaving my elderly mother and young children, but God urged me to go forward and prepared the road ahead. I dreamed that one day my husband, children and mother could join me in the United States, where we would have freedom to worship the Lord.

Freddie, Joseph and Daniel accompanied me to the airport.

Unbeknownst to my twin sons, who were playing happily with balloons and watching the planes flying overhead, I would be leaving them for many years. I hugged them tightly in my arms, but held back the tears until I boarded the airplane. I cried bitterly as I watched the city of Beijing fade into the distance. Eventually, my tears turned to prayers of protection for my family. I prayed that the Lord would grant me a family reunion before too many days passed.

I arrived at the University of North Carolina in the city of Chapel Hill, and was amazed at the beauty of the university's campus, complete with perfectly manicured green lawns, lush plants and vibrantly colored flowers. Amid the rolling hills and tall trees, I could see church steeples. It was autumn, and I was overcome with the brilliance of the leaves. Their red and golden hues evoked in my heart the gratitude I feel toward my Creator. My imperfect voice sang a lovely poem written by Alfred Joyce Kilmer (1886-1918), "Trees," in my praise to God:

"I think that I shall never see
A poem lovely as a tree.
A tree whose hungry mouth is prest
Against the earth's sweet flowing breast;
A tree that looks at God all day
And lifts her leafy arms to pray.
A tree that may in summer wear,
A nest of robins in her hair,
Upon whose bosom snow has lain,
Who intimately lives with rain.
Poems are made by fools like me,
But only God can make a tree."

I soon found my way to those tall steeples to freely lift my voice to God. How I longed for my family to share in my experiences. I wrote to my boys often, encouraging them to listen to their father and remind them that, even though I was an ocean away, I was still singing to them.

On the first Sunday after my arrival in the United States, I attended a Chinese church service in Raleigh. The hymns rang joyously in my ears as my eyes glistened with tears of thanksgiving to the Lord. When the pastor invited first-time guests to introduce themselves, I stood, tears running down my face. I told the congregation, comprised mostly of believers from

Taiwan and Hong Kong, about the tribulations faced by mainland Chinese Christians.

Studying my public health courses and conducting seminars was certainly a full-time job. Despite the workload, I soon became a member of this church, and spent many wonderful hours in fellowship with my newfound brothers and sisters in Christ in churches, Bible studies and prayer groups. I always made time to spend with these precious saints and my schedule was always full, trying to know more about God Himself, His grace, loving Him and serving Him more.

As a visiting scholar, I was assigned to a dormitory of medical students. I cracked open the door to my room to find it empty. As I was beginning to unpack, my new roommate, an American girl who introduced herself as Michelle, entered the room. She noticed the Bible I had placed on the table and expressed her delight in meeting me. She told me that she had earlier prayed for a Christian to be her roommate but never thought of one who was Chinese. We became fast friends, and she later invited me to share my testimony in her church and spend holidays with her family.

The next morning, Michelle accompanied me to the cafeteria for my first American breakfast. I noticed that everyone was eating cereal. I was surprised by the variety, and was unsure which box to choose. My roommate pointed to a box plastered with a huge, golden sunflower and said, "Take this, it is the best and I eat it everyday." Reading the label, I noticed that the cereal contained the husks and shells of sunflower seeds, barley and wheat. The brightly colored letters acclaimed its nutritional value, as it was supposed to contain vitamins A through Z and would improve women's skin with complexion-improving qualities. Memories of life in the hard labor camp suddenly came flooding back to my mind. For many years I was given nothing but bitter bread made from the ground husks of sunflower seeds. I now realized that the rough and coarse substance I was forced to eat was actually nutritious. God had amazingly sustained me with exactly the nutrition I needed to survive!

I began expanding my circle of friends and received many invitations to attend the fellowship and activities of both Chinese and American Christians. God also opened the door for me to work with a television program called, "Good News for All Nations." The close friendships I was establishing were a great comfort to me; however, late at night, when all distractions were removed, I would yearn to see my family again. I had to turn my eyes away from the mothers who took their children to play in the parks.

Time flew by, and after I completed one year at the university, I asked some friends, who were going to visit Beijing, to check on my family. When they returned to the States, I was delighted to hear about my well-behaved sons, but dismayed to learn of the disorderly state of my home. Freddie was traveling abroad doing research for the Chinese Academy of Science, spending three months each year in Tibet for geological expeditions.

I began to worry about my sons. I was also concerned about my mother. Every two weeks I wrote a letter to her, but she never responded. Then one Sunday at church I learned, through a mutual acquaintance of my sister's and mine, that my mother had passed away and my brothers and sisters had conducted her funeral.

I was shocked and hurt that no one had bothered to notify me. Once more, I struggled with guilt that I had abandoned my family. However, once more, God comforted me through my pastors, Reverend Peter Ning and Reverend Bruce Johnson, who conducted a beautiful memorial service for my mother. In the midst of my friends I was able to share her testimony, love and sacrifice. As people sang the hymn, *"Be still my Soul, Oh, love which would not let me go,"* healing flooded my heart. Oh, yes, Lord, You love my mother more!

The Lord Revived My Voice

Since my voice had been damaged and hoarse for over twenty years, I was so sorry that when I sang the hymns and shared my testimonies for the Lord, I had such limited use of my voice. However, when I thought of what pleases the Lord, it is the praise united with my mouth and my heart, worshiping Him in spirit and in truth. It didn't matter whether my voice was good or bad. So I obeyed the Lord and didn't ask for this particular healing. Amazingly, when I came to the U.S., I found my voice had become much better. I also frequently attended Chapel Hill Bible Church, just across the street from my college, UNC. The sermons of the pastors deeply touched me.

I made the acquaintance of Mrs. Peacock, a soprano vocalist. Although she did not know how to heal my voice, she invited me to attend her vocal lessons and hear her lectures. I was able to practice with her students who were learning how to sing and practice breathing. I learned a lot from her.

In October 1984, the rehearsals of the "Messiah" concert traditionally to be performed at Chapel Hill began. It was a performance composed of singing "The Hallelujah Chorus" in four parts together with the choir and an eight hundred-member congregation. The symphony orchestra was also fantastic. "Messiah" is my favorite opera and I sang it so many times when I was young that I could even sing it from memory. So, whenever the choir had rehearsals I went there to listen.

During the final rehearsals when the congregation joined with the choir, I could not control myself. I began to sing with them. My Lord, I believe that when You hear our praise, You are comforted. The "Hallelujah" chorus was so solemn, holy, melodious and perfect, it seemed that angels and a heavenly army also joined in singing with us. My tears tumbled down. I didn't care about my hoarse voice, since there were hundreds of people and nobody would hear my voice. But, suddenly I felt something eased and opened my throat so that I could sing notes higher and higher without difficulty. I could even hear my own voice and it wasn't hoarse anymore. I just couldn't believe it: Oh King of Kings and Lord of Lords, You are doing another miracle for me! You revived my voice!

After the rehearsal I told Mrs. Peacock, and she was very happy. She insisted that I sing a solo hymn, *"I Know that My Redeemer Liveth."* She originally planned to sing this herself but she let me sing this hymn in solo to witness for the Lord that He had revived my voice. It was only a few days before the performance, so with a grateful heart, I was a little bit nervous but practiced the singing seriously. During the performance of the "Messiah" concert, with a praising and grateful heart I glorified the Lord's name with my revived voice. After that I joined the Raleigh Chinese Christian Church choir and when I worked with "Good News for all Nations," on gospel TV, as I shared my testimonies I also sang. Ever since then I have been singing hymns with my revived voice in my ministry to serve, praise and glorify the Lord!

Chapter 34

Entering Canaan and Fifth Vision Revealed

While in the U.S., I was receiving spiritual training through Bible study, prayer and Christian fellowship. It was clear to me, however, that God was calling me to be the voice of the suffering Christians in mainland China. In 1985, I resigned from the medical department of the University of North Carolina to live for one year in New York City, where I hired an attorney to change my visa status. That year was especially hard for me. In contrast to the beautiful and friendly environment to which I had become accustomed in North Carolina, New York City felt cold and hostile, a place where money did the talking. I was also robbed on several occasions.

Working extremely hard in order to pay my attorney expenses, I was saddened by the American consulate in Beijing consistently denying visas for Freddie and the boys to visit me. Whenever I longed for my family, hymns I learned as a member of the Calvary Baptist Church choir comforted me. I was physically very weak and spiritually stretched and my faith was tested from time to time. The night when I learned that Freddie's visa application had been denied for the third time, I fell asleep complaining to God about my incessant trials.

During the middle of that night, I awoke in extreme pain. My head was pounding and my eyes were watering heavily. I recognized the symptoms as pointing to acute glaucoma and ran outside to find a taxi to take me to an emergency room. Once at the hospital, an eye doctor informed me that I needed immediate surgery. He told me that vision might never return to my right eye. I prayed to the Lord on the operating table that I might still serve Him, no matter what happened. Immediately, a phrase from the hymn, *"Amazing Grace,"* filled my heart. *"...was blind but now I see...".*

Three days after the operation, the bandages were removed. My left eye had fully recovered, and I still had some vision in my right eye. The doctors were very pleased with the success of the surgery, but I knew Who had healed me. It was at this time that the Lord revealed to me the fifth vision confirming the work He had been doing and had left to do.

A few days later I had an odd dream: I walked into Lincoln Center in New York City. I took a seat in the front row, a part of the audience, which was entirely comprised of my Christian friends from both Chinese and American churches. The curtain rose, revealing a carpenter's workshop. Suddenly, a strong, teenage boy with curly dark hair appeared on stage. With his left hand he grabbed a thin little boy with blue eyes and blond hair. The bigger boy emptied the carpenter's toolbox and proceeded to squeeze the little boy into the box, using a hammer and spikes to seal it tightly shut.

The audience began to scream in protest as blood poured from the little boy's arms. I ran to the front of the stage, but it was too high for me to scale. The dark-haired boy finally ran away and when I looked again at the blond-haired boy, there was no mark on him. He was sitting peacefully in the toolbox, smiling at me. I failed to understand what had just occurred, only that my heart seemed to connect with that of the young boy.

As my dream continued, suddenly, a great light shown through a stained-glass window, and I saw a huge staircase that stretched from the stage to the sky. A saint with long silver hair and a white robe slowly descended the stairs. He approached and picked up the toolbox with the little boy inside. The saint slowly walked, carrying the boy in what had become a beautiful basket with blue ribbons cascading down. The transformed toolbox holding the blond haired boy and the saint who carried him then ascended the staircase, as the brilliant light followed them. There was a strong, personal connection between us as the boy's blue eyes met mine. They bid me farewell, seeming to smile with a wink, letting me know he was fine. I cried out for the saint to catch and punish the curly dark-haired boy, but I was ignored. I saw the curtain go down, and "The End" appeared. Only a hammer and a few spikes remained on the stage.

I called my pastor, Reverend Bruce Johnson, to tell him about my vision. He told me that he believed the carpenter's workshop symbolized Christ's workshop. I then realized it symbolized the lessons of suffering and brokenness I had yet to learn. I made a commitment to the Lord and my faith was strengthened. I knew that God was preparing a mission field for me that would extend beyond my imagination.

In the spring of 1987, as I was recovering from eye surgery, I returned to North Carolina to stay with Jackie Wu, a lovely sister in Christ. While there I learned that Freddie, as a representative of the Chinese Academy of Sciences, would be traveling to the United States for a conference. After three years of separation, Freddie and I shared a tearful embrace and reunited.

When my congregation learned that Freddie and I had been married for nearly twenty years, my dear friend, Betty McGee, organized a celebration. Freddie and I shared our testimonies and I sang a hymn, *"In His Time, in His Time, The Lord Makes Everything Beautiful in His Time."* The Lord blessed us with a wonderfully inspiring celebration. That night in 1987, just as we had done almost twenty years earlier on our wedding night, Freddie and I slept on the kitchen floor. By the candlelight, we dedicated our hearts once more to God.

Christian Aid Mission, a mission organization in Virginia that supports indigenous missions worldwide, in the spring of 1987, learned of Freddie's and my testimonies through some Christian magazine articles that I had written previously. Dr. Bob Finley, founder, and then CEO and president of Christian Aid, who had been praying for the means to establish a China division for fifteen years, requested an interview. Almost immediately after the interview, I officially joined Christian Aid to begin working to support native Chinese missionaries.

I also evangelized local Chinese scholars who were studying at the University of Virginia. I took Freddie to meet Dr. Finley and the Christian Aid staff. Freddie flew back to China to make arrangements for the indigenous ministries there and for our boys' departure from China to the United States. I began sharing my testimony in churches throughout the United States. Finally, in October 1988, Freddie and our sons received the necessary permits to immigrate to America.

The Lord also placed upon my heart the desire to establish a Bible study fellowship at the University of Virginia for Chinese scholars, which came to fruition in a peculiar way. I asked the Lord to help me. For several consecutive days, the Lord placed a single word in my mind: "cook", (the first "C" that the Lord gave to me). Confused, I wondered if perhaps I was misguided about establishing a Bible study fellowship, and instead was I supposed to open a Chinese restaurant? All I could do was wait upon God for additional instructions.

The following weekend, I became acquainted with a young Chinese girl who was studying at the university. I began inviting her to my house for homemade dumplings, and she eventually became like a daughter to me. She noticed that I prayed before each meal and was naturally curious as to whom I was directing these words. I began to share about Christ and told her Bible stories, even though I knew that she thought of these as little more than fairy tales. But she loved to have dinners with me, which we both enjoyed.

Eventually I began hosting other Chinese students in my home for dinner every weekend, and a small family was born. The fellowship was wonderful. I cooked, they ate and we chatted and laughed together. However, the students showed no interest in learning about Jesus. Each time I attempted to share, they changed the subject, although our friendship continued to grow. I continued to host these dinners in my home, all the while seriously doubting the effectiveness of my Christian witness. One weekend, after three months of this, I decided to resign as "cook," believing I had misunderstood what God intended.

The students arrived at my home as usual the following weekend, and I told them that I had not bought groceries. To my surprise they had brought their own meat and vegetables and began to cook dumplings to treat me. As usual, I prayed before we ate, thinking that it would be our last supper together. My prayer lasted almost twenty minutes, and when I said "Amen," I was astounded to hear each student say "Amen" as well. I asked them why they said "Amen," and they explained to me that for the past three months, they were testing the extent of my Christian love.

They were curious to find out if I would continue to show them kindness even if they refused to respond to the message of Jesus Christ I shared with them. As we began to eat, they asked me many questions about Jesus and the Bible. I was humbled before God. I was going to give up on those students that very night. Once again, God showed me that He is faithful, even when I am not. To Him be the glory, great things He continues to do, even when we grow weary.

The Mustard Seed Bible Study Fellowship thus began. Later it became the "Chinese Bible Study Fellowship" (the second "C" that the Lord gave to me), which Christian Aid fully supported. The fellowship rapidly expanded, and five years later, the vision of the congregation became focused on converting the Chinese as a nation to God. Because of China's strict one-child policy, several Chinese students remained in the United States to marry and begin their families. Before long, I was a "grandmother" to twelve beautiful babies. The nurses became accustomed to my visits, smiling as I walked down the hospital corridors with armfuls of flowers and treats. I was always congratulated on my "latest addition" of grandchildren.

As the number of children grew in our Chinese Bible study fellowship, the need for child care became apparent. The Lord once again provided by bringing Dr. Stephen Cheng, his wife, Susan, and their two children to Charlottesville from Taiwan. Dr. Cheng was a visiting scholar to UVA, and Susan was the director of Overseas Radio and Television (ORTV) in Taiwan. Susan and I became fast friends, and began a children's ministry (the third "C"). Her help was invaluable to me, as I was attempting to lead worship, be the pianist, plus take care of the children. Before long, with Christian Aid's help, our Bible study fellowship grew into the Revival Chinese Christian Church (the fourth "C").

Susan and I also began a women's fellowship group, as well as prayer meetings and discipleship training classes. We emphasized the importance of growing in faith through studying the Truth of God's Word. New Christians were encouraged to enroll in Bible study fellowship groups to solidify their faith and mature from spiritual infancy to steadfastness; from wearing a decorative cross around their necks, to taking up their cross to follow Jesus.

Throughout the 1990s, the Lord broadened our horizons by expanding both Freddie's and my speaking engagements and our ministries from only in the United States and Canada, to mainland China, Taiwan, Singapore, Malaysia, Indonesia, Argentina, Brazil, Puerto Rico, Australia and the Philippines.

In every country we visited, our message remained exclusively: "...*Jesus*

Christ and Him crucified." (1 Corinthians 2:2.) Those who live in poverty and face persecution on a daily basis have humbled us. We have been encouraged by the bountiful storehouse of theological training centers, evangelical organizations and Christian media available in North America to reach Chinese who travel abroad. So, to join the great team of world evangelization, I see this is the fifth "C", "commission" that the Lord gave to me.

Because we were away more often than not, we called a full-time pastor, supported by Christian Aid, to shepherd our young Chinese church. The First Baptist Church in Charlottesville, which supported Lottie Moon in 1870 to live in China as a missionary for forty years, graciously allowed our church to use its facilities. But later, our fledging church lacked clear leadership and direction. Members of the church had very differing views pertaining to crucial issues such as church vision.

We experienced the typical splits, misunderstandings and confusion that reflect an immature congregation making imperfect decisions. However, the Lord was faithful to use each and every circumstance to break us and teach us how best to love one another. Even in the midst of difficulty, God's guidance and sovereignty were displayed. Nothing could have stopped Freddie and me from loving and walking with our Chinese brothers and sisters in Christ.

Chapter 35

Happy Family Reunion

In the summer of 1988, Freddie, Joseph and Daniel were granted an immigration visa by the U.S. government and on October 12, 1988 they were coming to America. The staff of Christian Aid drove me to Washington, D.C. airport to meet my family. I wondered how my sons would treat me. Would they still remember the songs that I taught them? Did they love the Lord and understand His grace? Did they truly understand why I had to leave them for over four years?

I clutched their photographs in my hands, the same ones I looked at every day, and I wondered how they must have changed. I nervously stood at the airport terminal, watching the long line of passengers exit the plane. Finally, I spotted them, my voice cracked as I called out, "Are those two tall, handsome young men my Joseph and Daniel?" Before I even stepped forward, my sons ran to me, grabbed me and swung me around and around. I laughed as tears streamed down my face, and I think Freddie's smile would have extended to the back of his head if he had no ears to block it.

The boys were delighted to arrive at our townhouse in Charlottesville,

Virginia, which was double the size of our small apartment in Beijing. They enjoyed all the conveniences of the new place. Our supper grew cold that evening as we extended our prayer of thanksgiving to God.

Joseph and Daniel faced a challenging cultural adjustment, as their English was poor and they struggled to understand their teachers. In China the students stay in one classroom while the teachers rotate with each lesson. In America my sons learned that they had to walk to different classrooms with each course. In Beijing they were accustomed to coming home for lunch, which was not allowed by their school. American students treated them like strangers, which was very hard for them. For the past sixteen years, they had been inseparable, always walking shoulder to shoulder, for which they were now ridiculed by their classmates.

I knew that the deep bond they shared resulted from the fact that Freddie and I could give them little attention during their childhood years. The problems worsened daily. They had to rely on one another for support and encouragement. This hurt me deeply, but I thought Freddie would help me. Now, at last, our family was reunited. Actually, Freddie and I spent most of our time and energy in mission work, and I struggled to balance my motherly obligations with my evangelical service to the Lord. Joseph endured the loneliness and hardship in his teenage years. He is very responsible by nature and took care of his six minutes younger brother, Daniel. As Daniel said, "Mom, after you left us we had to have daddy home. We have nobody to turn to, and I always feel that Joseph is my daddy."

What could I say? I cried out, "Oh, dear Lord, forgive me, please help me to be a better mother. Especially please help Freddie to wake up to see his sons and wife need his love and help."

My Lord heard my cries. He helped Joseph, Daniel and me in every way. The Lord took me through many tough times and more lessons in our married life. Praise His name! He's given me faith and understanding, obedience and endurance. I know He is in charge always. I know to trust only in Him. I have failed many times in so many ways over such a long period of time.

Praise the Lord, by His grace my sons soon adjusted to the American culture and graduated from high school as honor roll students in 1991. Joseph and Daniel also devoutly served the Lord in the Chinese church, offering to drive students without a means of transportation to church. Every weekend we hosted Bible study fellowships in our home. Joseph and

Daniel grew spiritually as they meditated upon God's Word. Both were accepted to Virginia Tech, and for the next five years I prayed that God would bring them to spiritual maturity.

Chapter 36

A Hundredfold Harvest

The tribulations suffered by the early church directly following Christ's death clearly illustrate the sacrifice required of the Christian life. During the Roman Empire, Christians were brutally massacred through sadistically creative methods. They were tortured for sport. Wild beasts tore them limb from limb in coliseums jammed with an audience savagely enjoying the carnage. They were thrown into boiling pots of water and burned alive. But in their last moments, these faithful martyrs did not protest, but instead glorified God through songs, prayers and peaceful silence. They even preached to the Romans and cried out, "Come down and join us! Let's go to heaven together!" Some Romans were so touched by their extraordinary boldness, peace and joy, they jumped down from the stands and were also killed.

In the former Soviet Union, under the Communist tyranny of Lenin and Stalin, Christians who refused to betray the Lord were exiled, imprisoned, tortured and killed. Many were sent to hard labor camps in Siberia where they starved to death in the bitter cold. Their youth was stolen and many never married, but their testimonies are a priceless reminder of the unshakeable faith for which we, as Christians, need to strive.

Over 12,000 western missionaries came to China to plant churches and establish compassion projects over the last hundred years. Thousands of Chinese Christians and western missionaries were murdered during the Boxer Rebellion in 1900 and endured civil wars and eight years of Japanese occupation before the Communists took over China in 1949. Instead of retaliating, around 800,000 or so remaining Christians prayed for the conversion of China. The following generation of Chinese Christians living during the past fifty years that followed the 1949 Communist takeover of China was unable to write down the true stories of the tumultuous Chinese church history without facing persecution or death. They were fired from their jobs, expelled from schools and imprisoned. Their homes were ransacked and they were publicly humiliated. They faced torture and inhumane conditions in hard labor camp prisons. Their countrymen rejected them as they were falsely accused of being American spies, counter-revolutionaries and criminals. However, persecutions and tribulations always bring great spiritual revival and harvest.

Today the underground house church movement in China is flourishing. China has experienced the fastest growing church movement in the world. There has never been a comparable explosion of church growth in all of human history. The testimonies of Chinese martyrs, both written and orally shared were preserved through the years and Christians in China today have reached more than 100 million. During the Japanese occupation of China, during the darkest hours for Chinese Christians, my father first shared his vision of indigenous churches in China with Bishop Hua-Qing Wang, affectionately known as Grandpa Wang to my siblings and me. The two promoted the Self-Supporting, Self-Governing and Self-Propagating movement to many churches in northern China, which were originally planted both by western missionaries and indigenous Chinese pastors. The vision was furtively expressed to Chinese ministers during meetings in my father's home.

I remember when my mother sacrificed all her jewelry and diamond rings which we had depended on to sustain our livelihood to start the "Chinese Christian Self-Supporting, Self-Governing and Self-Propagating Million Pound Foundation", my father recommended Bishop Hua-Qing Wang to be the president. When Bishop Wang heard this, he praised the Lord with tears. He knew that he was old but he was very clear that it was

God's will to be asked to help establish Chinese Christian Indigenous Evangelistic Ministries to be Self-Governing, Self-Supporting, Self-Propagating. Bishop Wang smiled at me and said, "Hi, you little ardent co-worker, do you want to succeed Grandpa Wang's ministry?" Bishop Wang went to be with the Lord before Christians were persecuted in China.

Pastor Zhen Wang was entrusted by my father to hand copy the Bible in Chinese calligraphy. The original hand-copied Bible in Chinese calligraphy was lost when the Red Guards destroyed Bibles during the "Cultural Revolution" in the 1960s. In the 1970s and early 1980s, a serious shortage of Bibles developed. After his release, a Chinese Christian who had been imprisoned for his faith made 200 handwritten copies of the New Testament for those who sought God's Word.

In 1980, after I was rehabilitated and moved to Beijing, Freddie and I were eager to visit the ministry leaders with whom we fellowshipped before my twenty-year imprisonment. During one house church meeting in China where I shared my testimony, Pastor Sheng-Yun Yang, who knew my father well, took my hand and expressed his delight on hearing my testimony. His fervor to serve the Lord had not faded through the years. The wrinkles on his face spoke of the many trials and persecutions he endured, yet the light in his eyes conveyed the joy of the Lord in his heart.

I later learned that before Pastor Yang died, he dedicated his entire savings, only five hundred Yuan, or the equivalent of two hundred and fifty U.S. dollars, to the poor churches in northwestern China. Here these faithful servants of God showed me through their spiritual love the essential truth of the gospel. *"Verily, verily, I say unto you, Except a corn of wheat fall into the ground and die, it abideth alone: but if it die, it bringeth forth much fruit."* (John 12:24).

My generation is now between the ages of sixty and eighty. We, the remnants preserved by God, have had the privilege to watch the next generation of Chinese Christians take up the torch and follow Christ Jesus to send the gospel light to every corner of the world and back to Jerusalem. Over one hundred million Chinese have given their lives to Christ Jesus, creating the urgent need for discipleship training. Thank God!

He prepared His faithful servants as a small but solid group through Christian Aid Mission. These serve Him by giving love, financial support and Bible teaching to help indigenous missions development, not like a father, but like a brother to the suffering brothers of all nations. This is the same vision that God had given my father, who was unable to finish the job. Now, all by His grace, I am able to serve Him along with all of the staff at Christian Aid Mission.

Chapter 37

Great Commission of God

Step by step throughout each phase in my life, God was faithful to continue the good work He started in training me by continually breaking and remolding me as He saw fit. Yet I fully realize that I am not a perfect vessel. By God's grace, He has used me as a piece of clay to join the mission team to accomplish His purpose among the Chinese. In every generation, the Lord has chosen a remnant of believers to serve Him.

Every year, Freddie and I are sent to China to help indigenous Chinese missionaries and workers to establish Bible schools, discipleship training centers, children's Sunday school ministries and orphanages as well as other Christian compassion projects. The exponential growth in the number of Christians in China has surpassed all other nations in church history and is due to those saints who have equipped themselves with the truth of God's Word. As the Bible tells us, *"The harvest truly is plenteous, but the laborers are few."* (Matthew 9:37).

Looking back on my life, I realize that the good work the Lord accomplished through me was only achieved after He broke me. He remade me into a worthier vessel of clay, even though I was badly marred in many ways. As His Word states in Jeremiah 18:4, *"And the vessel that he made of clay was marred in the hand of the potter: so he made it again another vessel, as seemed good to the potter to make it."* These words from the Bible have become my only source of joy and hope. Because He never threw me away, I am confident that I will be ever in God's hand. The gentle Potter will never grow weary or impatient with His creation, but continuously work to complete the good work He started in each one of us.

My prayer is that I may be submissive to the work He has yet to accomplish in me and through me. Yes, my body will grow older and weaker, but the child-like heart that God gives to those who love Him, who have been called according to His purpose, will never grow old.

"What shall I render unto the Lord for all His benefits toward me? I will take the cup of salvation, and call upon the name of the Lord. I will pay my vows unto the Lord now in the presence of all His people." (Psalm 116: 12-14).

Now as I recall the words from the song, "I'll Walk with God," they fill my heart:

> *I'll walk with God from this day on,*
> *His helping hand I'll lean upon.*
> *This is my prayer, my humble plea,*
> *May the Lord be ever with me.*
> *There is no death, though eyes grow dim.*
> *There is no fear when I'm near to Him.*
> *I'll lean on Him forever and He'll forsake me never.*
> *He will not fail me as long as my faith is strong,*
> *Whatever road I may walk along;*
> *I'll walk with God, I'll take His hand, I'll talk with God, He'll understand;*
> *I'll pray to Him, each day to Him and He'll hear the words that I say.*
> *His hand will guide my way, my life,*
> *And I'll never walk alone while I walk with God.*

Let my "Hallelujah" join the chorus of millions of angels that echoes throughout the universe forevermore to praise Christ Jesus, the King of Kings and the Lord of Lords, Who is coming back soon!

Dear Reader,

This book, which is part of a series on Dorothy's testimony, is not for sale. If your heart is touched by this book and you would like to support Dorothy's Chinese Ministry, your donation will be greatly appreciated. The Chinese Ministry at Christian Aid is primarily aimed at training Chinese indigenous missionaries to be mature and well-grounded. This ministry also helps orphaned and disabled Chinese children. Your intercession and financial support make up the foundation of this ministry and your contribution will be used to do tremendous work for God's kingdom in China.

Dorothy is available to travel to different states in the U.S. and to different countries to preach, to share or to lead retreat conferences. If you need to contact her, please get in touch with Christian Aid China Division.

If you feel led to contribute financially, please designate *Chinese Ministry* on your check.

Christian Aid Mission
P.O. Box 9037
Charlottesville, VA 22906

TEL: (434) 977-5650
FAX: (434) 295-6814
E-mail: freddie@christianaid.org

Patricia Taylor, editor, with author Dorothy Sun - October 2006.